The Severely and Profoundly Handicapped:
A Practical Approach to Teaching

The Severely and Profoundly Handicapped:

A Practical Approach to Teaching

Edward T. Donlon, Ed.D.
Director, Clay County Learning Center
Ashland, Alabama

Louise F. Burton, M.S.
Rehabilitation Services
Education Program
Talladega College
Talladega, Alabama

GRUNE & STRATTON
A Subsidiary of Harcourt Brace Jovanovich, Publishers
New York San Francisco London

Library of Congress Cataloging in Publication Data

Donlon, Edward T
    The severely and profoundly handicapped.

        Includes bibliographies and index.
        1. Handicapped children—Education. 2. Perceptual-
motor learning. I. Burton, Louise F., joint author.
II. Title.
LC4015.D59   371.9   76-17293
ISBN 0-8089-0952-5

Grune & Stratton, Inc.
111 Fifth Avenue
New York, New York   10003

Library of Congress Catalog Number 76-17293
International Standard Book Number 0-8089-0952-5

Printed in the United States of America

Contents

Preface   ix

1. **Identifying and Analyzing Problems**   1

   Introduction   1
   *Early Needs 3,   Where They Are 4,   The Children
   5,   Others Who Fit the Group 11*

   Observation for Evaluation   14
   *Observing Joe 14,   Setting Goals for Joe 24,
   Observing Sandra 28,   Goals for Sandra 32*

   Educational Planning   36
   *Establishing a Baseline 37,   Target Behavior 37,
   Learning to Observe 38*

2. **Recognizing and Implementing for Specific Needs   40**

   Introduction   40
   *Selecting a Teacher 41,   What Kind of Teaching 42,
   Who Can Teach 43,   Expectations 44,   Time Out 45,
   Realism 47*

   Infant Learning   49
   The Need for Input 49,   Other Suggestions 50

   Body Image   54
   *Forming an Image 54,   He Needs Help 55,   Getting
   Him in Touch 56,   Tactile Stimulation 57,   A Real
   Experience 58,   Realistic Expectations 59,
   Manipulating People 60,   Suggestions to Try 60*

   Experience with Objects   63
   *Relating to the Environment 63,   Observing Use of
   Objects 64,   Making the Use Positive 64,   Getting
   Your Attention 65,   Setting Goals 65,   Learning to
   Use Objects 67,   Other Suggestions 68*

   Tactile Stimulation   70
   *Encouraging Tactile Investigation 70,   Varying
   Tactile Experiences 72,   Defensiveness to Texture
   73,   Tactile Qualities 73,   Tactile Language 76,
   Materials 76*

Olfactory and Gustatory Sense Training   77
    Teaching: When and What 77,   Real Experiences
    Made Big 78,   Creating Interest 79,   Problem
    Solving 80,   Careful Observation 82,   Ideas for
    Activities 82

Visual Stimulation and Training   84
    Learning to See 84,   Rewarding His Efforts 87,
    Wearing Glasses 87,   Encouraging Independent
    Travel 89,   Checking with Vision 90,   Using
    Visual Clues 90,   Developing Concepts 91,
    Exploring 91,   Perceiving 92,   Sequencing
    Development of Vision 93,   Using Daily Experiences
    94,   Other Suggestions 95

Auditory Stimulation and Training   99
    Need for Auditory Training 99,   Learning to Wear
    an Aid 100,   Awareness of Sound 102,   Sound Games
    to Try 103,   Motivating the Child 106,   Voice
    Awareness 107,   A Personal Experience 109,
    Praising the Child 110

Movement in Space   111
    Training in Independence 111,   Mobility 113,
    Orientation 113,   An Experience 114,   Stimulating
    Reflex Movement 115,   Moving Forward 117,
    Developing Confidence 119,   Coordination 121,
    Varied Experiences 122,   Other Suggestions 124

Self-Care Skills   127
    Need for Self-Sufficiency 127,   When to Begin
    Teaching 129,   Toilet Training 131,   Ideas to Try 133,
    Eating 135,   Steps Toward Independence 137,   Some
    Suggestions 139,   Dressing 141,   Suggestions 142,
    Grooming 145
        Washing, Suggestions, Nose Blowing, Brushing Teeth,
        Suggestions, Combing Hair, Suggestions, Nail Care and
        Makeup
    Care of Possessions 150,   Problem Solving and
    Self-Care 151

Communication   152
    Finding a Method 152,   Using Unacceptable
    Communication 154,   Learning Manual Signs 155,
    Constant Input 156,   Other Suggestions 158

Language Development 160
*Language: A Major Goal 160,   Sequencing
Development 161,   Inner Language 162,   Building
Inner Language 163,   Need for Varied Experiences
163,   Receptive Language 165,   Building Receptive
Language 165,   Encouraging Small Approximations
167,   Expressive Language 167,   Building
Expressive Language 168,   Creating a Need for
Expression 169*

Speech Training and Oral Language 170
*Total Communication 170,   A Real Experience 171,
Teaching and Getting Results 172,   Amplifications
175,   Tongue Exercises 175,   Blowing 176,
Learning to Vocalize 177,   Beginning "Lessons" 177,
Early Speech Elements 179,   Attitudes 179*

Socialization, Play, and Use of Free Time 181
*Observing Use of Free Time 181,   Play 182,
Tolerating Toys 183,   Participation 184,   Cleaning
Up 184,   Homemade Toys 186,   Playing While You
Work 187,   Make It Fun 188*

Behavior 188
*Analyzing Behavior 188,   Using Behavior 189,
Changing Behavior 191,   Setting Limits 192,
Undesirable Behavior 193,   The Learning
Atmosphere 195,   Punishment 197*

3. **Family Concerns and Other Considerations 201**

Introduction 201
*Mobilization and Development of Family Effort 204,
The Family Needs Must Continue 207,   Being
Realistic 208*

Communication to Parents 209
*Making Parents Aware of Services 211,
Considerations for Placement 214,   Getting Parents
Aware of Laws 216,   Financial Help (Funding) 217*

Kinds of Programs 221
*Residential School Programs 221,   Day School
Programs 223*

Severely and Profoundly Handicapped in the Community   224
  Activities of Daily Living 225,   Leisure Time 226,
  Economic Needs 227,   Social Needs 228

Learning to Live Together   231
  Community Expectations 232,   Community Attitudes
  234

Vocational Rehabilitation   236
  Observation for Potential 237,   Essential Behaviors
  for Work 238

Advocacy   239
  Amplification of Child Advocacy to the Severely and
  Profoundly Handicapped 242,   Who Can Advocate
  244

Appendix I: Behavior Rating Form Communication
Adjustment Learning Instructions   246

Index 253

Preface

This is a book about children. They are individuals who have many problems now and will have many more as they grow and develop physically and mentally and as they, and we, fight for them to have a place in society. They are presently called severely and profoundly handicapped. In the recent past they have been classified under several labels: the multiply handicapped, profoundly retarded, severely disturbed, deaf–blind, idiot. A tour of any facility purporting to deal with any of these specific groups would find children who look and act the same.

The overriding characteristic of each is that there is no program designed to meet their needs or to develop potential and evaluate progress. Each child is an enigma to family and most professionals. The severity and multiplicity of their handicaps can be and usually is overwhelming.

There is not a large body of knowledge directed at treating or educating these children. There are two primary reasons for this. First, the development of medical technology has only recently reached a stage where they can be treated and nurtured through the hazards involved in early stages of development. Second, since most of these children have obvious abnormalities, the best advice was all too often "Put the child in an institution where you will get the best of care, and forget him." Thus the children were sent to institutions where, for many reasons, there was inadequate programming, or they were kept home, with equally inadequate programming.

A program that considers the strengths and weaknesses of each child is a necessity. This should be formulated immediately upon recognition of a problem and should be based upon as much real information as it is possible to obtain at that time. Our concern is that too often parents, teachers, and other professionals working with the severely and profoundly handicapped spend inappropriate energy looking into the general problems of the future and neglect the specific problems of the present. If the present can be analyzed, then goals for the future can be established. When this is done, information can be sought through consultation with experts, research of successful programs, and reading about theory and practice of others. If knowledge gained from these sources is combined with at least equal parts of energy and common sense, then an effective plan can be designed and implemented.

We are hoping that this book will help others to develop a plan that deals with the specific and important areas of concern in the child's early development. Many children who are severely and profoundly handicapped may be older but still functioning at a very low level. Again, we hope that the guidelines presented here will help these young people to begin a program that will lead to development and further progress. There is no one who cannot progress and be a more functional and contributing member of society. This is true of all children and adults and is certainly true of the children discussed in this book.

Before any treatment plan can be outlined, it is necessary to describe those behaviors that are of most concern. Chapter 1 is devoted to a procedure for providing these descriptions and to outlining some of the behaviors that occur in many severely and profoundly handicapped children. Since most children in this group cannot be tested on standardized scales, we must depend upon careful observation of behavior for clues. A system for structured observation is presented which has been effective in describing the child's development and providing a basis for prescriptive programming.

Since children vary both in type and degree of handicap and differ in learning patterns, it is possible to prescribe specifically for a child only when dealing with him as an individual. Before beginning to prescribe, it is important to know those techniques that could be used with some possibility for good results. Chapter 2 provides a number of categories and techniques that apply to many. Some are applicable to each child, but an attempt to use all of them would be inappropriate. We are not striving for completeness. Only a sample is included which has been useful in our work with other children. Acceptance or rejection of specific ideas and development of new ones depend greatly on the reader's creativity and ability to apply them practically and appropriately to the individual child's needs at that time.

One of the most difficult processes in working with severely handicapped persons is to maintain perspectives about the future. Many factors interact to determine the degree and kind of acceptance and involvement the child will have as he grows and matures. Special attention must be given to these factors so that he will have the best possible chance. The final chapter considers some areas that have been important to others and hopefully will help the reader to maintain perspectives and consider as many variables as possible.

In our concern to provide for the basic and immediate needs of a handicapped child, it is easy to postpone consideration of what may seem to be less pressing areas. Other areas of development may be avoided for different reasons. They may be too painful to think about or the necessity has not yet arisen. We hope that by talking about these beginnings, organization and direction will follow, and from this a child will develop with a better chance and more alternatives than he might have had before.

1

Identifying and Analyzing Problems

INTRODUCTION

The severely and profoundly handicapped child is easily identified. The results of his disabilities are evident. Visual problems have behavioral components as do auditory disorders, mental retardation, and brain injury. Other disorders can be described and diagnosed, but no amount of writing can adequately portray the severity and complexity of these conditions when they exist simultaneously in one child. For those who wish to work with these children, there are few guidelines and almost no description of behavior that is typical of the group.

It is also difficult for parents to know whether their child is developing as well as might be expected and even more difficult to obtain information on approaches that might be tried so that results may be predicted. A multitude of questions must be answered and problems solved before a family can develop directions to help the child. In many respects, one of the greatest concerns is the difficulty one has in stating the nature of the problem specifically enough so that it can be identified and attacked. Most problems are stated in general terms. He is severely handicapped. He has profound problems. He needs a special school. He will develop slower than others. These statements may be true, but they offer little or no direction toward meeting the child's needs today. Parents feel lost and alone; they feel that their child is different from any other in the world. There is almost no one who can help in teaching and planning for the future. It is our feeling that ap-

1

proaches have been tried and gratifying results obtained with these children. Some statements can be made about their nature as a group, even though the range and behavior of individual personalities and learning characteristics vary greatly.

We are attempting to describe this group in terms that will allow others to identify similar behaviors in children of their own. After this, behaviors will be categorized and discussed, and specific suggestions will be offered to correct the negative and reinforce the positive. Attention will be given to the fact that even though the children in question have multiple problems that may be specific in nature, it is possible to apply many of the principles and techniques to other handicapped children and even to children who have no identifiable handicap but demonstrate some of the behaviors described.

All of the techniques and suggestions presented here have been tried with success on some child. We feel that this is an important criterion for inclusion of any suggestion. Many persons confronted with a severely handicapped child for the first time have a feeling of total inadequacy, thinking there is no place to start and no way to establish goals for future work. This is not true. All children can make some progress, and if one is careful to observe and establish reasonable goals, progress may be predicted with surprising accuracy.

Specific suggestions are presented in Chapter 2. However, they are not given for the purpose of preparing a "cookbook" to be followed for each and every child. The reader should use any suggestions that seem appropriate, and it is hoped that others may serve as catalysts for developing more useful techniques. If a person has an ability to relate to children, is aware of their basic needs, and can apply ideas gained from others, then effective results can be attained.

Sometimes professionally trained personnel are needed. These times are usually evident as needs develop and will be recognized if there is communication between persons working with different groups of children. Our concern here is to provide guidelines for those who will accept the challenge of working with the severely handicapped child before he is ready to enter the formal educational process that will prepare him for a productive adult life.

All children need to reach certain behavioral objectives before they are ready for the next step in their search for self-sufficiency and productiveness. This is true for the severely and profoundly handicapped as well as the nonhandicapped. Realistic goals can be established for each group, although some are more difficult to attain than others. It is important to recognize that before we can work with someone, his assets and liabilities must be known, in addition to interests, habits, and motivations. Careful observation is especially important so that successes may be repeated and failures avoided.

Early Needs

The infant is almost totally dependent on adult supervision. His basic physical demands must be met by someone else. Soon, however, he begins to use his senses to interact with his environment. This leads to an awareness of an outside world which he will learn to use and control. We are interested in the development of children from birth and recognize the importance of providing extra experiences for the handicapped. Our main concern in this book begins when the child first uses his senses for gaining information. Our goal is to urge him to use information gained in these experiences for other learning. The use of senses for gathering information is refined and patterns of problem solving are formed. It is then possible for others to intervene and devise programs to guide the child in a desired direction. This direction will be toward a readiness for formal and productive learning beyond that which is necessary to satisfy basic needs. We do not believe that children should be exposed to serious and more abstract learning until a certain self-sufficiency can be attained. Ages of attainment may vary considerably. Much depends on previous experience and the direction that learning has taken. For instance, many of the children considered here are proficient at controlling parents and avoiding any form of directed experience.

We do not suggest that certain tasks need to be completely mastered before others may be presented. Children certainly do not have to be completely toilet trained, for instance, before they begin to count. However, it is important to consider the degree of supervision necessary before a child enters a certain type of program. If 75 to 100 percent of a child's activities need direct adult intervention, then it is probably inappropriate to place him in a group where the goals are directed toward formal activities. We do not, for instance, teach finger spelling to a deaf child who has no idea that words have the quality of symbolic representation. Our goal is to describe behaviors and offer suggestions to develop a child's functioning in many areas, with emphasis on skills that will contribute to future learning and adjustment. If some useful information is transmitted to those working with young severely handicapped children, then much of our goal will be achieved.

Where They Are

When we speak of severely and profoundly handicapped children, it is appropriate to ask where they are. What programs serve them? Who is responsible for them? The disease, the accidents, the factors that cause these disabilities are found everywhere. Neither race nor economic status nor even family health is an assurance that these disabilities cannot occur. There are some factors, of course, that can add to probabilities of occurrence. Some of these have been studied and are being brought under control, for example, the effect of Rh blood incompatibility and rubella infection during pregnancy. Disabilities can occur during and after pregnancy or even from disease or accident as the child is growing. While these are of concern to us, this book is not about causes or cures. It is concerned with alleviating the effects of the conditions and aiding the children to reach maximum development during their early life.

Individuals and groups of these children may be found anywhere. The identified groups become larger in more densely populated areas. Likewise, if there are services, they are usually centered in cities that have concentrations of professionals and facilities directed toward service. Because of the low incidence of these children in proportion to the total population, educational centers are frequently located in only a few places within a region of the country. Thus, children served are often placed in residential settings.

Many children are not in existing programs because of their age and inaccessibility. Numerous children are identified in this group, but it is generally felt that many more have not as yet been found. The size of this unknown group cannot be determined. We can only say that as programs are developed and children served there are always many more who are identified and ask for service.

We are concerned with the nature of the child who can profit by techniques suggested in this book. It seems useful to describe this group which has stimulated the development of these procedures. The following descriptions and case examples should therefore be considered as composites of children in the group from infancy to the time when they are self-sufficient enough to be able to maintain themselves in an academic and social setting. In this setting, goals will be directed toward preparing them for social and vocational skills leading to a self-sufficient and rewarding adult life.

This particular group has not been identified as being primarily physically handicapped, mentally retarded or emotionally disturbed. Many do have characteristics and behaviors associated with each of these categories. Some, perhaps too many, have been "diagnosed" and consequently given one of these labels. Perhaps the main distinguishing characteristic of the severely and profoundly handicapped is that the children do not respond satisfactorily to tried and true methodologies that are successful with others. A severely disturbed child, for instance, would be expected to respond predictably to a program which, in the past, had been successful with other children in the same diagnostic category. The situation would also obtain for other less profoundly handicapped children, the retarded, the physically handicapped, the deaf, and the blind. For some reason, they do not respond and most approaches do not work. The experienced person—the master teacher, the best therapist—gets better results than the less experienced, but frequently they do not know why. They can, however, articulate some of the differences these children have in their development and their learning and behavior patterns.

Confusing and frustrating as they are, there also seem to be directions for many, and there are common factors within the groups. Here we have observed others and borrowed from their successes and failures to add to our own.

Our goal is to offer specific techniques that have been effective. But even more than this, we are interested in developing a process, so that these techniques will fit into a pattern and become useful in developing others that are even more effective.

The Children

Most severely handicapped children are not known to educators until they are at least five years old. However, this situation is gradually being remedied. Early diagnosis and the development of programs have indicated to physicians and clinics that referrals can and should be made so that programs can be instituted and results accomplished as early as possible. At age two and above, these children are either just beginning to walk or have been walking for only a short time. Their motor coordination is not as well developed as might be expected, and frequently there are signs that some fine motor skills are almost entirely lacking. Eye–hand coordination is affected, but when one considers the fact that many have visual disabilities and motor incoordination, it may be that the eye–hand ability is even better than one would predict.

As they grow older, the role that experience plays in ability is evident. Those with adequate experiences become better coordinated and more mobile in their environments. They can climb, jump, and run as well as many nonhandicapped children.

Lack of practice affects the development of fine motor skills. The children do not always use all their senses. They may rely on vision entirely, even though it has been diagnosed as limited. They are not always aware of fine differences in objects, and unless specifically trained, other senses are not used to compensate for insufficiency.

The use of senses varies considerably. Some are diagnosed with sensory disorders. They have severe visual or auditory acuity loss or other disabilities in these areas. More often, though, it is difficult for the specialists to say exactly what is wrong with these important receptive pathways. Some certainly do have "acuity losses." They may need glasses or even a hearing aid. Many of the children we have seen are classified as deaf–blind. However, very few have such profound sensory deficits that no use can be made of these areas. Many do not respond, but that is the challenge—to determine effective procedures that can motivate the child to use all available senses to receive information.

Our observations indicate that for many in this group, vision is the major sensory modality used for gaining information about the social and physical environment. Children look at objects and concentrate visually on many things. This activity may be positive, but more often it is not. Sight is frequently used as a means of avoidance. They do not close their eyes to avoid, as many other children do when they are angry. They look at light or movement. They concentrate on their hands and move them in ways that make interesting visual patterns, at least to them. They look—but at something else. Whatever they see is interesting to them, although not necessarily to us.

When glasses are used, the correction may be of high magnification, which increases visual discriminative ability but decreases peripheral fields. The children can then locate small points and complete some tasks such as form boards and simple puzzles. They may not be able to follow a ball rolling on the floor and may even bump into small chairs and other objects that are out of their field of vision. This is especially true with those who move faster than their corrected visual ability allows. Therefore, it is necessary to provide these children with as many opportunities as possible to use vision and increase its efficiency. These opportunities must be presented in ways that will encourage the child to try several approaches to see better. For example, a child who receives a visual image from a small spot on the retina may need to turn his head away from the normal line of sight in order to increase his vision. Such tactics can cause concern to the uninitiated teacher and consequent frustration to the child, especially when the adult in authority forces the child to conform to normal behavioral patterns, such as "looking straight ahead like others do."

Those who have severe sensory disorders in both vision and hearing, but do not have a total loss in either, seem to develop primarily as visually oriented children. Their efforts at gathering information are directed more often through the visual modality. This is the sensory area through which they gain new information or avoid any directed activity. Their fascination with light or flashing objects, such as prisms, silverware, and other metal objects, can lead to almost ritualistic behavior as the child uses his sight in what appears to be a meaningless activity. Even after they develop communicative ability, they express an interest in light bulbs, the sun, or other bright objects. Such behavior is not restricted to children with multiple sensory disorders. Many children with mental and emotional problems display similar behavior.

In some ways, audiological characteristics are similar to visual anomalies. There may be losses in acuity as well as confusion in the central or interpretative area. Differences also occur. In addition, the child with auditory disorders may demonstrate a broader group of problems, especially those related to communication.

Many children have a demonstrable amount of hearing. They are attracted to some sounds and attend to a variety of noises, especially those they can manipulate. Some of the children have been fitted with hearing aids, and once they become conditioned to wearing them, accept them. However, this does not mean that the aids are used meaningfully. Some children do not understand even single words when presented only auditorially.

Hearing is often used in a self-stimulating fashion through sound levels, such as radio music or feedback from a hearing aid, or physically, in which case the child may hit his ear or his head in such a way that auditory stimulation is produced. Frequently, auditory stimulation has a tranquilizing effect, and the child will seek odd sound sources that are meaningless but which gain his attention for considerable periods of time.

The fact that these children do not use their obvious auditory ability for receptive communication is puzzling and frustrating to the family and teachers. Frequently, too, hearing loss is assumed to be so profound that even amplified speech is not received. This does not follow, however, when the child is observed "listening" to bells, horns, and noisemakers. Eventually, consistent responses to simple speech may be gained, and the child learns to recognize nouns and verbs, especially when gestures and signs are used in conjunction with vocalizations. Even here, though, it is difficult to maintain motivation to develop a large receptive vocabulary and to use words already learned.

Frequently there is little, if any, startle response to loud noises, and it is difficult to detect a situation where the child uses auditory reception as a way to gain information from others or to control his life better. Thus, many children who have comparable visual and auditory characteristics are visually oriented and use the auditory modality only in self-stimulation and for the most rudimentary communication.

The other sensory areas, tactile, gustatory, and olfactory, may be observed and used in a variety of ways. Some, at least, are used for their "intended purpose" as recognized in our nonhandicapped society. Other uses may be observed that serve a variety of purposes and may be considered creative if we accept the child's needs for stimulation as being more useful and important to him than those goals established for the educational program.

Many children have definite preferences for tastes and smells. This is especially evident with textures as in food. At times they would rather not eat than have a food that they do not like served with one that is a favorite. Some of these reactions may result from the anxiety of parents who are concerned that the child has enough to eat, particularly if there is a possibility that he may starve or become malnourished. In this case, the child is usually given as much as he can eat of soft foods and those that he enjoys. This habit does not easily change, and the child becomes "spoiled" from eating only a limited selection of foods. Likes and dislikes for certain tastes are also evident. These taste preferences are often unusual. Pickles and even vinegar have been noted as being preferred by many children.

Tactile experiences are also sought after by many. Some children seem especially to enjoy tactile experiences that would be abnormal in the nonhandicapped child, whereas they may reject such items as Playdough and clay, and even soft fuzzy toys may be repulsive to them. There may be an intensified reaction to some materials. Extreme negative signs and even fear of some objects and textures may be noted. There is usually no obvious reason for these reactions, but they are present in many children and can usually be extinguished when attention is paid to them. These reactions do not usually transfer from one item to another.

Although the children have strong likes and dislikes and demonstrate tactile awareness, they are not seen as dominantly tactilely oriented, unless the child is totally blind, of course. In that case, as with most nonseeing children, they do rely on touch, taste, and smell to add more dimension to their receptive system.

When handed an object, most of these children tend to handle it more and hold it close to their eyes. They then may taste or smell it to gain further information. If they find it useful as a new object, they may manipulate or play with it in some unique way. This is especially true if they have self-stimulating behaviors and if the object can be used for this purpose.

Motor behavior, both gross and fine, seems at first glance to be poor. Some might think the child is awkward. With closer observation, it may be evident with some that the basic gross motor patterns have developed and movement has become useful to the child. Description is difficult, but many of the traits come from a looseness and seemingly relaxed pattern of gross motor activity. The child probably has good balance even though he appears to be falling. Orientation is good even though there is little evidence that the child knows where he is, he frequently has an excellent sense of danger, although he gets into seemingly precarious situations.

At least some of the well-developed gross motor movement patterns can be attributed to the child making the most efficient use of his residual sensory modalities. If it is necessary to touch the wall several times to maintain a path, then the means of touching could end with what appears to be a meandering walking pattern. This allows for touching with the hand and orientation with the feet to sense different textures on the floor. Visual and auditory cues are also used at these times, and the combination of them with motor cues and learned responses to varying environments allows the child to function efficiently in his own realm.

Fine motor patterns combine hand movements with auditory and especially visual receptive capacities. There may be considerable motivation to find an object and manipulate it for a specific purpose. This purpose is often meaningless to the adult observer and may serve as self-stimulation rather than meaningful play. A toy car, for instance, is not used as a car but may serve as a way to focus a spot of light or make a clicking sound for the child.

Many fine motor patterns are noted without objects. Although these are not often the same patterns noted in nonhandicapped children, they give the impression that the child must have good coordination and a sense of motor memory which could be used in developing a program for other acceptable learning. Indeed, one of the frustrations of parents is the fact that the child will not carry out simple motor tasks that may be used in eating, dressing, or some of the other common daily living skills.

The inability to communicate about the simple basics of living, including daily living skills, is frustrating. Imitative behaviors, which for other children are usually easily developed, are also most frustrating, as these children frequently either cannot or will not imitate our behavior. The child needs acceptance, but it becomes difficult to reward him for "right" behavior if it is seldom exhibited and especially hard if we do not even have an effective reward that we know he understands.

Some of the simplest motor communication techniques work at times with some children. A hug is accepted but not sought after. Clapping the hands or patting the child on the head may or may not bring desired reward effect—which is to encourage repetition of the behavior. Sometimes, he behaves as though he cannot perceive the simplest words and phrases. If they are accompanied by some meaningful reward, then after many repetitions the child may respond. It is difficult, though, to accomplish the next step and transfer this behavior to other situations or to generalize the responses and use them at other times or places and with other people.

Communication is often noted when the child is doing what he wants and "conditioning" the adult. If he has a certain movement or sound that becomes meaningful to others, then that is accepted as his "language" at the time. Other movements and utterances are developed, with the child serving as the developer. This leads to a closed communication system between the handicapped child and his immediate acquaintances—the family. Along with this, the child offers considerable passive resistance to accepting new communication systems, no matter how they are introduced. The only thing that is usually evident is that he is thinking and does have definite desires and needs. He can communicate these and will change his behavior as necessary to make his wants known, but this is accomplished only after considerable resistance.

Most communication is by gross motor movement. Vocalization may accompany this, but these sounds are sometimes not based on imitative speech patterns. These expressive communication efforts are consistent and generally meet the needs of the child.

Even though expression is at a low level, many of the children behave as if they are even lower in the receptive category. However, there is usually evidence that they are receiving more information than they will admit. It is, for instance, difficult to get even the simplest response after many tries at giving commands in a variety of forms. Once we have become "acquainted," then a set of words can be developed for the specific child-adult interaction.

The adult is the person who most often socializes with the child. Unless the adult is part of a large family where older children take over some of the parent roles, the child usually does not have intensive or long-lasting interaction with peers. He may play side by side with them or may fight over a certain object, but he seldom goes further unless considerable attention is given to promoting such interaction. If the child does not socially interact, then his chances are limited for appropriately using his time during waking hours of the day. He can play with objects, as he frequently does, but this play is often for the purpose of self-stimulation. At such times, he uses his teeth to bite a comb, or flicks a spoon to produce light reflections on his retina. If no objects are present, he may be equally proficient at self-stimulating activities without objects.

Adults and children may find a basis for interaction around some objects. Sometimes the interaction comes when the adult becomes exasperated and tries to remove the object, which then becomes a game to the child. He usually wins. With persistence and some ingenuity, the adult can substitute other objects and play a slightly more meaningful game. Usually the attempt at interaction fails if the adult tries to discourage some unacceptable behaviors without gradually encouraging the child to substitute more acceptable acts.

Socially, then, this child generally does not interact with other children. He may further be described as being neutral in temperament rather than usually happy or unhappy. He enjoys playing with objects of his choice and using these for purposes of sensory stimulation rather than meaningful, symbolic, or social play. He will interact with adults, often for the purpose of satisfying his own needs—generally for food—but he will also interact at the adult's insistence and will continue so long as the interaction is not entirely counterproductive to his own activity. He will change his behavior for us if approached properly, but this is usually specific to one adult and not transferred to others. These specific behaviors are usually remembered over time, so that after a day or even a week, many of the same reactions can be elicited by the same adults. These specifics can be reported and described to others, but it is not usually the case. Unless there is observation and direct communication, these behavior changes do not occur.

Others Who Fit the Group

There are other groups of children who can and often do benefit from some of the teaching procedures used with severely handicapped children. Some are occasionally placed in facilities designed for the severely and profoundly handicapped child. This placement or similar treatment may occur because the child at an early age exhibits some of the characteristics previously mentioned. It can also occur because those concerned feel the child can fit into the particular situation. At still other times, the placement may have just been a convenient solution to the problem as to what to do with the child who had no other place to go. Also, certain characteristics exhibited early by the children have sometimes led to the misuse of labels such as deaf, partially sighted, mentally retarded, or emotionally disturbed. For example, a child who is unresponsive when auditory stimuli are presented early in his life may appear deaf, when actually his hearing mechanism is intact. Thus, while such placement may be of benefit to children who are severely and profoundly handicapped, the decision must be based on several factors.

In order to identify some of the behaviors most frequently seen in these children, a few will be discussed here. The most obvious is usually an inability or refusal to communicate with others within the environment long past the time when most children are speaking fluently. Many appear to resent any intrusion upon their privacy and move away when approached. The child may sing or chant to himself. This behavior most often occurs when he seems content with his world. Chants are usually made up of more vowel than consonant sounds and may have the rhythm of speech; however, recognizable words are usually missing. Some of the children we have seen physically manipulate people to satisfy their needs or desires. This can be seen when the child takes an adult's hand an places it on some desired object that he could have gotten for himself.

One young boy drank water from a mud puddle when thirsty and would snatch food from the kitchen when hungry. One could assume that this child did not feel a real need for adults and was unconcerned about what adults thought of him. He appeared to have developed some level of self-sufficiency and daily accumulated more knowledge about how to survive *all alone*. He had created a "little world" and became self-reliant enough to satisfy his basic body needs without help from others.

The fact that the prescribed treatment for a child with such behavior has often failed to accomplish the desired results has substantiated the assumption that there is "little hope." Our experiences have shown that there is hope. These children do not always fit into any exact diagnostic category, and it is often difficult to find an appropriate, descriptive label. Labels are often arbitrary and fail to offer solutions to the real problem. Frustrated and confused parents often shuffle their children from one "specialist" to another, finding labels but little actual help as to what can be done. Such confusion can also be detrimental to the child's eventual adjustment.

Children need security, a stable home environment, and relationships with adults who are capable of handling them and confident in their ability to do so. However, once behavior problems arise, environmental conditions often deteriorate, possibly at a comparable rate. Therefore, when they need even more stability, they get less. Such conditions compound the problem.

With some children, progress seems to be normal during the first few months or even the first year; then something happens to alter their behavior. A new baby may arrive in the family; the mother may go to work, leaving the child with a babysitter; or problems may develop between the adults within the home. Regardless of the cause, at some point, the child changes. He may regress by reverting to behaviors he had long since outgrown. The child slowly and carefully builds a wall around himself, within which he creates a little world that is more acceptable to him, one with which he can cope. His world is now made up of *self,* and the child takes what he wants from others, giving nothing in return. In time, environmental pressures build up, and the child begins to realize that things have gotten out of hand. He then increases the pressure by trying to take charge, such as when he attempts to manipulate people. Since people are not easily manipulated, the situation begins to reach a crisis stage. The child either strengthens the wall around himself or he relates only to those he can manipulate. Any intrusion on his privacy, any attempt to get him to cooperate, or any refusal to obey him may cause him to react aggressively (scratch, pinch, pull hair, kick, or bite). He is trying to control. Because he is difficult to understand and communication is almost impossible, people may interfere with him less and less, which reinforces his antisocial behavior.

Sometimes such children are placed successfully in existing programs designed for children with other "problems." However, if specific goals are not established to help the child adjust, then little is accomplished. Merely to place the child in a program is of little use, unless, of course, the goal is to get the child out of the house. What would be helpful is a program or a situation that could meet specific goals, such as communication, group adjustment, socialization, certain daily living skills, and simple visual-motor tasks. The physical facilities are unimportant at this time. Emphasis should be placed on locating available services and evaluating them for potential contributions rather than searching for nonexistent "schools" that would be perfect for the child's total adjustment.

One of the most important factors in evaluating the available services is the person who will be working with the child. If the person who is to do the teaching can relate to the child, then the location is un-important. The selection of professional help is discussed in another section.

OBSERVATION FOR EVALUATION

Although verbal descriptions are often inadequate in evaluating children for whom standardized tests are inappropriate, there are times when such descriptions can serve certain purposes. Composite verbal pictures of two typical children (Joe and Sandra) are included here for the purpose of better defining the child who is our target in this book. Our comments and suggestions are not limited to this particular "category" of child, but they have been stimulated by knowing such children.

Observing Joe

Joe, a four-year-old, is severely and profoundly handicapped. He enters the room with all the eagerness of any interested, curious child in new surroundings. He quickly sizes up the situation, locates a light bulb, and proceeds to manipulate his environment and the people in it so that the light bulb can be his. It soon becomes clear that he is ca-pable of communicating immediate desires when motivated and in one way or another usually succeeds in getting what he wants. When first attempts to reach the light bulb by himself fail, he leads a nearby adult to it, as if to say, "You get it for me." If necessary, he places the adult's hand on or near the desired object. Any encouragement from the adult results in demonstrated excitement and a decrease in frustra-tion. Failure to be granted the light bulb leads to extreme tantrum behavior, including screaming, head banging, and refusal to be physi-cally removed from the area.

Several encouraging behaviors are evident during this short period of observation, substantiating our opinion that this child would benefit from an approach similar to the one described here. To give more structure to our evaluative description of this child, we will select some of the categories used in a behavior rating protocol.[1]

This procedure involves the application of an observation sched-

---

[1] Curtis, W. Scott and Donlon, Edward T., *Telediagnostic Protocol: Behavior Rating Form, Communication Adjustment Learning.* University of Georgia, Division for Exceptional Children, 1973.

ule to eight different situations designed to present a child in his average day. The rating of these observations involves the application of judgment based on the child's methods of communication, adjustment, and learning.

The situations observed include children in structured and non-structured settings that are both familiar and unfamiliar. They also include the child's reaction to a variety of sensorially stimulating materials. The ratings on a child vary from the most primitive behavioral response to one in which the child's behavior is considered satisfactory in that category.

Another primary concern of those working with the severely and profoundly handicapped child has to do with his ability to function independently in the activities of daily living. We feel the behavior rating protocol is also useful in describing the child's behavior in this area. Figures 1–4 display the average rating of ten observers as they perceived Joe and Sandra after viewing the eight behavioral situations videotaped for the rating protocol. See Appendix I for a description of the procedure followed to make these videotapes.

Joe indicated a functional ability in most of the activities of daily living, requiring up to 50 percent supervision in some categories and less than 25 percent in others. In the area of eating, Joe could feed himself independently but refused to eat many foods. He limited his preferences to foods that were either seasoned with tomato flavor (catsup or spaghetti) or those that were sweet, such as candy, cookies, cake, ice cream, and sugar-coated dry cereals. Attempts to encourage him to taste other foods were met with the same tantrum behavior noted when desired objects were refused.

Little help was needed in dressing. Joe required assistance only with buckling, buttoning, and occasionally zipping. He also had difficulty in getting his shoes on without help. His ability to accomplish these tasks was rated as nearly normal. However, all were accomplished in a dilatory way.

Elimination and bathing also presented few problems. Joe would cooperate when placed on the toilet; bathing time usually developed into play time and, although obviously capable, he seldom assisted the adult. As for ability to learn these skills, Joe was rated as normal. We felt that he could, with proper guidance, learn to perform all daily living skills at a normal level with little or no help from outsiders.

Joe's functional vision varied with the situation. At times, he did have well-developed fine discrimination. He could recognize desirable and undesirable foods, probably both by color and form. There was also an ability to recognize objects from a moderate distance (10 to 15

BEHAVIOR RATING FORM

COMMUNICATION

BEHAVIOR	Absent (1)	Primitive (2)	Emergent (3)	Usable (4)	Satisfactory (5)
Receptive System					
Auditory Reception	✓				
Visual Reception				✓	
Tactile Reception					
Gustatory/Olfactory Reception			✓		
Referent System					
Object Centered Communication					
People Centered Communication				✓	
Expressive System					
Tactile/Motor Expressive			✓		
Oral Expressive					✓

ADJUSTMENT

BEHAVIOR	Observed	Liability	Asset
Cooperativeness			✓
Purposefulness			✓
Manageability		✓	
Independence			✓
Attentiveness		✓	
Responsiveness			✓
Flexibility			✓
Persistence		✓	
Physical Activity		✓	
Curiosity			✓

INTERACTION PATTERN	Initiator	Mediator	Recipient
The Subject	✓		
A Child			
Child Group			✓
An Adult			
Adult Group			
Mixed Group			
An Object or Task		✓	
Object Group or Tasks			
Agent			

LEARNING

BEHAVIOR	Observed	Liability	Asset
Affective			
Curiosity		✓	
Flexibility			✓
Perseverance		✓	
Attention Span			✓
Reaction to Reward			✓
Reaction to Punishment		✓	
Self Concept			
Energy Level			✓
Sense of Humor			
Motivation and Interest		✓	✓
Self Control			
Sensory Motor			
Mobility			✓
Gross Coordination			✓✓
Eye-Hand Coordination			
Sensory Discrimination		✓	
Spatial Orientation			✓
Intellectual			
Vocabulary			
Creativity		✓	
Problem Solving Skill			✓
Ability to Generalize		✓	
Abstracting Ability			
Sees Relationships			
Memory			✓
Symbolic Ability			✓

Situation _____ Date _____

Subject _Joe_ Age _4_ Agency _____ Observer _Summary of 10 Judges_

Fig. 1.

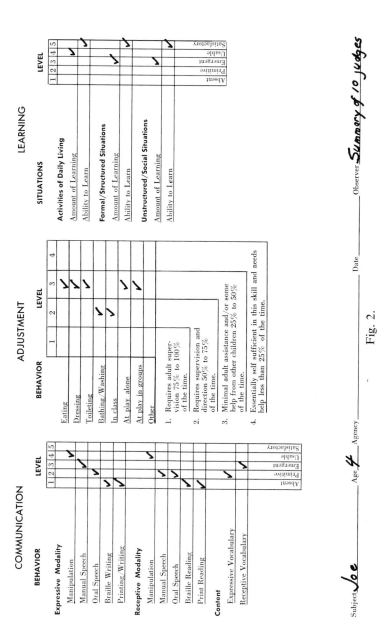

SUMMARY RATING FORM

COMMUNICATION   ADJUSTMENT   LEARNING

Fig. 2.

17

BEHAVIOR RATING FORM

COMMUNICATION

BEHAVIOR	Absent	Primitive	Emergent	Usable	Satisfactory
Receptive System					
Auditory Reception			✓		
Visual Reception		✓			
Tactile Reception		✓			
Gustatory/Olfactory Reception					
Referent System					
Object Centered Communication		✓			
People Centered Communication		✓			
Expressive System					
Tactile/Motor Expressive		✓			
Oral Expressive		✓			

LEVEL 1 2 3 4 5

ADJUSTMENT

BEHAVIOR	Observed	Liability	Asset
Cooperativeness		✓	
Purposefulness		✓	
Manageability		✓	
Independence		✓	
Attentiveness		✓	
Responsiveness		✓	
Flexibility		✓	
Persistence		✓	
Physical Activity		✓	
Curiosity			

LEVEL

INTERACTION PATTERN	Initiator	Mediator	Recipient
The Subject	✓		
A Child			✓
Child Group			
An Adult			
Adult Group			
Mixed Group		✓	
An Object or Task			
Object Group or Tasks			
Agent			

LEARNING

BEHAVIOR	Observed	Liability	Asset
Affective			
Curiosity		✓	
Flexibility		✓	
Perseverance		✓	
Attention Span			
Reaction to Reward			
Reaction to Punishment		✓	
Self Concept		✓	
Energy Level			
Sense of Humor		✓	
Motivation and Interest		✓	
Self Control			
Sensory Motor			
Mobility		✓	
Gross Coordination		✓	
Eye-Hand Coordination		✓	
Sensory Discrimination		✓	
Spatial Orientation		✓	
Intellectual			
Vocabulary			
Creativity			
Problem Solving Skill			
Ability to Generalize			
Abstracting Ability			
Sees Relationships		✓	
Memory			
Symbolic Ability		✓	

LEVEL

Situation _____ Age **5** Agency _____

Subject *Sandra* Observer *Summary of 10 judges* Date _____

Fig. 3.

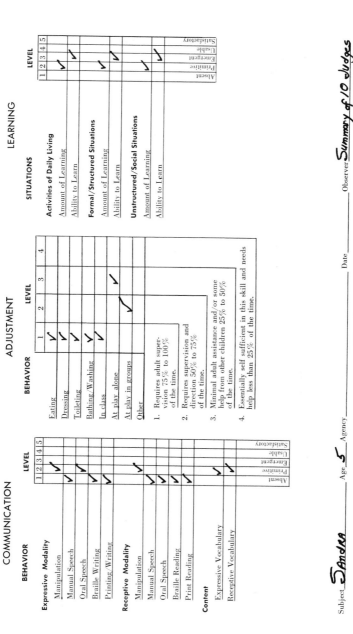

SUMMARY RATING FORM

Fig. 4.

19

feet). He could select objects that interested him and move toward them, maintaining visual contact. There seemed to be little, if any, awareness that most objects had meaning other than their visually stimulating quality. A toy car was not played with as such but was desired for its potential to reflect light and produce shadow patterns. Joe could also visually recognize people from a moderate distance. It is doubtful, however, whether he could discriminate facial features indicating an emotional attitude, unless he was very close.

It was difficult to keep glasses on Joe. At the slightest provocation, he would remove them. Sometimes he showed anger by throwing them with considerable force and accuracy.

Much information was received through the visual modality. Because Joe's needs were simple, he did not require the visual ability to do more than recognize highly stimulating objects, such as light bulbs and shiny or high contrast items. Glasses with high magnification restrict the visual field. Although this could have been a reason for rejection, it is more likely that throwing them offered an excellent way to demonstrate anger.

There was little obvious indication that Joe was receiving usable information through the auditory channel. He responded minimally to sounds within the room such as slamming doors, whistles, and objects being dropped. This auditory response was usually indicated by changes in behavior, such as a momentary pause before continuing the activity in which he was involved, a change in facial expression, or an eye blink. He did not attempt to localize the source of the sound. He refused to wear his hearing aid and therefore did not have amplification to assist him in hearing the room sounds. At this time, rejection of the hearing aid would cause one to believe that he was afraid of the aid, possibly due to a previous experience. The eye blinks and body changes did supply evidence that this sensory area could be further developed and become a way for Joe to get more meaningful information about his environment.

There was no reason to believe that the tactile, gustatory, or olfactory senses were impaired, although observation indicated that they were not being used much above the primitive level. These senses were used to gain basic information which allowed for low-level avoidance or selection of sensations. They could also be brought into use in emergency situations or when extreme emotions, such as fear or anger, existed. These senses could have been used in a greater variety of ways but were not.

Joe showed an almost exclusive visual response to any goal-directed behavior. The systems of touch, taste, and smell were used but not as much as might be expected of a child with a visual and auditory disability. He would move to an ojbect of interest. Then, if the object was not clearly perceived, he would either pick it up or move even closer. Tactile perception was not generally used to obtain more information about the object. In some instances, such as with food or where size and consistency were of interest, Joe would touch, smell, and taste to obtain more information; with clothing, he might tactually test for texture. While he did not have phobias of textures, smells, or sounds, he was attracted to hard shiny objects, probably because of their properties for reflecting light and providing visual stimulation.

Generally, Joe communicated by using objects as referents, and therefore objects were important in the communication process. This communication was observed in many instances, but ratings were below normal, since the objects served as goals rather than more abstract symbols. Thus he would "communicate" with an adult to obtain a shiny car. The car was then used for visual sensory stimulation to reflect light rather than symbolically as a toy miniature of an automobile.

People were part of the object-centered referent system. If the person offered some highly motivating service, such as providing him with objects, foods, or light bulbs, Joe communicated. He became a people-centered communicator when he manipulated the adult to satisfy his needs to obtain a sensory-stimulating object. People-centered communication was at a level between primitive and emergent. The fact that Joe was successfully manipulating people when motivated was evidence that he could, with guidance, move to a higher level of communication.

Tactile motor communication, which made up a majority of his observable expressive communication, was at a primitive level. Expressive attempts were designed to satisfy immediate needs, whether sensory or biological, and not for the purpose of communicating ideas and thoughts or for sharing experiences. Joe particularly enjoyed communicating with objects through manipulation. He resorted to oral expressive communication only to emphasize his objection to adult interference. At these times, his vocalizations were screams, yells, or cries at the primitive level.

As Joe is observed in a variety of situations throughout his day, several statements can be made about the way he interacts with his environment. Observation of his behavior also allows us to understand the priorities that he may have for any specific situation.

Environment here is a general term that includes physical and social variables. We assume that all children interact with many parts of their environment, in any situation. It is not usually possible to interpret a cause-and-effect relationship under these conditions, but we can, after careful observation, predict a child's preferences and have better than average accuracy as to how he will behave in any specific situation.

If we think of any interaction as involving, at least, an initiator and a recipient, then statements can be made about the usual and hence predictable patterns of these interactions. Frequently, in addition to the initiator and recipient, there is a mediating variable that is also recognizable through the observer. When one frequently observes any individual child in a certain type of situation, it should be possible to predict general patterns regarding the initiator, mediator, and recipient.

Joe seldom initiated an interaction with an adult unless it was for the purpose of obtaining or experiencing an object. If the object was readily available, then Joe would use it in a personal nature rather than as a way to adjust interpersonally. He would play with a light bulb, even though unlit, and happily exclude any peer contacts or adult interactions. Joe would characteristically initiate the interaction and the object would be the recipient. Whenever Joe used an adult to obtain an object for that interaction, the child would again be the initiator, the adult the mediator, and the object the recipient.

Another characteristic pattern for Joe involved the adult's initiating certain behavior, with Joe being the recipient. At such times, a mediator was not usually observed. A great majority of Joe's interactions would fall within these two patterns. He seldom interacted with peers and would not seek out adults unless it was for a specific purpose. When one considers the varieties possible for these interactions to take place, it becomes evident that Joe is making very little use of the opportunities available for interaction with his environment.

It is possible to apply this procedure to a variety of situations and compare observations so that one may determine similarities and differences between situations. If a child functions much higher in one situation than in another, then this information should be recorded so that it may be used at a later date to modify and further develop his program.

In addition to analysis of the areas of communication and adjustment, we are also concerned with observing characteristics of learning, which includes the process of learning as well as the content. It is our feeling that most learned behavior can be observed from the various situations involving the communication and adjustment patterns of the child.

If an adequate sample of behavior has been originally observed, then changes can be identified after a time period has elapsed. These changes we define as learned behavior. They may be brought about through a formal teaching experience, where another person directs the child through certain tasks that lead to changed behavior, or they may also occur through the child's experiences, which are not directed but are experienced during his average day. Learning probably occurs as a combination and direct result of these two conditions.

One of our first goals with Joe is to help him develop the ability to communicate with others. If he interacts with people and occasionally initiates this interaction in an appropriate way, then he can move toward independence in many areas. If he is capable of functioning independently yet does not have the needed skills to communicate expressively with others, then desire and motivation may be useless. Without the ability or understanding of the necessity to enter into communication with others, Joe will continue to devise other ways to accomplish his own limited goals. These goals may be the satisfaction of personal needs, such as increasing sensory stimulation, and may not be appropriate to normal, functioning society. Such goals set by Joe cannot lead to complete independence. Therefore, one concern is to motivate him to establish contact with others leading to rewarding, expressive communication.

By observing Joe, we have been able to gauge his potential and to establish baseline behavior that can be used to evaluate future progress. During the observation, we have begun setting long-term behavioral goals that will lead him toward a more rewarding life in his home, school, and community. This is part of the purpose of effective evaluation, not merely to describe behaviors but to do so for a purpose. We record present behaviors in a consistent way so that they may be used to further the child's development. By doing this, we use evaluative information to set future educational goals.

Another important area to be considered in evaluating a child is social adjustment. The opportunity to observe him in a variety of situations provides valuable information about his socialization patterns.

Much can be gained by observing the child's adjustment to new situations. A new room, a different table arrangement, a change in schedule, or new approaches by new people are all "new" situations to the child. Reaction to these changes provides a more complete picture of his ability to adjust flexibly. Joe was flexible; he enjoyed a change. Curiosity was exhibited when new people entered his surroundings, and new objects were a source of challenge. He did not approach these new people, however; he seldom approached others unless highly motivated. He did watch with interest. Responses to adult-initiated interactions were easy to obtain, particularly if there was a motivating object involved. The fact that the person was a stranger made little, if any, difference.

Joe's reaction to group play was significant. He would play in the same room with other children but did not interact with them. He preferred to be alone and was adept at manipulating the situation so that he was "alone," even when others were close by. He only approached adults or children when they possessed an object he desired, and he was aware of all interesting objects within the room. Joe demonstrated the ability to size up a situation quickly, select articles of interest, and pursue them with determination. If it was necessary to interact briefly in order to investigate the object or to secure it, then he was willing to do so.

Another area of interest when observing a child is his use of free time. These observations gave further evidence that Joe preferred playing alone. When given free time, his favorite activities centered around window play. During these periods, he would often discover objects of interest to him and take them to the window for further investigation and manipulation. The objects he selected were those that could be used to create a pleasing silhouette in the light; he would grasp a block, a wire triangle, a large comb, a plastic cut-out, or any other object that satisfied his needs, and quickly go to the window. When the new shadow was pleasing, he responded by squealing and dancing a quick little dance.

Setting Goals for Joe

By observing Joe in a variety of situations, we were able to establish goals that would lead him toward more independent functioning in the home, school, and community. These initial goals were revised several times as we learned more about his learning patterns. The following statements, which were among those originally recorded, led to establishing program priorities.

Experiences creating a need for socialization should be developed so that Joe can begin to interact with adults and peers in a variety of ways. These experiences can develop from normal daily occasions that are highly motivating and create a need to interact. For example, when Joe is interested in going outside to play or for a ride, he will be willing to take coats or wraps to others. Other daily experiences may be used in similar ways to encourage Joe's participation and interaction with his peers. During a meal or tea party, he may enjoy passing napkins, candy, or cups to the others. Then, as other children have their turn, he will begin to see the need to share.

Motivating objects can be used to attract his attention and can be introduced through stimulating group activities. Gather several objects, such as a flashlight, a bicycle reflector, colorful foil, a whistle or horn, an egg beater, and have share time. Joe can help pass and collect the objects. These same group sessions can be developed into interaction games such as marching, dancing, and other rhythm activities. Puppet play or ''smell and taste'' parties and craft activities can be used in a similar fashion. Mobiles can be created together while sitting or standing near the window. If the activity is rewarding, the desire to repeat it will lead to other opportunities for interaction.

Joe needs a variety of experiences. Therefore, it may be necessary to insist on brief exposures to activities of low interest to him. If, however, such experiences seem important, they could occur more frequently. Structured activities that are highly motivating and are accomplishing certain goals can be lengthened but should not become too demanding.

Task orientation and task completion can be integrated into daily activities. These tasks need not be puzzles, pegboards, blocks, or color cones. Joe can be encouraged to pick up shoes, take someone an object, move a chair, turn on the light, help stack the dishes, or feed the dog. Gradually more complicated tasks can be added that give him opportunities to experience success.

Visual discrimination activities lead to increased use of vision and also accomplish task-orientation needs. Picking up pennies and putting them in a piggy bank, helping pick up trash on the floor, pasting, and various art and craft activities can be stimulating. Imitating block patterns and grouping furniture in a dollhouse, lining up toy soldiers, simple hide-and-seek games with desirable toys, and similar play activities can create a need for more efficient use of vision. Rewarding visual discrimination activities will increase Joe's desires to repeat and expand visual experiences. He should begin wearing his glasses for close-up work during short periods and for activities requiring a greater degree of visual identification and discrimination. If he finds his glasses useful, he will soon recognize the need to wear them.

Tactile discrimination ability can also become useful to Joe and should be developed. Encourage tactile exploration. Motivate him to investigate tactually articles in a handbag, pocket, or grocery sack. In this way, he must feel it before he can see it, and tactual discrimination becomes valuable to him. Tactual discrimination can also be incorporated into auditory and visual activities by encouraging him to gain information in a variety of ways during daily experiences.

Language development should be a primary goal. Joe should be given every possible opportunity to participate in meaningful experiences, as these will be valuable to increase inner and receptive language. Experiences in each sensory area are important. Daily occurrences can offer valuable opportunities, and Joe should be included in as many activities as possible. Trips to town, helping cook, making popcorn, watching TV, going to movies, looking at books, taking nature walks, and enjoying family meals are valuable to Joe and provide many opportunities for language experiences.

All attempts to express himself, however primitive, should be encouraged. Joe needs to know that his voice does something, that his gestures are useful, and that his every attempt to make his wishes known are desirable and worth the effort. Expression of needs and desires should be encouraged when motivation is high. If Joe wants an object or food, he will be more stimulated to communicate by verbalization or gestures. By rewarding his gestures or primitive vocalizations, he can be led to increased development of expressive communication and eventually move to higher levels.

Constant exposure to others using language is also important. Joe needs visual and auditory language. For the present time, the most appropriate method of communication should be a total approach, which combines the uses of gestures and manual signs with the appropriate words. Total communication also includes facial expressions (sometimes somewhat exaggerated), body language, and pantomime. All opportunities for growth through language development are valuable. Begin using manual signs that are most meaningful and frequently needed on a consistent basis. These can serve as a beginning vocabulary: toilet, no, yes, good, bad, after a while, stop, go, come, play, eat, water, and bed.

Auditory training can best be carried out by taking advantage of opportunities to develop voice and sound awareness as the occasion presents itself during the day. By calling attention to slamming doors, whistling tea kettles, falling objects, and voice sounds, Joe will become more aware and gradually begin associating the sound with the source.

Joe should begin learning to make use of his hearing aid and other forms of amplification. Start with short periods and help him see the advantage of these devices in making his environment more interesting. Let him feel the vibration of a record player, alarm clock, and television. Place his hand on his throat when he is vocalizing. It will also be useful for him to feel your mouth and throat occasionally when you speak. As awareness develops and motivation increases, he will gradually begin attempting to initiate vocalizations. Imitation skills will need to be developed. Begin with gross movement and later move to tongue gymnastics; blowing activities (windmill and bubble pipe); and babbling, imitative games.

Daily living skills can continue to be developed. The best time to work on these skills is as they normally occur and when the knowledge is needed. More socially acceptable eating habits can be encouraged during meals and tea parties or at snack time. Dressing can be "practiced" after accidents, water play, at bath, or at clean-up time. The need for good grooming can be emphasized before going on a trip or to a party.

Joe can be encouraged to dress more quickly if the coming event is one of high interest to him. This may be accomplished by having him dress or undress for a fun activity such as swimming. He should be allowed to suffer the consequences for his delay in being late for the activity. Then as he begins to understand and respond more appropriately, his attempts should be rewarded by getting into the pool or to the tea party at the same time as the others.

A normal diet should be encouraged. High preference foods need to be withheld until he samples low preference food. Between meal snacks and tea parties should not provide him with enough nourishment to make avoidance at regular meals easier. Become aware of ways to help him make better use of gustatory and olfactory discrimination. Increased taste experiences during meal time will be helpful. Encourage him to smell flowers, foods, new toys, and materials. Occasionally insist that he smell or taste before looking. Let him taste ingredients being used to make a cake or casserole. He can help spray the bathroom or experience new perfume or cologne. These and other opportunities will occur frequently and require little time or effort.

Observations are useful in establishing beginning points. A record of behavior should be made as it is seen and can be the basis for establishing specific goals. Later, continued reference to this recorded information will be helpful to evaluate procedures and progress. More specific goals may then be defined and ways of reaching these goals established. As the goals are reached, more advanced ones can then be set.

If, within the designated period of time, a particular goal is not reached, it must be reevaluated and a decision made as to whether it is appropriate at this time. If inappropriate, it can then be removed as a teaching goal for this child, delayed for the time being, or modified to become more meaningful.

Joe is a child with a group of characteristics, abilities, disabilities and learning patterns that are unique to him. His abilities are high compared to many severely and profoundly handicapped children. Sandra, the other child we will describe, is in a lower functional group and is also severely and profoundly handicapped. Later, examples of behaviors seen in other children will be included when it seems important for clarification.

Observing Sandra

Sandra was lying on the bed, her head dangling off the edge, with an empty bottle in her mouth and a blanket clutched to her. Her face was red, her eyes were fixated on the window light, and an adept index finger was flicking the bottle. Total contentment would best describe this five-year-old. Nothing more was needed to make her life complete. This behavior was representative of Sandra's way of life. She constantly used her environment for simple sensory stimulation. Hours could be spent lying on her back watching a light. This occurred whether she was alone or with people close by, even with children playing games and talking beside her. If anyone moved near enough to touch her or if her light source was "cut off," she might move. More often, though, she would stop and wait for conditions to change again. An intense effort by an adult produced some change. She would conform passively to some directions. Simple and very specific motor patterns could be taught. She could drink from a cup, for instance, but could not be depended on to do this consistently. Just as frequently, she might pick up the cup and dump it on the table or pretend that her flaccid hand could not grasp an object. However, there were just enough times when something happened during the contacts that would encourage an adult to keep trying.

Categories that we used to describe and rate Joe may also be applied to Sandra. In Figures 1-4, we have compared ratings of these two children summarized from a group of ten judges. The average of the judges' opinion on each rated item may be useful in recognizing differences in the behavior of the two children.

Sandra was on a bottle and seldom ate solids. She would not chew and quickly shoved solid and lumpy foods from her mouth. We put cookies on the table and helped her discover them; however, she showed no curiosity and refused to pick them up. Our attempts to put candy in her hand were also futile. She would not feed herself. When the spoon was placed in her hand and pushed close to her mouth, she still watied for more assistance. Only if the spoon touched her lip would she open her mouth.

Dressing and bathing skills were at the same level. She would cooperate passively but failed to assist in the most elementary way. For example, she would not straighten her arm into the shirt sleeve, and when her shirt was pulled down almost over her head, but still covering her face, she would wait indefinitely until someone pulled it down further. If Sandra was encouraged to pull up her pants by bending her body over and placing her hands near them, she would remain in that position. The same was true if her hands were placed on a sock to complete the task of pulling it on. If Sandra was sitting on the bed and someone lifted her foot toward a sock, she held her foot in that same position for longer than seemed possible. She reacted the same way when her hands were placed under the faucet for washing. She continued no action once begun but remained pliable and waited patiently for more assistance.

Toilet behavior was similar. Sandra would stand near the window engaged in finger light play and wet herself with no apparent awareness. Whether soiled or freshly cleaned, there was no change in her behavior. She was not disturbed by the soiled pants nor was she curious. When placed on a toilet, she would sit for a short period, then get off and move toward the window for more light play.

In the activities of daily living, Sandra required adult supervision more than 75 percent of the time in all skills. As for ability to learn activities of daily living skills, we felt Sandra could, with assistance, move to a higher skill level and would then need adult supervision between 50 and 75 percent of the time.

During observation it was noted that Sandra was using her vision at an emergent level. Pupil size did change with different light intensity. There was always the impression that Sandra was staring, not focusing. She seemed to be looking beyond the object or person, even though there was a feeling that her attention was directed to that object.

When she moved from one place to the other, more information could be obtained. She would miss chairs and tables and exhibited an ability to see some smaller objects in the room. This happened regardless of whether the object was between the child and a light source, such as the window. The way that Sandra used her feet to gather information was even more significant. As she moved across the room, she would almost at random touch a fairly small object with her foot. She would occasionally pick it up and look at it. If there were enough reflective properties or other desirable characteristics, she would use the object for further visual or tactile stimulation. Here Sandra was using combined visual and tactile senses to experience an object. Even more enlightening, though, was her consistency in locating the object. When she touched an object with her foot, it looked like an accident. The consistency of the act, however, made it obvious that she was using visual cues from a great distance to locate the object.

While Sandra was using her sight as a major sensory area for gaining information, this area was rated emergent. This is a low classification, but the rating is based on the fact that she was obtaining information at a nearly primitive level. The emergent category suggests that this modality should be used in a program based on her needs.

Sandra's auditory reception seemed almost nonexistent. There was no response to verbal commands. Even shouted commands of "Don't," "No," and "Stop it" brought no observable change in behavior. There was no jumping or other startle response at loud sounds, and she did not seem to notice music. Noise from group activities did not seem to make her nervous, but she did tend to select a remote area of the room when there was much activity.

Less observable and certainly less consistent were other small signs that some auditory sensations were experienced. There were times when voice quality and emotional tone did make a difference. Sandra occasionally seemed nervous if arguments were going on around her. She became even less active if an adult spoke to her in anger. Other sounds sometimes evoked reactions. If the television or radio were loud, she would hit herself and cry. While she did not usually seem to be aware of music, there were times when she would move toward its source and touch it with her body. Generally, though, there was an almost nonexistent response to sound. It did not seem to be changing and for the present was not a useful priority in a teaching program, but auditory experiences should continue as should further observation. Auditory receptive behavior was noted as primitive.

Several olfactory-gustatory stimuli were introduced during the observation. Sandra responded negatively to sweet and sour tastes. She also rejected most items with an odor. If it was new, she rejected it, yet there was no obvious pattern that could be used to introduce new sensations. She did occasionally discriminate and sometimes indicated preferences. Frequently, the preference was shown before she was allowed to taste. This suggested efficient use of another sense to obtain an impression. She was encouraged to taste chocolate, sugar, a pickle, peppermint, lemon, and salt. Even force was difficult when she had decided not to taste. She immediately generalized from a negative experience. If she found one food undesirable, all remaining samples were refused.

Tactile reception always involved self-stimulating behavior. Sandra would move toward the floor fan and rest her chin on it to feel the vibrations. She sometimes moved her whole body to the fan for additional sensations. When her hand was placed on the record player, she lowered her chin to rest it on the edge of the player. She did not usually use her hands to reach out or investigate objects and refused objects presented; she was using other parts of her body for this purpose. Her face, chin, and feet all functioned as tactile receptors. It is difficult to surmise what information she was receiving, but certainly time and temperature differences were discriminated. Behavior that might analyze form could not be noted. In fact, there was little evidence that Sandra had any motivation toward using form discrimination in a purposeful manner. A spoon for instance had no more functional use to her than a pencil or a nail. This behavior was also noted as primitive, even though one could see that, with appropriate motivation, her ability in this area might be directed to promote learning.

There was almost no vocal communication and only a little motor expression. Gross body movements might be interpreted as primitive behavior. So might crying and screaming. There was little else, though, that would indicate either desire or ability to move outside of herself and communicate with others.

Sandra seemed much more aware of environmental situations than could be objectively recorded. It did seem worthwhile to note that if a motivating source could be found, Sandra might move to satisfy a basic need, such as hunger. However, our initial observations indicated that, for whatever reason, she could not or would not communicate beyond the primitive level.

Sandra interacted positively with almost no one. If other children were close by, there was little indication that she recognized them. If they entered her territory, she would move away or cry. In these situations, she was either passive or negative in her response. Much the same behavior was observed interacting with adults. It was possible, however, for an adult to structure the situation so that some degree of conformity was exhibited. This was not done by Sandra's choice, though, and she would usually object violently if forced to produce.

The most typical pattern of adjustment for Sandra was to be totally interested in a closed behavioral system, including only herself or an occasional object. She hit and bit herself during some periods and gouged her eyes at others. Masturbatory behavior was evident. However, none of these behaviors were constant and uninterruptible.

Sandra had almost no observable goals, even at a primitive level. She was not essentially a social or aggressive child. She was more nonsocial and unwilling to put forth any effort in her behalf.

Goals for Sandra

Growth in independence, including all activities of daily living, should be the area of major concentration in goal planning. The bottle should be withdrawn completely and Sandra should be encouraged to drink from a cup with assistance. This sudden change will probably bring strong demonstrations of anger. This is Sandra's way of expressing her opinion and should be met with understanding accompanied by confidence and determination. When she realizes she cannot "win," she will adjust to the cup. If appropriate, she might be held in the lap to eat or drink, then as she moves toward the table and chair for feeding, rewards can be used so that she will continue to change her behavior.

For the first period as she adjusts to the cup, foods should be mashed. After the initial adjustment, the consistency of her foods should be gradually changed. Favorite foods work best as starters. She may prefer applesauce, sweets, or tomato flavors. If so, select a coarser variety of these foods. When she spits out the food, be ready to catch it with a spoon and give her another chance. Avoid food in solid lumps such as beans, heavy meats, or even rice. These come later. Food textures and odor will probably make a bigger difference than taste. Awareness of this will make the transition to solids easier.

Gradual introduction of foods that require chewing is important. The more work she has to do to handle food in her mouth the better, as this will lead to oral muscular development. Sticky foods, such as peanut butter, or crusty foods, such as dry toast, can be useful. These should be introduced soon. If necessary, the peanut butter can be put on a spoon and eased into the roof of her mouth. No doubt some activity will be required for Sandra to get the peanut butter out.

Assist Sandra during mealtime by covering her hand and helping her bring the spoon to her mouth. Help her touch the spoon to her lip. Then decrease assistance for a few moments and allow her to complete the task. Over a period of time, she will begin helping more and more as she is given less and less assistance. Begin requiring more help from Sandra at the end of the task rather than the beginning. She will be more motivated to cooperate when the foods are her favorite tastes and consistency and may refuse to help when the food is not desirable.

Feeding should be on a regular schedule. If she eats less one meal, she will be hungrier at the next. She can learn to make these changes. Sandra is a husky child and missing part of a meal should not be a major problem.

Sandra should be dressed in loose, comfortable clothing for easier access during the training period. Continue to "help" her dress by covering her hand and gently guiding it. Awareness of her body will lead to beginning responses in dressing and toilet training. Play tactual games by touching and tickling her stomach, legs, and feet, both with and without clothing. She can occasionally wear only panties, if the weather permits. Going barefoot is also helpful to develop body awareness and offers her additional possibilities for tactual receptive experiences. Sandra should be dressed and undressed at appropriate times, such as before a shower, after soiling her clothes, and at bedtime. It is not necessary to remove her clothes only for the purpose of teaching her to dress.

Toilet behavior should be scheduled for several weeks. Chart her "activities" so a pattern can be established. This will also record progress. When patterns are noted, toilet schedule should be changed to meet her needs better. Also, as she learns to control herself and eliminate less frequently, progress can be recognized even though there has been little success in "catching" her. Stay with her in the toilet for now and do not demand that she sit for long periods. The beginning goal is to set up a routine and frequent, short periods are best. Require her to sit on the toilet until she is told to get up. Five minutes can be a long time. The goal now is to decrease the 100 percent supervision required in all activities of daily living, not to perfect the skills. Other goals may be set as progress occurs.

Sandra's use of vision can be developed through activities and experiences that increase her need to see. Opportunities for visual experiences must be planned frequently. A dark room with a small flashlight and several shiny objects should prove successful in directing Sandra's vision and developing more ocular control. Interesting objects can also be used to increase mobility. If she sees something desirable or wants to go to the window, she will be willing to look to see how to get there, even when obstacles are in her way. In the same way, a flashlight within her visual field may motivate Sandra to go up or down the steps. Other problems can be solved in the same way by giving Sandra the opportunity to use her vision as motivation to direct herself. The environment should be visually stimulating whenever possible. The windows, walls, and ceilings provide backgrounds easy to decorate with stimulating materials.

Hearing should be developed through a multisensory approach.

While seeing and feeling, she also needs to have appropriate auditory stimulation. For example, while performing household duties, the adult can use this time to talk, laugh, or sing to Sandra. When she touches the record player to feel it, she also has the opportunity to hear the music. A noisy toy used to "tickle" can also be heard. Isolated experiences, involving only hearing without vibrations or accompanying sensory experience, will probably be meaningless at this point. Concentrate on awareness through stimulation of all sensory areas.

A variety of tactile experiences is important. This calls for additional planning and energy expenditures. Use a variety of textures on Sandra's bed, rub her briskly with a towel after the bath, massage her with lotion or powder, comb her hair vigorously, and give her tactual stimulation through close body contact. Plan experiences such as rolling on the floor or grass, feeling warm and cold water, playing with ice, walking in wet sand, and bumping into a leafy hedge. Other daily experiences can provide additional ideas for sources of tactual–kinesthetic stimulation. Many of these experiences will occur spontaneously, but it is important to be aware and plan others. Tactual stimulation is important for all children, but particularly so for Sandra, as she has demonstrated an ability and some desire to gain information through the sensory area.

Gustatory-olfactory experiences also need to be incorporated into Sandra's daily schedule. Most can be experienced at normal eating periods. Other exposure to taste and smell can be made available as situations occur spontaneously. The room can be supplied with flowers, Sandra can be taken to areas of the house with unique odors, and various trips to the grocery store or neighbors' houses can increase olfactory awareness. Some sensory experiences may not seem appealing, but these will help her learn to gain and profit from the additional information received.

Since Sandra seems to have a low, almost primitive, level of reception in all sensory areas, she will need many experiences in each before motivation will be recognized and discrimination developed. The stimulation as outlined is mostly single sensory in nature. That is, one sensory area is stimulated at a time. Attention should also be given to ways where joint sensory experiences may be presented and used. The use of two or more sensory areas to "learn about" objects is especially important in concept development. Sandra does not do this in any observable way. Reward for using all possible senses can be given just for attending at first. If she picks up an object and smells it, she should be encouraged to taste and feel it. A brightly colored bell also rings and may be cold or warm depending on where it is found.

Signals should be developed so that Sandra can begin to anticipate daily activity. Touch her mouth before feeding periods, pat her pants when being changed or seated on the toilet, hold her closely for a few moments before bedtime, and rub her hands together when they are to be washed. The signals are always accompanied by appropriate verbal expressions. Signals appropriate to Sandra's daily schedule can be invented and used by all who work with her. If it seems useful, similar kinds of signals can be used to "name" familar individuals for Sandra. A soft pinch on the cheek can be Mama and a pat on the head can be Papa. This might provide another way to associate experiences with a signal, which is the beginning of receptive communication. Signals should be consistent. Everyone must agree on this so that the pat on the head is Papa and not "good girl." It is always important to talk to her with the signals. Attention to sound is important. Even if Sandra cannot discriminate the connection of sound and gesture, it is still valuable.

In providing all sensory experiences, gross materials with a highly motivating quality are first used. Two or more different objects offered at the same time give a choice and aid in developing sensory discrimination. Later, more similar objects can be used to develop this ability further.

Sandra's pattern of interaction with her environment must be modified. Since she is adept at "turning off" any attempts at change, it will be necessary at first to find ways to enter her system. If she is motivated toward a specific object, than an adult might share that object or even bring it to her and leave—but on a frequent basis so that any signs of anticipation may be recognized and reinforced. If she remains predominantly object oriented, then an approach using variety might help. Acceptance of variety gives a broad base for use to work and develop motivation. Even if Sandra refuses to accept some objects, this will be useful information in order to establish differentiated responses for other items. It will then be possible to predict still other objects that might be used. The objects can be used to promote more meaningful experiences. They will also aid in the adult–child interaction process.

While it is possible that Sandra will relate to other children, this part of her development is not of immediate concern. Her communicative skills are too low for other than the most rudimentary type of play and socializing. For the future, exposure to children is needed and should be observed, but no structured program of interaction is recommended immediately. A primary concern with Sandra is the fact that she is her own social system. Interactions with both children and adults are either neutral or negative. She seems perfectly content to stimulate herself in only the most basic ways and thus there is no motivation for growth or change. She is content to vegetate, to allow her basic needs to be cared for, and to withdraw from previous attempts. Most socialization will need to be initiated by an adult. This is a step beyond her most common interaction pattern, which is to be both initiator and recipient, frequently with an object as mediator. The adult, at first, will find it easier to work with an object, such as a flashlight, and in that way become involved. If this works, then less stimulating objects may be used, with the person becoming more stimulating. This develops social awareness, which is a necessary initial step.

Sandra's severe and profoundly handicapping condition and her low functioning behavior in all areas makes her a most difficult child with whom to work. This is further compounded by habit patterns accumulated over a period of time. These patterns are inhibitory to development and are especially so in her ability or desire to form social relationship at even the most primitive level. The lack of motivation toward any task except-self stimulation is an area of major concern. This prevails over all areas of development that require direction. It will need much consideration and careful analysis for progress as a program is developed.

Most of this initial program plan will focus on activities of daily living and use of free time. Maximum adult-child contact occurs when basic needs such as elimination, eating, and dressing are being met. The free time period also offers situations when an adult can enter in at the child's level. Most of these contacts will be physical. The adult should continuously talk but not expect response.

Observation is, of course, important. Any inkling of cooperation, imitative pattern, or anticipating behavior should be recorded and attempts made to reproduce them. It is difficult to predict areas of progress, but with careful observation and analysis, it should be possible in a short time to specify several and to use these in plans for the future.

EDUCATIONAL PLANNING

Educational planning for the child, setting goals, and deciding what must be done to reach these established goals must be preceded by evaluation. A goal cannot be selected until one is thoroughly familiar with the developmental age or functional level of the child. By establishing a baseline through observation and evaluation, we can know where the child is and what he is doing. Evaluation and goal setting is best accomplished by persons who are experienced and trained in working with the severely and profoundly handicapped child. It is possible, however, for others to identify behaviors that are important in developing a plan for each child.

In doing this, it is necessary to be aware of many variables. The child's use of senses is important, as is his source of motivation and his interests. Observation of these characteristics and organization of the observations make it possible to learn a considerable amount about the child and to establish initial goals which can be used to change his behavior and increase his potential for further development.

Establishing a Baseline

A baseline should be established. In order to plan adequately for the child, it is necessary to know his levels of functioning. In addition to helping set goals for the child, this baseline information will be valuable in measuring progress. Progress can only be measured from a starting point, and if some progress can be observed, then priorities can be set up and other goals identified. The baseline information should be recorded. As the child progresses, it may be easy to forget the behavior demonstrated when work began. Being specific about what is seen now will be helpful in the future.

It is not helpful to say that the child cannot manage the toilet by himself and therefore the goal is to get him to do so independently. This is far too broad. It is better to say that he does not appear to control his bladder and that he urinates approximately once an hour, apparently unaware of what has happened. In this case, awareness might be the first step to accomplish. Another example may be that he is observed opening his mouth for a bite of food only when it touches his lip, not when it is held close; therefore, he is probably not using his vision or the sense of smell to give him information. This observation will be helpful in planning the next step.

Target Behavior

In establishing a baseline, it is also important to be aware of and record behaviors that might be called "targets." We often speak of a target behavior as one that has high priority. What behavior is seen that needs prompt attention? This will vary from child to child. One child may click everything he can grasp against his teeth. We now think more specifically about this behavior and observe carefully when, why, and how it is exhibited. By recording "when" and "why," plans can be made to change or prevent the behavior, and by recording the "how often," we can keep track of our progress. The behavior may still be clearly evident at some later date, but if it is occurring less often, then we know we are progressing toward our goal.

Learning to Observe

Observation has been mentioned several times as being most important in evaluating the child. Some of the ideas we have found helpful have come from recent research using videotape for evaluation. This research gives us substantial evidence that it is possible to train observers to assess certain behaviors of severely and profoundly handicapped children. These same techniques can be applied to "live" observations. In this way, effective plans can be made and goals set for the child as a result of the structured observation of behavior in a variety of situations.

As observations of behavior are categorized, differences in levels of the child's development will be obvious. There will be times of the day when he is obviously more productive. The process of identifying these times and situations should give considerable direction to his program's development.

In this section, variables have been discussed which are important in observing and working with children. Much of Chapter 2 is more specific in outlining techniques and methods applicable to modifying the behaviors and allowing for maximum development in each. Chapter 3 outlines other factors and goals necessary in developing plans for the severely and profoundly handicapped child.

It is our premise that the ultimate goal for the severely and profoundly handicapped person is to live in an integrated society as independently as possible. For this to be realized, those involved with the child's program must agree and make plans early with this goal in mind. Considerable effort must be put forth with the child early in life to stimulate him and develop his interests. Then as he progresses and steps are made toward integrating him into society, the goals will become more realistic and specific.

The following sections deal with the development of specific skills and behaviors, such as how to make the child aware of sound, ways to increase use of vision, and methods of developing independent mobility within the environment. Even though these areas are treated individually, we realize that each is a part of the child. They continually overlap and most are areas of normal development for any child.

BIBLIOGRAPHY

Ambron SR: Child Development. San Francisco, Rinehart, 1975

Anderson R, Wolf J (eds): The Multiply Handicapped Child. Springfield, Ill, Charles C Thomas, 1969

Bateman BD: The Essentials of Teaching. San Rafael, Calif, Dimensions, 1971

Bayley N: Bayley Scales of Infant Development. New York, The Psychological Corp, 1969

Cruickshank WM (ed): Psychology of Exceptional Children and Youth. Englewood Cliffs, NJ, Prentice-Hall, 1971

Curtis WS, Donlon ET, Tweedie D: Deaf-blind children: An examination procedure for behavior characteristics. Educ Visually Handicapped 6 (3): 67–72, 1974

Curtis WS, Donlon ET, Wagner E: Deaf-Blind Children: Evaluating Their Multiple Handicaps. New York, American Foundation for the Blind, 1970

Diebold MH: A comparison of two approaches to the assessment of deaf-blind children. Unpublished doctoral dissertation, University of Georgia, 1975

Dunn LM (ed): Exceptional Children in the Schools. New York, Holt, Rinehart and Winston, 1973

Findlay J, et al: A Planning Guide: The Pre-School Curriculum. Chapel Hill, NC, Chapel Hill Training-Outreach Project, 1975

Gesell, AL: The First Five Years. New York, Harper and Row, 1940

Hammer EK (ed): Behavior Modification Programs for Deaf-Blind Children. Dallas, Callier Speech and Hearing Center, 1970

Haring NG, Schiefelbusch RL (eds): Methods in Special Education. New York, McGraw-Hill, 1967

Joiner E: Graded Lessons in Speech. Danville, Ky, Kentucky School for the Deaf, 1946

Kirk S, Lord F (eds): Exceptional Children: Educational Resources and Perspectives. Boston, Houghton Mifflin, 1974

Mery BD: Developmental processes in a congenital rubella child. Doctoral dissertation, Syracuse University, 1976

Sanford AR: Learning Accomplishment Profile. University of North Carolina

Tweedie D: Behavioral change in a deaf-blind multihandicapped child. Volta Rev 76 (4): 1974

2
Recognizing and Implementing for Specific Needs

INTRODUCTION

Where do we go from here? Up to now, the major emphasis has been directed toward describing the children and some of the problems confronting those concerned with the severely and profoundly handicapped child. But what happens now? Much can be done to help this child. Some mistakes that may have already been made can be corrected and certain other negative aspects can be avoided. Important decisions must be made. Who will "teach" the child? Who is going to accept the responsibility of planning for this child? Who will carry out the plans? Who can?

Programs for preschool handicapped children have developed in some areas. However, relatively few programs are accepting young multiply or severely handicapped children. Also these programs may not be available to many families because of geographic location. Many programs will only accept children who are "school age," yet training of these children must begin long before this. Too much valuable time is lost when it is necessary to wait until they are six. In addition, many learned behaviors will have to be unlearned. Thus, much of the first teaching efforts may be spent in helping the child unlearn certain behaviors: backing up rather than going forward. Almost no "program" will accept the full responsibility of severely and profoundly handicapped infants. Who then will teach this child?

Selecting a Teacher

If we can assume that a child is always learning, then the person who is promoting the learning is the teacher. Therefore, the person who is going to be spending a great deal of time with the child will be the "teacher." The decision, then, as to "who will teach" is answered; the one who will teach is the one who is there.

The decision as to who will do the planning may be another matter. The person who is responsible for the child will need some assistance and advice consisting in part of how to make educational plans, how to set and reach developmental goals, how to stimulate the child, and more. Medical diagnoses, such as hearing and visual evaluations, will be needed. Recommendations for corrective measures that might be beneficial to the child's auditory and visual input will be valuable. Orthopedic correction may be necessary. Other medical specialists may be needed. The service of a family counselor may also be advisable as the family tries to make the adjustments necessary to accept this child into the home. Primary concern here is focused on the person who will be teaching, whether this person is a professional teacher, early childhood specialist, a volunteer, or a parent.

We cannot say that anyone can teach, but a person who sincerely *wants* to teach can do an amazing job with some basic information and an experienced person to call on for additional assistance and leadership. For teaching to be successful, some knowledge is necessary, some experience will be valuable, an opportunity to observe others working with similar children is helpful, and an educational consultant is almost imperative. Most of this is available in many communities.

The titles of such persons may be different in each area. A child development specialist may be a Head Start teacher in one community and a nurse or a social worker in another. Because of this, it is necessary to be familiar with those persons who have interest, experience, and professional commitment. Programs will also vary in their names and objectives. These variations offer alternatives that are valuable and necessary.

There are times when a parent or teacher cannot accept a child. When this happens, the condition should be recognized and alternatives presented. Foster placement and special short-time residences are two of these alternatives. These problems are not easily solved, and their solution may require expert consultation. This is discussed further in a later section.

What Kind of Teaching

When one approaches the problem of teaching the severely and profoundly handicapped child, it is necessary to shift in perspective more than in any other field of education. Many avenues usually open to a teacher are closed when working with these children. One needs to know techniques that have been successful in teaching children with other handicaps. It is also important to be familiar with developmental sequences and normal teaching practices. In the final summary, however, these techniques do not work and the knowledge of normal and abnormal development is to little avail.

Many of the incidents and examples that follow are not presented in traditional education jargon. They are not meant to be. They are designed to stimulate the reader to think as a new teacher might when faced with the complexity and loneliness that comes with working with these children. Or, if the reader happens to have lived through this situation, perhaps there will be a chance to recall the unique but satisfying efforts demanded in working with and planning for the severely and profoundly handicapped child.

The following methods are not necessarily designed for a school type program, but it is hoped that they will be beneficial to anyone who is interested in the severely and profoundly handicapped child. We are addressing our discussion toward stimulating the child and finding ways to make him more aware, even during his first weeks. Suggestions are concerned with ways to wake the child, to help him begin to know at a very early age that there is something going on. This "teaching" begins in the bed or on your lap, not in a "school." It is necessary to help the child out of his "shell," if he is in one. He should be active and involved with himself and his environment in appropriate ways. Ideally, intervention begins before wrong habits are formed (e.g., self-stimulation, avoidance), but if this is not possible, some of these habits may have already developed. Then ways must be found to extinguish them and develop substitute uses of his energies.

Some wonder how working with a severely and profoundly handicapped child could be appealing. Perhaps it is because this kind of teaching requires intense effort and imagination and gives one a feeling of being totally involved. At first there may even be a feeling of surprise that this child can be "taught" anything. When progress seems slow, it is assumed that more time will be needed or that perhaps there is another way to approach the problem. For those who love to work with a child who has far to go and needs so much, the challenge is great. There is always one more thing the child needs to learn, and being involved in this teaching process can be exciting. Some are even selfish about teaching, even when someone else can do it as well. The successes are rewards beyond description.

On the other hand, there are disappointments, frustrating experiences, and rough days. Not every day is smooth sailing. There are times when it is difficult to get the response wanted from the child. Responses do not always come as soon as you might expect. After working hard to prepare for a lovely experience, everything may backfire. The child may vomit or soil his pants at the most inopportune time. Or he may persist in masturbating while you are trying to direct his attention toward a planned activity. Every door may seem closed when trying to find help and all may seem impossible. In addition, there may be little encouragement from others. An outsider's sympathy and pity for you and the child can be irritating. However, these disappointments and frustrations can be overcome.

Who Can Teach

It is not necessary to have a college degree to work with a child. A master's degree in special education with emphasis on education of the severely and profoundly handicapped child might be useful; however, much can be done without this. Training, education, and experience can be beneficial, but a person who has not had these educational experiences can still be a valuable asset to these children.

Young teacher aides with little or no college training and no preparation for this kind of teaching have been placed in classrooms with experienced teachers and have quickly become valuable additions. Perhaps these teacher assistants were familiar with normal child development, perhaps they were endowed with good, workable common sense, or maybe they merely loved to work with children; whatever the reason, many of them learned quickly and were immensely helpful.

Mothers can teach. They have been doing it for years, and one could guess that they may have succeeded more often than the "school." These mothers use different approaches; some are inconsistent and they make many "mistakes," but look at the number of children who enter regular school apparently well prepared and eager to learn. If we did not feel that mothers, fathers, grandparents, and other close relatives could teach, then there would be little reason for this book. These are the people who are needed. We must have their support, their attention, and their best efforts. These are the ones who will probably be with the child from the beginning; therefore, they must become knowledgeable. They must learn how and what to do with the severely and profoundly handicapped child. Those who have devoted years to the study and education of these children have other opportunities to contribute. Our interest is directed toward the person who will be spending a great deal of time with this child during his early developmental years, the one who will be responsible for guiding him toward independence.

Assuming we are addressing the "teacher," whether mother, home teacher, volunteer, or grandparent, there are some general statements that may be helpful. First, it is necessary to realize that there is no one way to teach. There is no magic formula. Each severely handicapped child is unique; his needs are different and his degree of handicaps is different from that of any other child. A technique and a way of working with the child that is best for this particular situation must be developed. It is important, though, to begin training the child as early as possible, so you cannot wait until this technique has been developed. Also, if the child is several years old before you first have the opportunity of working with him, it is necessary to begin as soon as possible. Today is a better day to begin than tomorrow will be and mulling over yesterday will accomplish very little. Appropriate early training, not necessarily infantile, prevents the need for much unlearning and will save time later.

Expectations

Developmentally, the child may be infantile in many areas. Knowing the developmental age, his functioning age, is more important than his chronological age. Little will be accomplished by comparing him to children who are developing normally for their ages, but it will be useful to know at approximately what level he is functioning. Once his developmental age is known in several areas, plans as to where he goes next can be made. Also, depending on many factors, some severely and profoundly handicapped children seem to progress faster than others, and more time may be required to learn most skills than is normally expected. Therefore, comparisons are often discouraging, frustrating, and damaging to enthusiasm.

Progress can be slow on a day-to-day basis, as this child has to be taught much that other children learn incidentally. Look further into the future than tomorrow, and after several weeks or months look back and recall all he has learned. Comparing him to himself and noting progress over long periods of time can be encouraging, particularly when miracles are not expected.

Teacher expectations are important. Expect nothing and probably nothing will happen. Believe he can reach some particular goal and keep working at it; never give up! There is a way to reach any child. If he does not seem to want to do anything but lie in bed, think of ways to get some reaction, even if it is an objection (scream). This is a start. He will not learn much if he stays in bed all day. It is important to remember that no matter how hard you try; it will still take a little longer. Once a working relationship is established with the child and some results are attained, the next stage may be a little easier. When he takes his first small steps forward or begins to come out of his world, progress may be somewhat faster. The first steps are the hardest because not only does he have to learn to know and develop confidence in you but he is also expected to *do* something.

Remember that the child will not have confidence in you if you lack confidence in yourself. You must be sure of your goals before requiring a certain behavior, then later look back and evaluate. If your efforts have not been successful, then mistakes may be recognized and analyzed. Once a plan has been developed, it is important to move positively and with confidence. The bond or trust that has been developed is made stronger by this action.

Time can be lost by being overly critical. Occasional feelings of fatigue, disgust, self-pity, and anger are normal. It is easy to make mistakes, and everyone falls short occasionally. There are times, though, when you are proud, and as the successes add up, then this pride is felt more often.

Time Out

The child cannot have all of your time. He will require a one-to-one relationship for many of his learning experiences during the first few months, but you must also think of yourself. Occasionally, sit down for a cup of coffee and say, "I'm tired and I am going to sit here and relax for a few minutes." This may seem more trouble than it is worth at first, but by sticking to what is said, the child will soon get the picture. All children have an uncanny way of knowing when someone is tired and they are often good at capturing one's attention one way or another. You must be more determined and smarter than the child, and there are times when you may wonder if you are. This determination is good. Persistence on the part of the child will be a valuable asset as you learn to use it to get him to do the things you want.

You must occasionally get away; this is beneficial both to you and to the child. Day-to-day life may change considerably when you become involved with a child who needs so much, but everything cannot change completely. The child must know that he is loved, but that all is not his. A schedule is planned with him in mind but also with the consideration of others. This child needs and will require much attention, but others, your family and friends, deserve some attention, too.

The ability to maintain objectivity and a perspective is always important in working with children. It is especially so in the intense, individual relationship that must be established with the severely and profoundly handicapped child. One way to do this is to get away regularly. That is why we have stressed this point. There are all too many cases where one may observe an adult and child becoming so involved that it is their only life. This relationship can be so strong that it hurts both parties. This is not desirable and should be avoided or at least recognized early so that corrective measures may be taken.

Letting others help will be useful in several ways. We learn from watching. When others try to accomplish the goal you are emphasizing, the child benefits from opportunities to transfer his learning to other people and situations within his environment. It is useless if he learns to respond only to one person and exhibits no real learning when he is with others. Helping the child transfer his learning will lead to adjustment in a variety of situations, but this may come slowly. He will probably test each new person, but the testing must not keep others from entering his life.

The importance of a block of time for yourself and for others has been emphasized; however, this is not to say that the rest of the day belongs to the child. The child, also, needs some time of his own. He does not need structure all day long. There are times when he should be allowed to "do his thing" even if it is nonproductive. One goal for the child is to help him learn to entertain himself independently, and this cannot be learned if someone is constantly controlling him. As the child is taught more productive forms of self-occupation, he will move to higher levels, and these undesirable behaviors will be extinguished. He will not improve faster if you spend every minute of every day with him. The progress is developmental and will, with consistency, occur gradually over a period of time. Too much effort at one time will be confusing and frustrating to everyone.

The length of time spent with the child will vary. There is no ideal time allotment for each situation; however, nothing will be accomplished if the child is pushed beyond his limits. You must know your goals and watch for responses, then when the child has done what you feel he can for the moment, stop and try again later.

Realism

An enthusiastic, enjoyable, fun-filled atmosphere is best for all concerned. An optimistic attitude about the child and what he is and will be doing is important. He needs the same feelings of belonging and acceptance as other children. He needs to be treated the same as other children in as many ways as possible. He needs the same experiences other children have as they grow and learn, even if it means he may fall and skin his knee. He needs the opportunity to go to many of the same places. By treating him differently and not expecting the same from him, he becomes increasingly different. Your relationship with the severely handicapped child should be similar to the way you relate to other children. He does not need pity, sympathy, or overprotection. Attitudes will play a major role in his success and development.

It is easy to feel you are "spoiling" the child, but if he is accomplishing many of the established goals, then it is not a cause for concern. He may even feel he can have all of your attention when he wants it. If he is trying to find ways to manipulate you, he is thinking. For example, at bedtime he may object violently to being "put away." This kind of communication is good. He is saying, "I don't want to be here, I want to be there where things are happening." He needs to know you understand, but you must be consistent.

The child will have to learn new things that may seem very difficult at first. He may object violently. Certain things will be harder for him. That is his problem; your problem will be to design ways to help him become more self-reliant, even if it does require a maximum effort on his part. In the long run, he will be a much better adjusted individual if he becomes more dependent upon himself and less dependent on you.

This child, as much or more than other less handicapped children, needs firsthand experiences. He may have difficulty integrating experiences for various reasons. For example, he may be hearing one thing and his eyes may be focusing on something else. It seems hard for him to tie it all together. If he hears a dog bark but is looking at the light, he may be receiving unintegrated information. Varied and repeated experiences will assist him in integrating what all the different sensory modalities are telling him. Opportunities that are stimulating can be used to help the child increase his awareness and help him learn to integrate his experiences. Situations he enjoys, such as parties, close body contact activities, rides in the car, and water play, or objects that he likes, such as a vibrator, a radio, or a battery-operated back scratcher, can be used to accomplish these goals. These fun times also help to develop a relationship with the child and build language skills. Objects, activities, or experiences he enjoys can be used as rewards. Use anything that works.

He needs love, attention, play time, and as many of the normal experiences as possible. Your best efforts are required, but by failing, you can learn. Then after reevaluation, new plans and attempts can be made. This is a good way to learn. The child cannot be expected to be perfect and you will not be perfect either. That is what makes it so interesting. One can make a mistake, find out what is wrong, and make plans to get better results. Others can also be used to help point out mistakes. Often, when a concept fails to be understood or a certain behavior cannot be elicited, one can turn to a teacher assistant, another teacher, or just a friend and ask for help. "Watch and see what I am doing wrong," or perhaps "What is the child trying to tell me?" This may work, since people not actively involved with the child can often get a better perspective. If this does not help, then at least it is recognized that the answer is not obvious and more evaluation, observation, and analysis will be required.

It is the combination of the many parts that count in building a program for the severely and profoundly handicapped child. Most children seem to have a resiliency far beyond expectations. They can handle your mistakes better than you think. In fact, it may be good that things do not always go "just right." It is important then to be sure there is variety—a good combination. This allows the individual to develop by giving him new experiences. As you recall the events of the day or the week, there should be many pleasant reminders that indicate this variety.

It is helpful to look back over a short period of time and answer a few questions concerning the child's experiences. For example, after one week, one could ask questions concerning the child's new or especially meaningful experiences. Where did he go and what did he do this week? Did he go to the grocery store? Was he included in the trip to a friend's house? Did he "help" prepare and taste a new food? Was he given several opportunities to experience community life? It is easy to recall several fun experiences that stimulated interaction with the child. If it cannot be determined that the child's opportunities to learn and experience have been broadened, then adjustments need to be made.

INFANT LEARNING

The Need for Input

A newborn baby immediately begins to receive sensory input through his ears and eyes. The child who is severely handicapped starts life with problems that limit this input. Therefore, other ways to get information to him must be found. This input, or stimulation, is needed as soon as possible. Each day the child is isolated from his environment causes him to be more different or developmentally delayed than the normal child. The difference between the two children, the normal child and the handicapped child, is not nearly so great at birth as it will be with the passage of time. This difference will depend greatly on how much information can be relayed to the child and how early it can be done.

Many who have observed or later recalled the behavior of severely and profoundly handicapped infants report that the children seemed more normal during the first few weeks and months than was later the case. Others also report that because of the children's early behavior, it was difficult for them to believe some of the medically diagnosed problems actually existed. Some described a child as being hyperactive during the first months of life and then, before the child reached his first birthday, he became passive and was content to lie in his bed and "be a good baby."

Possibly this child is trying early in life to compensate for stimulation he is not receiving. Perhaps by moving about and waving his arms and legs, he is trying to prevent boredom and isolation. Perhaps he later tires of his movement or is no longer challenged or stimulated by it and begins to withdraw. At this point, the child may begin to find other avenues of self-stimulation, such as eye-poking, finger–light play, gross vocal stimulation, or other peculiar mannerisms. If this is true, then it seems obvious that early stimulation, attempting in some way to compensate for sensory deprivation, might help keep him alert, active, and interested in the world around him. This is especially true for the child with severe sensory handicaps, but it is also important to recognize this behavior in any child who may not have had opportunities to use sensory information meaningfully.

The problem is to find ways to increase the sensory input or teach the child to make use of it so that he will not stop his exploratory efforts or decrease his receptivity. No two children are alike, normal or otherwise, and no situation is like another. Those who know the child best may be able to develop ways to prevent the child from being iso-

lated that are unique and more useful than any suggestions we might
make. However, a few suggestions might serve as a starting point.
They are included here for that purpose. These ideas are for whoever
will be teaching the child, whether parents, friends, relatives, or a professionally trained teacher; therefore, they may or may not apply to
any one situation.

Other Suggestions

1. If the child is very young, hold him close during feeding time.
    Some feel that the mother should nurse the baby if possible, to
    create a closer bond and help the child begin to develop a body
    image.
2. Cuddle the child close to your neck; vibrations can be felt as you
    speak. This will also give you an opportunity to talk close to his
    ear.
3. The child's father or others closely involved can be encouraged to
    hold the child close to their face. A "five o'clock shadow" has
    texture.
4. Hold him, rock him, and cuddle him close so he can feel your
    body warmth.
5. Treat him as normally as possible. Don't be afraid, he won't
    break.
6. Include him in every experience possible. Pity is not needed but
    acceptance, warmth, and love are.
7. The child should know that he is loved and accepted as he is.
    Feelings toward him will be recognized by the way he is held,
    picked up, and put down.
8. Other children should be encouraged to play with and talk to him.
    Brothers and sisters, friends, neighbors, or other older children
    who are interested can become involved and contribute. Tell
    them specific ways in which they can help. Your enthusiasm and
    pride will be contagious.
9. Respond to behavior that is pleasing, even if it is only tiny
    progress. He needs to know you think he is great. Laugh a lot.
    Fuss occasionally. Remember, he needs to be treated as normally
    as possible. Always say, "Good boy," more than "No, no, that
    was bad."
10. He should not be allowed to stay in his bed or playpen alone more
    than another child would. Cut out some of his naps. Encourage
    him to stay awake like any other child so he can learn. Provide a
    play area for him, one especially suited for his needs.

11. Let him be around other adults and children. Show him off. Once involved, teachers and others can develop this kind of pride and the child will sense it.

12. Make the child aware of his senses by providing him with a variety of sensory experiences.

13. Talk to him constantly in a normal voice.

14. Sing to him, humming little songs while holding him or working near him. If this is a nursery setting, your work with other children can also provide him with extra opportunities to learn and experience.

15. Use routine words and signals when possible, as he will learn to anticipate the next event of his schedule this way. Occasional variations from the routine are normal.

16. Play with noisemakers and help the child learn to manipulate them to make a sound. Hide one behind your back or manipulate it to his side or behind him; he will gradually become more aware.

17. Do not forget to use "natural toys." Pots and pans make good cymbals and drums. Other homemade toys are mentioned in another section.

18. Help the child learn that his body parts have names.

19. Rub him briskly with a soft bath towel after a bath, swim, or cleanup time. Name each body part as you rub.

20. Rub him with a variety of textures. Touch his hands, wrists, and face with them to capture his interest. Tickle him with something (this is not advised for some children who are having difficulty relaxing their muscles, such as with cerebral palsy). Make the activity fun for him.

21. Encourage him to touch your eyes, nose, and mouth; talk to him about it. Then help him touch himself. He needs to learn to understand himself and his body before he can fully understand his environment.

22. There are many children's records that emphasize body parts. Use records and sing along or just sing your own songs while you and the child touch the body parts as they are named. Sometimes the records will be more help to you than to the child.

23. Teach the child that different objects and textures *feel* different.

24. Touch cool or warm things to his skin. Try warm lotion or baby oil. Touch your cold hands to his cheek. Let him play with ice cubes or empty them from a bowl.

25. Help him play with sand or small stones in a bucket.

26. Give him various textures to hold: soft, hard, fuzzy, and sticky objects.

27. Name the textures he feels. Hard: the table is hard, the wall is hard, the floor is hard. Soft: the carpet is soft, the cover is soft, his clothes are soft.
28. Use different textured blankets, spreads, and pads for him; do not always use smooth, tightly fitted sheets as in a hospital.
29. Put a warm diaper or blanket fresh from the dryer against him. Later let him help you remove them from the dryer.
30. Take him outside daily. He needs to experience temperature change.
31. Play simple tactual motor games with him such as "pat-a-cake" and "I'm gonna get you." Lightly cover his head with the blanket and say, "Where are you?" Then uncover his head and say "There you are!" Constantly look for and be aware of developing communication cues. These may be indicated by facial expression or gross motor movements and vocalizations.
32. When moving the child from place to place, help him learn where he is.
33. Put him close enough to the side of his bed so he can feel and occasionally touch the rail. The same can be done when in a stroller, high chair, or wheelchair. This way he is given a point of reference which helps develop environmental orientation.
34. Help him learn the specific furniture and materials or equipment that belong in different rooms as orientation clues. With visual problems this is especially important. "Here's the stove, we're in the kitchen," "the TV is in the den," and "the tub is in the bathroom."
35. Let him lie or play on the rug, the floor, and the grass.
36. Always be sure his clothing fits loosely.
37. Remove his clothing occasionally. In this way, he can then use all of his body surfaces to gather information. It will also increase awareness of his body and make it easier to move on his own.
38. Get him off his back. He cannot learn to crawl from that position. Place him on his stomach. Put him in a semisitting position in an infant seat. He sees more when up. If he can sit, the seats that bob up and down while fastened in the doorway are good.
39. Try a "baby backpack" to get him up and seeing more. If he does not walk, this is better for your back than constantly carrying him in your arms. Then, if you are in a nursery, you can better handle an extra child with two free arms.
40. Stimulate the child's vision.
41. Use bright colors to attract his attention. Wear colorful clothing to catch his eye and make him want to move. Encourage others to do so.

42. Bombard the child with one bright color at a time. Use seasonal colors; red for Valentine's Day, yellow for Easter, or just choose a color for decorations and call it to the child's attention. Say, "Red; the picture is red," and "Let's find more red things; the cover is red, the pillow is red, your Jello is red." Decorate his room with various posters, pictures, and other materials that are the color you are emphasizing. This need not be an expensive project.

43. Attach pictures or shapes to the window for him to see when he is looking toward the sunlight.

44. Hang objects for him to see from the ceiling or light fixtures. It is better for him to be looking at things that move than to be moving things so he can look at them (i.e., flipping an object or his hands).

45. Teach the child that certain smells and tastes have special meaning.

46. Wear a special perfume he can learn to recognize as yours and encourage frequent visitors to do so. This also applies to men who are important in his life. The same shaving lotion used consistently can make an impression on the child.

47. Certain smells are found in special places. Food smells come from the kitchen and fresh air smells come from the open window. Take the child to the source of the smell so he can learn to associate the odor. Always give him names for what he smells.

48. Have tasting parties at snack time. He can try a tiny taste of food new to him or one prepared in an unusual way.

49. Be sure to constantly expose the child to a variety of experiences.

50. Let him go barefoot.

51. Do not try to spend too much time "working with him." Do take advantage of daily situations and be sure he is present to experience them.

52. Let him enjoy water play, both in the bath and with a pan or pail.

53. He needs to feel things that move or vibrate, such as the faucet when water is running or the washing machine when it is on.

54. If he is home much of the time, put him on a floor pad nearby as you move around the house or apartment doing your chores. If he is in a day program or nursery, there will also be times when it is important to move him with you and also accomplish some other task at the same time. Walk around with him. Take him for short walks in and out of the house or building.

55. The more you treat him differently, the more different he will be. Encourage others to treat him normally. This includes roughhouse play and occasional falls. Explain his handicap casually to curious

onlookers; you will be more comfortable, and they will be less curious and more accepting.

56. Do not avoid places you would go if he were "normal." Cookouts, visiting friends, shopping trips, fishing, and picnics are normal experiences for any child. This is important in the family setting and also in the school or nursery situation. Never say "He probably won't get anything out of it anyway," and leave him out.
57. Find ways to help the child gain meaning from experiences.
58. Develop an early signal system so he will begin to anticipate what is happening. For example: touch his mouth before you feed him or close his eyes when it is time for a nap. (See other suggestions in the section on Communication).
59. Constantly think of ways to help the child understand what is happening to him and around him. This will require awareness and effort on the part of others.

It is important to realize that each sensory modality needs maximum stimulation. Visual efficiency can only improve through use. It is better to think of our visual sense as a muscle and practice with it whenever possible. All sensory areas could be considered in this same fashion. Our senses of hearing, touch, smell, and taste become better and more discriminatory with constant meaningful use. Emphasis on development of all sensory areas is time well spent.

BODY IMAGE

Forming an Image

For the child who is severely and profoundly handicapped, learning to understand himself and his body is often difficult. If there are visual problems, people moving around him cannot be clearly seen. With auditory problems, he will not hear what would help him form an image of himself as a separate, capable human being. Other physical limitations, such as crippling conditions, restrict experiences within the environment. In addition, the child may have missed the normal mother–child body contact because of various problems during infancy. He is less active and has been treated differently from the normal child. He seems fragile and is given more protection. Control of himself and his environment needs to be learned, but this has not been encouraged. Because of his dependence on others, he may form an inadequate self-image which leads to further dependency.

With little motivation to develop into a self-reliant individual, he becomes increasingly more dependent. Although to develop this confidence and self-reliance, *more* encouragement is needed than with the normal child, there is often far less. If he is handled and talked to as if nothing is expected of him, he responds by expecting nothing of himself. When he is wet, someone supplies him with clean pants. Food appears and is put into his mouth, even before he has indicated hunger. There is little reason to develop curiosity or independence. His only requirement is to receive the food or dry diapers when furnished. If he looks at himself as a recipient of attention, knows his bodily needs will be taken care of and that nothing is expected of him, he will not try to do more.

The child who receives this treatment will have an inadequate image of himself. He will become more dependent on those who attend to him, and since there is almost no experience by which he can differentiate the parts of his body and realize that they are all a part of a functioning whole, he will remain at an infantile level.

He Needs Help

A normal child often develops an acceptable image of himself with little awareness or help from anyone. The severely handicapped child needs help in developing a body image, and help must begin at the earliest possible moment. When a child lacks self-understanding, there is no way for him to reach out or communicate with the world and no motivation to do so. If he fails to learn that he is a person and capable of doing as others, then he cannot go far. For example, if he does not understand that he has an arm and that it is a useful part of his body, then he cannot and will not physically reach out; if he is unaware of his mouth as a source of sound, then he cannot reach out vocally, and if he is not aware of his body, the learning normally gained through imitation is beyond his reach.

A child cannot function in a vacuum. Nor does he learn from being in a physically nonstimulating environment. If he is totally familiar with his living area and there is no variety, then boredom will replace curiosity. In the same way, a nonstimulating, routinized social environment will lead to boredom. Eventually, if these conditions remain, the child will "tune out" and live in his own make-believe or self-stimulating world. For this type of living, the mind and nervous system can accomplish their purposes with only a minimal amount of help from outside stimuli. If the only stimulation required is to rock back and forth, or to push on the eyeball, then the demands on the child's concept of the body are minimal.

However, if the child is to experience a well-differentiated body, the social and physical environment must be varied. This differentiation allows the child to experience his sensory areas and body parts as separate units which bring him stimulation. He also realizes eventually that the parts can be synthesized into one integrated, functioning, and efficient body.

There is no single way to encourage this development, but by trying different approaches, it is possible to develop a technique that will get results. The approaches taken must revolve around variations in the social and physical conditions so that the child will be required to use his body more and more until he is functioning at fullest capacity and until he knows what each part can do. In this way, an integrated concept of body image will eventually develop naturally. Unless there is much practice in all areas, it will be difficult for any learning to take place. Suggestions are given in the following sections for development.

Normal parent–child relations are important in developing within the child an awareness of himself as a useful, functioning individual. It is necessary, then, that we emphasize the importance of allowing the child to have as many experiences as possible with his parents or parent substitutes. The close contact of nursing a baby or holding him during feeding is important. The way the baby is picked up is also important. He can learn a great deal by the way he is touched. Rough, smooth, soft, hesitating, loving—all of this will come through to the child and make him aware of the feelings toward him. The infant must not be left alone or isolated in his crib. He is already experiencing enough isolation through lack of sensory input or difficulty in attaching meaning to sensory experiences. A child should be made to realize he is important, capable, and loved.

Getting Him in Touch

For the child to understand himself, he must be in touch with his environment through all his senses. This will be more difficult for the child with severe and profound handicaps, since some of the ways a child normally reaches his environment or is reached by it are not possible. He cannot easily entertain himself by watching others move around him, and he cannot always gather needed information or stimulation through his hearing. He sees someone come toward him but cannot see well enough to tell that they are coming through the door; then suddenly the image disappears. He hears sounds that are not clear and has difficulty understanding the source. The physical contact important for all children is even more important to this child. He must feel himself being held close to a human body; held tightly and securely as he is being talked to, stroked, patted, or stimulated in any other appropriate way. Awareness of the source of visual and auditory stimulation will require help.

Many children have not had the experiences necessary to maintain perceptual contact with the environment. Lack of meaningfully stimulating situations has allowed them to develop ways to maintain contact within themselves and to use objects in the immediate environment in unique ways so that they will not be faced with new challenges or frustrations. So these children rock, twirl, or develop bizarre gross motor patterns which sometimes incorporate other sensory areas. They are not concerned about being in touch with the rest of the world.

It takes considerable rapport and physical contact before the child will begin to be interested. Sometimes "parallel play" by an adult playmate is the closest a person can get. At these times, the only cue that there is recognition of the adult may be the fact that the self-stimulating activity increases in frequency. If there is enough motivation and an object is being used, the child will sometimes relate at a low level if the object is taken away for a few seconds. At other times this removal will only be a cue to enter into a different level of withdrawal and self-stimulation.

The conditions surrounding any small act of investigation must be carefully observed. If similar situations can be presented frequently, the child will become increasingly interested in a new world, and he will then be locked into a new system dependent upon the contact he maintains and energy he puts forth. Interpersonal contact at these times is primarily adult-oriented. Most children who are severely and profoundly handicapped seldom interact with peers. In these situations, it is usually necessary to provide an adult who will react to even the slightest cue and will serve as a model for developing responses.

Tactile Stimulation

It would be difficult to overemphasize the importance of tactile stimulation for these children. Some come to us very involved with themselves and with self-stimulation and have even been labeled "unloving." We do not feel this withdrawal is an overall characteristic of any other particular group. However, the lack of response could result from the combination of many events. Many hospitalizations, a period of adjustment for the family, conflicting advice as how to handle the child, and a child who often seems to want to be left alone are all events or situations not conducive to the relaxed, confident, loving atmosphere recommended for normal early adjustment of the child. Many severely and profoundly handicapped children are tactually oriented in that they use touch to maintain orientation with their immediate environment. They do not, however, use it to gain new information. Their tactile ability, while seemingly well formed, is frequently only capable of gross discrimination. The child does not recognize this deficiency in himself. He cannot know that some materials feel better than others or that there are degrees of fuzziness, some of which are tolerable. With encouragement and a variety of tactually stimulating meaningful objects, more efficient use can be made of this modality.

With all sensory areas, it is important to be aware of any possibility to use other senses in a supportive manner. Thus, if a child orients himself to an object visually, it may be important for him to use tactile cues for further analysis.

A Real Experience

Much time must be spent hugging, rubbing, holding, or swinging a child who may look as if he wants to be left alone. One little girl responded to loving gestures like a slippery eel—she wanted to get away from everyone and almost everything in her environment. She could not use her body to imitate any activity or relate to anyone appropriately. She would much rather swing on the curtain or remove a doll's arms and legs than interact appropriately. This child could never fit into the home, school, or community as long as she related to no one. Stimulating experiences were planned for all sensory areas. Play activities were encouraged and speech was emphasized for months. Finally, there was some evidence that our efforts would be rewarded, and we kept pushing.

One day the breakthrough came when this little girl realized that she could play "follow the leader" with us. Suddenly, she found that she could use her body to copy the behavior of others. She followed the group around the table, down the hall, and back again, as the adults who participated both laughed and cried at the same time. She was so proud of herself, and she knew everyone was proud of her. The program and progress continued and within weeks she was learning signs and words for objects in her environment. She had to "find herself" before she could learn to put names on things. At times, she would try to do as she was told and gleefully climb in her teacher's lap for a social reward (a big cuddly hug). This child weighed 55 pounds and may not have looked like a "lap baby," but at some developmental stages she was just that. She wanted love and approval and was willing to cooperate to get it. If a feeling of mutual love and acceptance can be established, then progress can be predicted. Later in the year, we witnessed this same little girl pantomine and gesture for pictures in her book and then reach proudly for her mother's hands, as if to say, "Now you copy me!" That was a beautiful sight.

It is doubtful if Rosy would ever have interacted with another person if she had not first learned to understand her body. Without these close, physical contacts and concentrated efforts to develop a body image, the freedom to move and desire to communicate would have been difficult to stimulate, and if it developed at all, it would have been severely delayed.

Realistic Expectations

We must avoid expecting too much from the child too soon. One little blue-eyed blonde boy of several years ago comes to mind. One goal was that he wave goodbye when leaving school. Each afternoon we stood facing each other and waved while someone (mother or teacher) stood behind him to help. He seemed to be the most stubborn child in the world. He could always do the things *he* wanted to and often refused to do as asked. This was to be our starting point. Some day he was going to wave. A few days later, it came to our attention that this was not stubbornness but rather an inability to understand his body well enough to imitate body movements. He had no awareness of himself as a conforming member of the classroom, and he did not know that we were waving to him so he would wave back. We also realized he had never imitated a clap, stomp, or jump and never pointed or gestured.

We began working harder than ever on a variety of activities to encourage imitation and body awareness. One day while a teacher was encouraging him to clap, with almost numb hands, the change came. She would clap, ask him to do the same, manipulate his hands, clap again, and wait. Incidentally, she was rewarding her own behavior by eating a piece of cereal each time she clapped (he loved cereal). He looked longingly at the bowl of cereal, which was gradually disappearing into her mouth one piece at a time, and then back at the teacher. The months of effort were rewarded. He touched two fingers together and cereal was popped into *his* mouth. Was it an accident? Would he repeat this behavior? He did it again. More cereal. Within minutes, Jody was clapping. The next day he learned to imitate extending his arms above and to the sides of his body. Before the week was over, his father taught him to imitate a praying position with his hands. Within weeks, this child could use sign language to indicate the names of objects, and he soon developed expressive language that he used during daily activities. A teacher must constantly be aware of reasons for lack of response. This time the mistake was mine, but we can learn much from our mistakes. He was not stubborn, he was just not ready.

Manipulating People

Many children go through stages that involve manipulating people to satisfy their needs. If the child has just begun to do this, it may be acceptable; but if he constantly gets exactly what he wants by using another person, he must be assisted in progressing to a higher level of communication. By pulling an adult to the door and placing her hand on the knob he can convey a message. For some children this is good and indicates progress. However, he must learn that there are other ways to communicate this desire, and if this manipulation brings continued success, he will have no reason to move to a higher level of communication. Also, if a child takes a person's hand and extends it up and toward an object out of his reach on a shelf, that person knows what he wants. He is, however, manipulating and using the person as a part of himself, not as a separate individual. He needs to learn gradually that others are not part of him but separate people. This should develop with the development of body image and is part of the child's increasing ability to understand his environment.

Suggestions to Try

Below are some suggestions we have tried and found helpful. Some may seem unusual, as we are concerned with stimulating areas that develop normally with most children. Those interested in teaching will enjoy creating numerous other ways to get a point across, but perhaps these will trigger a thought.

1. Encourage any kind of imitation (voice, motor, etc.) by imitating what the child does. When he coughs, sneezes, or the like, imitate him. The same can be done with motor responses. He will eventually imitate you and this is a fun learning activity.
2. Put a piece of tape on his fingers. If he removes it, maybe he will discover his fingers.

3. Put a hat on your head and then on his. Repeat. Say, "Hat on my head," then "Hat on your head." He will gradually learn that you both have heads and that objects transfer from one person to another.
4. Look in a mirror. Hold him up. If he is small, hold him up so he can see both of you, and see that you are separate beings.
5. Play "up and down" in front of a mirror. Movement may attract his attention. Talk constantly.
6. Touch his eye, then the eye in the mirror. Follow the same procedure with other body parts. Talk about what you are doing.
7. Let him see himself in the mirror with a hat on, then with the hat off. Repeat. Do not expect immediate results. Keep trying—otherwise you can expect nothing. With repetition there is hope.
8. Try gross movements in front of a mirror. Raise one hand, then help him raise his hand. Other similar exercises can be performed with the mirror and will encourage body imitation.
9. Play games. Try "peek-a-boo" with a blanket or towel over your head. Say, "Where am I?" "Here I am." If he ignores you, don't be concerned. Repeat. Laugh and make it fun. If you don't enjoy yourself, he won't either.
10. Encourage him to explore your arms and face. If he is interested in you, that's great!
11. Imitate his vocalizations. When he says something (makes a noise), then hears you say it, he will more readily become aware of what he is saying and realize your interest.
12. Touch his hand to your face and its parts, then to his. Repeat, naming the parts constantly. "My nose," then "Your nose."
13. Help him to learn to imitate gross movements such as clapping, stomping, jumping, turning, sitting, standing (while you also tell him to clap, stomp. . .). You may have to manipulate him.
14. Later, when he has progressed, work on fine movements, such as face, tongue, and mouth control.
15. Exercise with the child. Lie down on the floor and raise your leg and your arm or other similar gymnastic movements. Manipulate his body to do the same.
16. Get down on the floor and crawl beside him. Let your bodies touch. Try crawling on top of him (your body over his in a crawl position). Move your arm forward, then help him move his. Next, gently shove his leg forward.
17. Walk with him with his body touching yours. Try having him stand on your feet, facing forward. Walk this way.

18. Sit close together on a porch swing. Swing back and forth to feel the movement. Find other ways to move with him.

19. Imitate his spontaneous movements and encourage him to repeat them.

20. Put a piece of paper over the top part of a full length mirror so what he is seeing can be better controlled. We don't want him merely looking up at light reflections.

21. Encourage a favorite activity seated in front of the mirror, such as eating candy, playing with a favorite object, or drinking juice.

22. Stand in front of him and wave "Bye-bye" while someone stands in back of him and helps him wave. He will eventually realize he is doing the same as you.

23. If he has a tantrum and flings himself on the floor, imitate him. If he looks at you, that's progress. He is looking and you are doing as he has done. That is body image.

24. Do not smother the child. Feelings of pity of guilt will retard his development. Laugh and relax with him, then he will too.

25. Expect him to perform. Constantly doing for him removes incentive. He will be encouraged if you exhibit confidence in him.

26. Teach him to imitate your body position. Work toward eventual imitation of large dolls and later pictured body positions.

27. Imitating the image formations of a doll will be fun for the more advanced child and can lead to many group play activities.

28. Play games such as "follow the leader," "this is the way," or "Simon says." You may need to modify the game somewhat.

29. Draw around the child's body on a large piece of paper taped to the floor. Cut it out, fill in the features and fasten it to the wall. Talk about it. Say, "This is you, Sam." Enthusiasm helps.

30. Draw his shadow outside on the pavement with chalk.

31. Draw around his image on the mirror. Use crayon, lipstick, magic marker, or the like.

32. Pantomime silhouette action pictures. For example, if you have a picture of a child in bed or a boy marching with a flag, provide him with simple props such as a blanket or a flag, and let him act out the pictured activity.

33. Try the following more difficult activities with a group of children. Let one or two who learn more quickly be first. The others may then become more aware through imitation and association.

34. Play with masks, costumes, and discarded dress-up outfits. A stocking over the face is always good for a laugh.

35. Rub parts of his body with lotion to help him become aware. Let him rub the lotion on you.

36. As the child advances, he may be capable of more complicated manipulative body image activities with a doll. Verbal commands such as "Wash," "Sit," "Stand," or "Go to bed," can be given to the doll.
37. Be aware of the possibilities that *you* may be tactually defensive. When he tries to explore your facial features, do not insult him by drawing away.
38. When playing in the tub, splash water on him and encourage him to sprinkle or splash you.
39. Let him complete a picture. You draw a face or stick figure and leave off something obvious (nose or mouth). Help him fill in the missing part.
40. Play with body puzzles. Cut arms, legs, and head off a picture. Let him put it back together. This works best if the picture is clear and if it is first pasted on cardboard.
41. Large paper bags can provide endless ideas for activities. Make a mask, play facial "hide and seek" or "guess who," and crawl through the sack. This is fun when the child is required to "break out" the other end to make a tunnel or to celebrate his "appearance."

EXPERIENCE WITH OBJECTS

Relating to the Environment

Along with developing an understanding of himself as separate from others within his immediate surroundings, the child must also develop an understanding of objects as separate parts of his environment. Children with multiple problems often have difficulty developing an understanding of the permanence and constancy of objects. If the object is moved, they do not know where to look for it, and many lack the curiosity and initiative to try. For example, when the child pushes his bottle from the high chair tray, he may not realize that it fell to the floor and stayed there. Perhaps he feels that it disappeared from where he last saw it or that it continued to move into space. For him to understand the constancy of objects, he must be shown over and over. Help him down and encourage him to find the bottle. Later, when he pushes an object from the table or chair and looks for it, it a sign of progress. More of these understandings will be developed if you are aware and use daily experiences to help him in the learning process.

Object manipulation is one way the child learns to relate to and interact with his environment. He must learn that objects are to be manipulated and that this is a pleasant and worthwhile way to spend his free time. The child will do *something* when he has free time, and it is important for him to learn constructive, self-entertainment activities. This learning will require planning, as he will not begin using toys constructively without help.

Observing Use of Objects

The parent or teacher must become an astute observer, as this child will devise many creative and interesting ways to use objects unacceptably. The objects should not be used for self-stimulation since this will prevent the child from relating appropriately to his environment. Some examples of this type of "play" have been mentioned earlier. Nonproductive manipulation of objects can be seen when the child is given a flashlight and he shines it into his eyes or when he clicks a comb against his teeth. To use the objects to stimulate himself as he twirls around the room is not the desired goal, yet this behavior is often seen. These ways of using the object will gradually change to more constructive use if the child is programmed so that he moves forward to a higher level of development and learns other satisfying new ways of activities. Changing this type of behavior will take time. It is not recommended that objects are constantly removed from the child; it is better to *use* his desire for self-stimulating objects to develop a more acceptable behavior. This will require observation and analysis before the behavior can be modified.

Making the Use Positive

There are many ways to begin using undesirable manipulation of objects. If the child is flicking the comb against his teeth, say, "That is a comb," "This is what we do with a comb," and help him run it through his hair. Then give him another chance. He must learn to make choices.

If objects are continually removed with no opportunity to understand what was unacceptable, he may misunderstand the reasons for taking away his playthings. For example, if you jerk the comb away, he may feel it is dangerous. It would be more helpful to say, "You want to click something on your teeth? Let's get a toothbrush." Then, go into the bathroom, find the toothpaste and toothbrush, and help him brush his teeth. Another approach might be to reason with him. He may know what he is doing. Take the comb and flick it against your teeth and say, "No-no", shake your head and frown. Then take the comb and comb your hair and his, smile, and say, "Yes" while nodding your head. As long as you have what he wants (the comb), you may be able to keep his attention, and this can be a step forward.

Getting Your Attention

Most children are socially oriented toward an adult, even though the end results may be predominantly negative. Thus, a child may carry out inappropriate acts in order to get attention. Even though the attention is frequently negative or punishing, this still may be classified as a success experience by the child, since someone did come to him. The object-oriented child may do this by manipulating objects in such a way as to be pleasurable to himself and also make the nearby adult do something to stop him. Therefore, if the child is hitting his teeth with a block, he may win both times—he is stimulated by the act and rewarded by the adult's attention in stopping it. This is one form of object-oriented behavior, and an in-depth knowledge of the object is not required to bring it about.

One child cannot have constant attention every moment of the day. Sometimes it is best if you pretend not to see what a child is doing each time he wants attention. If he has learned to be sneaky, then perhaps he is learning right from wrong. If he tries a variety of behaviors to get us to relate, then at least he does want attention. This desire for attention can be used later when it is the child's turn to work. Sometimes the child will try almost anything to capture the adult's attention. Purposefully soiling pants often works. With some teachers, this behavior often backfires, and after a few tries the child usually finds some better way. By the time he finishes a cool shower and dresses himself completely, then returns to the same classroom with the same situation, he may begin to realize that getting attention does not always bring the expected rewards. He will begin to make better use of his time as these experiences help him learn to make the right choices.

Setting Goals

It is important to have specific goals for each child and to realize that one person cannot do everything for every child. Perhaps one goal will be for the child to learn to entertain himself. Having him reach for a shiny object on a desk can be motivating. Some may say this object is too tempting for a child who is obsessed by light or loves to "flick" shiny things. However, if the goal is for the child to reach out or to amuse himself alone at the desk (rather than on the floor), then the shiny object can be used to accomplish it at this time. Later, when this goal has been reached, a switch can be made to less tempting toys. This may have been the first time little Johnny stayed in a chair and amused himself alone. It is sometimes acceptable to allow a child to purposely manipulate an object inappropriately when the goal for him includes other behaviors.

We feel it is important to use as many objects as possible, moving progressively toward using them meaningfully. Therefore, he must have access to objects. Some teachers may try to arrange their school-room so that the child will have an ideal learning situation. One teacher reported that when a child discovered something she felt was too tempting, she placed it out of his reach. It soon became obvious to her that she was putting many things on the top shelf or in the closet. One day, she and a fellow teacher looked around the room to see how many objects could be manipulated in a self-stimulating way and discovered that almost everything except the fixtures and furniture could be "used." Most objects could be flicked, waved, or twirled, and more things are shiny than you dream (even flash cards and coloring cards with a slick finish). So she made a decision. This was her room. She was there first and might be there last. The child had to adapt to this sit-uation. All could not change because he had not learned to control him-self. She would help him adjust to the room as it was and not constantly try to change things to suit him.

It takes time to develop a way of working with children that works best for each person. There are obviously many ways to accomplish the same goals. It is important, though, for the person working with the child to establish specific goals and then decide what would be a first step forward toward reaching each one.

Goals must be different for each child. If the goal is to get the child to play with a toy, it may be acceptable to allow him to use it inappro-priately as long as he does not use it to stimulate himself. For another child, this same behavior may not be acceptable. When Rob is given a hammer and waves it up and down occasionally hitting a person or ob-ject, he may be rewarded. If Jimmy does the same thing, he may be scolded by saying "No! Mistake! That is not what is done with a hammer." In another case, a child may pick up a block and put it in her mouth. She is rewarded because this was the first time she has shown any interest. If another child did this, she would not be rewarded since she knows more acceptable ways to play with blocks.

Helping the children learn to play with objects and relate to them in an appropriate way can be time-consuming and sometimes frustrating. One's attitude will play a very important part. On the other hand, it can be challenging to discover ways to use behavior, such as self-stimulation, to reach a desired goal. There may be no other teaching situation that offers such a challenge.

Learning to Use Objects

Severely and profoundly handicapped children have difficulty understanding that objects are representational. They do not realize that a toy car represents a big car, that a doll represents a baby, and that a stuffed dog is like a real dog. They need help in gaining this knowledge. It is best to begin with real objects. Later, help him learn to associate the real with the representational object and even later with a picture. For example, when presenting a toy car, do not expect the child to pretend he is driving a real one. This association is difficult. Also, when introducing "toys," real ones, such as large balls, blocks, or bells, are best.

The child will need to begin learning to identify objects as he progresses developmentally. It is important to name familiar objects. Eventually he will begin understanding that objects have purposes and also that they have labels. He will not suddenly wake up one day and realize that objects have names and begin asking the name of everything in the house. However, sometimes children do make remarkable progress when this understanding is gained.

Progress sometimes occurs in spurts and great leaps. After many weeks of holding a bell up to Beth's ear and telling her about it with no apparent interest on her part, one teacher was rewarded (Beth was diagnosed as deaf). While playing a game we called "guess which instrument" (sound an instrument behind a screen and the child is required to "name" it), Beth observed one of her classmates give the correct manual sign for bell, as it sounded. Success finally came! It was obvious she was thinking about the task. She waited excitedly for her turn and gave the correct sign not only for the bell but for other instruments as well.

This was a beginning for Beth. Within days a box of objects (bell, ball, candy, hat, comb, toothbrush, Coke, etc.) had been accumulated that she could identify. Several objects would be placed on a chair beside the teacher, and Beth would sit waiting for a sign. When the sign was given, indicating one of the objects on the chair (and we always talk as we sign), Beth would grab the correct object and give it to the teacher, hoping for a reward. She usually got one, too. Within a few days she could "name" each object in the group. This soon led to expressive use of language in daily situations (i.e., if she saw candy, she immediately signed "candy"). Thus, after many months of hard work in several areas, we were rewarded by a few days of real progress.

Another common difficulty often seen in severely and profoundly handicapped children is the problem of understanding that parts of something make a whole. For this reason, we provide many experience activities to develop this understanding, such as encouraging them to put the removable arms and legs on a doll or cutting up a picture of an object or a piece of fruit and helping the child to understand how it all goes back together. It is always exciting when a child first tries to fit a wheel back on a small broken car. He is learning that things go together to make a whole and this is important information.

In addition to this learning, as the child progresses he should begin to learn how to make selections of parts of a whole when there are alternatives (parts that belong and others that do not). In order to choose the correct alternative, he must use other sensory areas as a means for discriminating the essential differences. For example, if the child is replacing tires on a car and there are five tires, one of which is somewhat different, he may need more than tactual cues in examining the tire to identify the one that does not belong. Then he will need to call upon the use of vision to help him solve the problem. If he has no usable vision, he may need to examine more carefully the tire treads or the size through use of a higher level of tactile discrimination.

Other Suggestions

The following suggestions are offered to help the child develop object awareness and a concept of objects in order for him to gain meaning from them, which will aid him in relating to his environment. Some of these ideas may be appropriate, others will need to be adapted. They should be used in any way that seems helpful.

1. Place a ball, block, or doll in his lap and then take it away. Repeat. You want him to realize the presence and absence of objects and therefore become more aware.
2. Pass a ball from you to him and back. Try sitting on the floor and putting your feet close to him so he can feel as the ball goes from one person to another.
3. Mix up shoes and see if he can find his. Do the same with coats and sweaters. Help him at first.
4. Try to find objects for play that are appealing to him. It's all right to let him play with a flashlight or shiny object for a few moments, but be aware of your own goals and watch for self-stimulating play. Replace objects that are too tempting with those

less tempting. However, if he is only interested in the self-stimulating toys, use them for short periods for motivation while gradually lengthening the time he plays with more appropriate ones.

5. Build things with blocks. Work toward teaching him to copy simple block designs.
6. Folding paper into shapes can eventually become a way to interact with a child.
7. Let him help complete a place setting. You fix one correctly. Next leave the fork off and help him put it in the correct place on the napkin. He can learn to help. Later you can try this with a small tea set. Always go from big to small and from real to copies.
8. Hold objects within his reach and call them to his attention. Encourage him to reach out. In the beginning, he will need assistance.
9. Help him put objects in a container or take them out. Try plastic eggs in a basket, rocks in a box, or beans in a jar.
10. Water play is excellent. Put a boat or ball in the tub for him to find.
11. Work on independent skills such as opening and closing the door, flushing the toilet, holding his own glass or spoon, and turning on the light or the water. A good place to begin may be by teaching him to turn the light on and off.
12. Put something he likes within his reach on a table (i.e., flashlight, cookie, candy, baby bottle). Encourage him to find it. Motivation may be increased if he is allowed to see, touch, or smell the object first.
13. If he knocks something from the table or pushes it away, look for consistency. He does know something is there.
14. Covering part of a toy and helping the child discover it is a good way to work on visual memory of objects. Let him see you cover it and call attention to the part that can be seen. Play ''Where is it?'' Later you can completely hide articles he enjoys and help him find them.
15. Occasionally include objects briefly that stimulate other senses. A radio, a vibrator, a back scratcher, mechanical toys, and windup fuzzy animals are usually appealing. The more ways he can investigate or be made aware, the better.
16. Constantly observe how the child spends his time. Watch for self-stimulation rather than meaningful use of objects.
17. Tap out rhythm patterns on the table or desk and help him imitate you.
18. Make paper chains together.

19. Try designs on felt board.
20. Play "peek-a-boo" with a puppet or doll. This can be fun for both of you. This activity is fun in a group with other children.
21. Start with real things you can find around the house, such as the telephone, hammer, broom, shovel, or electric razor.
22. Remember to go from large objects to small ones. The smaller the child, the larger the object.
23. Use objects to help him discover himself. Tickle him with a puppet. Play "I'm gonna get you" or "I'm gonna get your nose."
24. Later try the above games with a doll.
25. Roll a ball across the floor to him.
26. Don't forget household objects such as a manual hand mixer, a pocketbook filled with surprises, a hole puncher, a coffee can, and boxes.

Remember that the child's use of objects begins very early. Sensory contacts stimulate this and lead to investigation. The more he can be encouraged in these experiences and be rewarded when he reaches out, the more his curiosity will be developed and learning promoted. As he goes from the beginning stages of chance contact, to total sensory experience, to manipulating the object, he will be developing in many ways that will be necessary to his future.

Objects have fascination for everyone. They form the puzzles that occupy our mind and time. Their mastery and manipulation provide occupational possibilities for many people. Their acquisition and display provide us with the symbolic signs of status, which are so important to many and necessary to re-create the cycle of work, use, and enjoyment.

We must then recognize these factors so that they may be applied to severely and profoundly handicapped children. Other children with more sensory ability can begin and carry on with experience as the only teacher; these children need more encouragement than the non-handicapped and must be taught.

TACTILE STIMULATION

Encouraging Tactile Investigation

The joy of discovery that comes with tactile investigation is something that is within the reach of the severely and profoundly handicapped child. However, he cannot and will not develop the correct use of this channel of input without help. Frequently we see children who are tactilely oriented, but these children may be using this as a way to stimulate themselves and to keep from getting new information. It is our goal to use the tactile sense as one of the remaining ways to gain meaningful information. We often see children who are relying on vision as a major means of sensory input. Visual training for increased visual efficiency has recently been emphasized quite heavily. Other times we see auditory training as the major program emphasis. Although this use of vision and hearing is important and certainly beneficial to the child's learning, it concerns us that the child is not being taught more systematically to use the sense of touch as a way of learning about and recognizing things within his environment.

The problem clearly results from the fact that in order for a child to touch an object, a definite effort on the part of an instructor is often required. The child may make use of vision or hearing with less outside effort. To touch requires more effort. There must be purposeful planning and intervention if the child is to develop this sense to a usable extent. Someone must take the child to the stimulus, put his hand on it, talk about it, rub it on him, and then repeat the whole process over and over. For example, if we want the child to realize that the house is surrounded by bushes and that they have certain tactile qualities, then we will have to take him to them many times. He will have to experience the unique way a bush feels, be encouraged to investigate it, and so on. One of our goals in exposing the child to many textures and forms is to develop his awareness that these differences are important and useful. Another goal is to develop this sensory area so that it will be useful as a supplemental system for the input of information. On occasions where vision and hearing are severely limited, the modality then becomes the primary means of gaining information.

Some children have problems accepting a variety of tactile sensations. One obstacle to overcome may be intolerance. The child may not tolerate different textures, temperatures, or movements. He may even reject efforts to place his hand on the object we want him to experience. Many rubella children display this tactile defensive type of behavior, but tolerance to textures can be developed. If the child does rebel, there may be ways whereby he can receive the stimulus in conjunction with a pleasant experience and thus be desensitized. It is important to realize that there may be a reason this reaction has developed. We should be careful not to force him, as we want him to be curious and motivated for the new experience.

Varying Tactile Experiences

Tactile experiences need not always involve the child's hands nor be limited to them. It makes little difference what part of the body is involved. Walking barefoot on different textures may mean more to him than feeling the same things with his hands. He can go barefoot or wear very little clothing when the weather permits. We have often joined in this activity and removed our shoes, too, so that we could communicate our shared feelings.

Some children respond well when given as many "total body" experiences as possible. This may be rolling up in a small rug, being rubbed briskly with a rough towel, rolling on the grass, body log rolling, swimming, or many similar experiences. The hill behind the school became our favorite body rolling area. We listened to the children scream and laugh as they rolled down and almost forgot that this freedom and pleasure was not always their reaction. With some groups, we tried this activity many times before they could even *begin* to relax and enjoy it. Another similar fun activity begins with finger paint and ends with a shower.

Tactile experiences should be multisensory. The child touches, smells, and tries to see and hear us talk when he is touching. In this way, he connects seeing, smelling, hearing, and touching. Eventually, he will learn to verify the information he receives from other senses through tactile investigation.

Encourage exploration and investigation. It is wrong to push the child's hand away when he is checking; he may stop. If he is stopped from reaching, other problems are created. Severely and profoundly handicapped children especially must feel their food, their wet pants, their messy faces, or your mouth. They learn from these sensations. It will be necessary to direct some of this investigation later, but we cannot discourage his initial interest. A hand that has just left applesauce may not be appreciated on your face, but this is much better than a limp, uninterested child who lacks the motivation and curiosity to investigate his environment.

There are many interesting multisensory experiences. Try covering a flashlight with something colorful or an unusual texture. He may want to touch and feel the light; if so, he will be receiving information from more than one source. A small vibrator wrapped up in cellophane or soft material is good. Shine a light on an object. A dark room is good when it is difficult to direct his attention. If the only thing visible in the room is the object you want him to attend to, then your chance of success is greatly improved.

Lights that brighten and dim to variations in sound intensity are great. The child can see, feel, and with practice can learn to make sounds that cause the light to change.

The bigger the experience, the more it will mean to the child. He must be exposed many times before he can go further. It may be necessary to show him continuously the same things before he indicates any beginning awareness. Eventually he will learn to recognize and discriminate between objects by using the tactile sense. Remember that if he is going to gain useful information in this way, much must be taught.

Defensiveness to Texture

In our experience, some of the children who seemed to be tactilely defensive were also picky eaters. Upon further investigation and analysis, we found that the children who were often sensitive to food objected to the texture rather than the actual taste. This problem can be overcome; however, recognizing the problem is the first step.

While providing a variety of tactile experiences, it is best to emphasize the real. Symbolic representatives of real objects should seldom be used, since the real is more meaningful and usually available. In the beginning, do not confuse him by calling a small toy car a "car." It is a toy. A real automobile is a car. Artificial greenery is not a leaf, a little tea set is not a cup, a stick with leaves on it is not a tree, and a stuffed toy bunny is not a real rabbit. Better to show him the real objects and label them for him often. Symbolic toys come later. For now, each effort to increase the child's awareness should involve real, meaningful information that will be useful to him. It is important to spend time and energy helping him tactilely learn about the objects conveniently found in his surroundings and available at most times. He will be more motivated to feel and touch such things as food, water, the floor, and animals than to touch what has little meaning to him; repetition will then be easy as these objects are so accessible.

Tactile Qualities

Objects have qualities that some may not feel are tactile. However, for the purpose of this discussion, it is practical to include them to emphasize the variety of experiences related to this sensory area.

Temperature is fun to investigate through the sense of touch. The stove, heater, or fireplace will feel hot. Enthusiasm, excitement, and exaggerated facial and vocal expressions can help direct the child's attention to the source of heat. Ice is cold and can be fun to manipulate. When exposing the child to various stimuli, always use appropriate words, gestures, and signs. The refrigerator can provide opportunities to experience cold as can the water faucet, swimming pool, lawn sprinkler, or ice cream cone. The heating pad is warm, as is the bath water or a cup of coffee. Some foods can be hot, and the television, tape recorder, and record player are also warm. All opportunities to expand experiences with heat and cold should be utilized. Knowledge in this area is useful; it may also lead to personal safety as the child's independence increases.

Resistance and pressure can also lead to a variety of experiences. Play tag games with the child by pushing and pulling him, encouraging him to do the same. Pull at his crayons or a small object in his hand; tease him. Give him a desired toy and then try to take it from him, encouraging him to hold it more firmly. Other tug games can be developed in similar ways. Help him to lift and move objects of varying size and weight. Small objects are easily moved and lifted, large ones, such as furniture, will not move even when pushed hard. Tape wound round his fingers may be difficult to remove, rocks and logs are hard to lift, doors must be pushed hard, and people shove against each other in a crowd. These and other experiences will increase the child's perception and provide him with the initiative to go on with further investigations.

Since some objects will not move, these can serve as reference points. Others are easily moved and should be thoroughly investigated. The child can learn that he has to pull hard to open the refrigerator door, yet it requires little effort to close it. Some objects stretch. A rubber band, piece of elastic, a balloon, or a nylon shirt can be stretched. A trampoline or set of old bed springs will give in when pressure is exerted and can provide other opportunities to stimulate interest in various tactile experiences.

Movement can be tactilely experienced and often provides a way to motivate independent investigation. Balloons on a string move, as do soap bubbles, small windmills, mobiles suspended from the ceiling, and playful animals. Place the child's hand on the object or hold the object against some part of his body. Swings move, doors open and close, and wagons and some chairs roll. These experiences are valuable. Running water moves and water play is often a fun way to vary experiences. Vibrations should be tactile experiences. Help the child feel a vibrator, small radio, safety fan, television, air conditioner, and hair dryer. Discover other ways to expose him to movement as daily events present the opportunity.

Exposure to a variety of sizes can also increase the child's awareness. Large objects that are easily manipulated are best in the beginning and provide many opportunities for investigation. Big balls, blocks, pots and pans, boxes, plastic jars, and pocketbooks can be used to stimulate curiosity. As tactile development increases, the child can learn to categorize and discriminate between large and small objects. Other large objects within the room can also be used to increase learning experiences.

Shape can be important. Is the object round or square? Does it have sharp points or curves? Teach the child to investigate the shape of various objects by moving his hands under yours as you feel the shape. Find ways to motivate him to examine objects. The experience must be pleasant and rewarding so that his attempts to learn in this way will be repeated and bring additional satisfactions.

Extension also has tactile quality. How far does the table extend? By discovering the length of the table, bench, wall, or floor, the child becomes more aware of his surroundings. As motivation increases, he will learn to make use of this method of investigation, and in other new experiences this knowledge will be valuable.

Surface must also be investigated. How does the surface of the driveway feel? This information will eventually give him a clue as to where he is in the yard. How do the front steps feel? The ground has one surface, the floor in the kitchen has another. Some surfaces are flat, others are round; some are sticky or slippery, others are fuzzy. The wall in the family room has one surface, the bathroom wall has another. This information can become meaningful and helpful in orienting the child within his environment.

Many surfaces have texture, which is another tactile quality. Expose the child to textures that are rough, such as asphalt, tree bark, and rough bricks; smooth such as glass or silk; soft as pillows, cotton balls, or an old blanket; hard, such as the floor or the sidewalk; spongy; wet; damp, as wet sand; and slick or slippery, as the bottom of the bathtub. Constant exposure and variation of experiences will bring increased interest, and the child will be motivated to continue using tactual investigation as a way to gain additional information.

In increasing the child's tactile experiences, include bumpy and wrinkled textures; a variety of rugs (shag, rough, or outdoor); various materials (satin, net, cotton, burlap, velvet, corduroy, and oil cloth); cement and gravel; parts of the body and face; a variety of animals; windows and doors; also foods, flowers, boxes, brushes, paper, grass, and many others to be discovered.

Tactile Language

The use of touch can be important in developing language. We often develop a tactile signal that becomes meaningful communication to the child. If we want the child to get his shoe or to realize that we are now going to do something with shoes, we touch his hands to his feet so he feels them as we tell him to find his shoes. This becomes a way to communicate that it is time to get his shoes or to put them on, and this can eventually be remembered as a signal. Another example is to take the child's finger and touch it to his front teeth, like a toothbrush, when it is time to brush. He will eventually learn that this touching means "time to brush teeth." Always talk constantly about what you are doing. More suggestions can be found in the section on Communication. Tactile signals can be developed and used consistently.

Materials

The following materials have been helpful in working on the development of appropriate use of the tactual sense.

1. A texture board can be made from cork, sandpaper, emery cloth, sponge, rug samples, cotton, and a mirror fastened to a piece of plywood.
2. Shape puzzles or form boards are fun to make and use. Cut two thin pieces of wood approximately 1 foot square. Cut shapes from one piece then nail the cut-out piece on top of the uncut piece. The shapes that have been cut out now fit right into the open forms.
3. Make your own nesting boxes by gathering together different size boxes or cans that will fit into each other.
4. Make a zipper board by nailing a large zipper to a strip of wood.
5. Sew a little vest that has snaps or hooks on to it to use for practice.
6. Large items are best in the beginning. The smaller the child, the bigger the block, ball, or box should be.
7. Rods of different lengths are easy to find and can be sorted or lined up consecutively.
8. We enjoy sewing cards, when the child has developed to the point that he can handle this fine motor task. Buy some inexpensive ones or make your own. Draw or paste a simple picture or shape on a piece of cardboard, then punch a few holes around the outline of the picture and provide the child with a long colorful shoestring.

9. Gather objects of various shapes in a can and teach him to sort them. These can be screws, nuts, pegs, or marbles. Later, finer discrimination can be used to separate large and small pegs, marbles, nuts, and screws.

10. Make cookies of different sizes, shapes, and textures. The textures can be varied with nuts, raisins, icing, and other edible decorations.

11. We occasionally enjoy a commercial game we happen to discover.

12. Make up a big box of objects that go together, such as clothing, playthings, edibles, pencils, crayons, and markers. Help the child sort by function.

13. Squares of post board can be covered with different textures such as cotton, Scotch tape, sandpaper, and various other materials. Others can be covered in glue and sprinkled with sand, corn kernels, grits, and peas. These can be fastened to the wall so the child can discover them as he moves around the room.

14. Squares can be made into consistent sizes and put in a box. Then the child can take them out and stack them, spread them out, or make designs on a desk.

15. The grocery store provides many inexpensive sorting materials. Noodles, spaghetti, and dried beans provided unlimited opportunities for actual experiences (care must be taken, however, to keep certain raw edibles out of the mouth as they may lodge in the throat).

Continuous exposure to various tactile stimuli will give the child some needed contact with his environment and help him to understand himself better. The effort it requires will be worthwhile as experiences will gradually become more meaningful.

OLFACTORY AND GUSTATORY SENSE TRAINING

Teaching: When and What

The child with limited use of one or more channels of input (vision or hearing), or the child who has not learned to use information received through these senses will need to develop the use of other sensory areas to help compensate. The sense of smell (olfactory) and the sense of taste (gustatory) are two areas that may be developed and used in a compensatory fashion to aid the child in getting more information. These two channels of input should be remembered during the occurrence of normal daily activities to help increase the child's understanding of what is happening.

Many daily experiences may be used to develop these senses. However, these situations should be meaningful; otherwise, the child may not understand what he is tasting or smelling and will have no way to relate what is happening to an actual daily activity such as eating or bathing. The experience should be planned so the child can see, hear, and feel what he is tasting and smelling. He will then learn to use odors and tastes to learn even more about his experiences.

If the child is to recognize the many things around him, the best way to teach him is to do so as the activity occurs. For example, while washing he can experience soap. He should be encouraged to smell, feel, rub, and even taste the soap before it is wet. Then it is put in the water and he feels the difference. Introduce these activities in as normal a setting as possible. Food may be best introduced in the kitchen or grocery store; flowers and grass in the yard; bath powder in the bathroom. As his experiences are broadened, he will become better able to use the senses of smell and taste to gather even more information about his environment.

Real Experiences Made Big

The bigger the experience, the more it will mean to him. Merely handing him an apple or a cookie is not as much fun or as meaningful as carrying out a planned "lesson" around the experience. This can be done by beginning with a trip to the store to buy a potato (while doing other weekly shopping, of course) and ending with hot French fries right out of the pan.

Likewise, if you want to help the child learn more about apples, you can plan an activity around the concept you will be emphasizing (apple) and include many opportunities for him to smell and taste the apple. This might be done by going to the store or to an apple tree to select some apples, then returning home or to school to wash, cut, peel, and finally eat the apple. The child is always allowed to help as much as possible. The understanding can be strengthened if a *real* apple tree is available, of course, but this is not always possible or necessary. During this time, constantly talk to the child about the apple and what he is doing or helping you do to the apple. Use words and gestures; with hearing-impaired children, also use signs. Encourage him to smell it, if he does not do so spontaneously. After repeating an activity such as this one several times, he will learn to relate the apple odor to meaningful experiences. In the beginning, the child may have little, if any, interest. He needs many experiences before evidence of progress will appear. Other fruits or sweets, such as candy, cookies, cake, ice cream, or peanut butter, can also be presented in a similar way. You may also enjoy following through by occasionally cooking such edibles as potato sticks, cubed carrots, peas, or stewed apples. If he does not like to eat it, at least the odor will fill the kitchen, and he may have learned something such as "I do not like carrots, and next time I smell them cooking I will know that it is carrots and get away!" That can be meaningful information too!

"Guess what is in the sack" is another fun activity that will encourage the development of smell, taste, and touch. This can be played following a trip to the grocery store. While emptying the sacks, encourage the child to see and feel what is inside. In the beginning, let him put his hand inside the sack and help empty the groceries. Later, this can work into a guessing game. A display of enthusiasm will stimulate curiosity.

One little boy learned to use odors particularly well and now relies heavily on this information. Recently we were playing "surprise" with a group of children and some potatoes in a sack and knew the children might not guess what was inside. We kept teasing—at least we had their attention. After several of the children had a turn reaching down into the paper sack and feeling but not seeing what was inside, it was James' turn. This little boy gingerly poked his hand in the sack and tried to pull out one of the potatoes. When this effort failed, he tried to peep inside. This too was impossible as we were not going to cooperate. Finally, he pulled his empty hand out of the sack and smelled his fingers. "Pomato," he said as he gave the correct manual sign for potato. (James was only beginning to pronounce words with any clarity but we understood his oral communication attempt.) This is using odors to gain meaningful information, and these responses come only after continued efforts are made to emphasize odor awareness. Incidentally, we later washed, peeled (the children were great with a little help and a potato peeler), cut, fried, and finally ate those potatoes. You can be sure they are all more aware of the full sensory value of a potato.

Creating Interest

Although it is best to give the children the opportunity to experience different odors and tastes in meaningful situations, we have had fun during group get-togethers playing "games" with distinctive odors and tastes. This activity is a good attention getter, helps to develop an enjoyable relationship, assists the child in learning to take turns, and is also good for visual discrimination and language development. In groups like these, we use total communication (see Speech section) if there is any possibility that at least one member of the group has an auditory problem or a related language disorder.

We gather everything "smelly" we can find around the room and a few things from the kitchen and bathroom, then put them all in our "surprise" bag. Next we sit down in a semicircle and take the articles out one at a time. We let each child examine the objects—in *any* way they wish. Cotton balls that have been soaked in vinegar, lemon juice, whiskey, turpentine, or perfume sometimes bring interesting reactions. We usually put the cotton inside discarded medicine bottles so they can be easily manipulated and also reused. Also be sure to try coffee grounds, pepper, salt, sugar, vanilla, chocolate, and spices. Countless other ingredients can be smelled and tasted.

To begin the activity, the teacher, adult, or volunteer opens a bottle and smells it with enthusiasm to encourage interest and curiosity. She looks excited and talks about it, while each child has an opportunity to smell or taste what is inside. If a child wants to put his fingers in the bottle, encourage this exploration. If he does not seem curious, we always put a little dot of what we have on his finger or palm. Then he may look for it. He may even try to rub it off. Fine. This indicates an awareness of what has happened. He is feeling and probably smelling. Also he may eventually happen to get a little in his mouth. He is learning. Another child may be eager and try everything. Red pepper looks pretty on the palm but does not taste so good. The next time round he may reject some things he remembers as not so pleasant. This is what we want—discrimination between what is good and what is not.

Problem Solving

While playing with tastes and smells, we are constantly aware of every opportunity to develop problem-solving skills. Development of this skill is important and requires us to be alert to situations or planned lessons that offer an opportunity to present a little problem for the child to solve. This can be fun. For example, introduce the child to marshmallows, and after he has thoroughly examined them and eaten several, perhaps a cotton ball could be substituted. Is it the same? It looks similar, but it is *not* good to eat. Later this activity can be extended by offering a mixture of cotton balls and marshmallows for choice. Another time when we know the child likes something very much (candy, potato chips, dill pickles), we put it in a place that necessitates problem solving. It can be candy inside a snap-top jar, a pickle in plastic wrap, or potato chips in a bag. Sometimes we put the surprise sack on a shelf or barely beyond his easy reach. We have tied things on a string and hung them from the overhead light fixture, put the "surprise" that smells so good in a tightly tied sack, or let them see the goody and pretended to run away with it. Sometimes two of us "big children" even sit down at the table and slowly begin eating our surprise. You should see them trying to come up with the language that might work or trying to manipulate our hands so we will share. When working with children, we laugh a lot, and the children usually get what they want, but we get what we want, too. What we want may be a little language, curiosity, socialization, group play, or simple problem solving. We make them do the *thinking* whenever possible, as they will eventually have to rely more on themselves and less on us.

One day Carolyn, a teacher assistant, brought some delicious homemade cookies to school. We decided that these cookies would be used to make a big experience for the children. After recess, Carolyn let the children "discover" the cookies in a sack on the table, then she grabbed the cookies and started running around the table. Naturally, everyone fell in line too, and one teacher pretended she was going to grab those beautiful cookies. You should have seen the children. They chased her and almost got the cookies. The language was rapidly coming out. Judy was signing, "get," which meant "I want to get that." Roy was laughing and pulling at Carolyn. James was saying "Surprise," and Rosy was running and laughing aloud, very much as part of the group. We had their attention and interest. They were motivated to get those cookies, we used that motivation! One teacher grabbed the cookies and balanced them on the corner of the cafe curtain rod. Now how will you get the cookies? The children looked, reached, and tried to get an adult's arm to reach them. Roy pushed Carolyn over to the window. Those grown-ups would not cooperate. Then one of us pushed a chair toward the children, and they got the picture. Two of the children quickly climbed on the chair and tried to reach the cookies. Still too far away. They climbed down and moved the chair closer to the window. Still not tall enough. What now? We handed James a broom. "Oh, I see," he seemed to be saying, and he immediately started swinging the broom toward the cookies. The task seemed impossible. Then Judy came up with an idea. She grabbed the broom, climbed on the chair, and finally knocked down the cookies. The children were thrilled and their faces beamed with success.

We all sat on the floor and ate cookies, while we encouraged language such as "cookie," "more," "thank you," and "finished." Later we saw several indications that the children had learned much that day. It is good to plan as much as possible in order to be prepared, but we cannot let a chance slip by to try something new. What is tried spontaneously may work better than anything. With lots of enthusiasm, a real love for this kind of work, determination, a sense of humor, and some good basic knowledge, many things will happen that never seemed possible. That is what makes these children such a challenge and a joy to teach.

Careful Observation

Watch for slow reactions when working with taste discrimination. We often decide to let a child have another taste of red pepper or vinegar if he wants it; but we observe carefully and go about this slowly. Often it seems to take a long time to develop recognition of the taste and whether it is pleasant or unpleasant. This can occur because of lack of development, so we help him learn. The child can have a little more, but slowly; we do not want to make him sick. We have seen children try a seemingly unpleasant taste several times before later learning to discriminate. This may take several sessions. Some children seem receptive to anything, and we sometimes wonder if they would drink a whole bottle of vinegar or eat a tablespoon of pepper if someone did not intercede. The children do learn to discriminate, but it often takes longer than we thought.

The multisensory approach works well. Encourage the child to examine an object by utilizing all possible senses. He can feel as well as smell Papa's pipe; be placed on a pad near the freshly cut grass; or feel, smell, and taste a banana. We must continuously develop ways to assist him in utilizing every possible channel of input.

Ideas for Activities

The following additional suggestions might help to increase your awareness of ways to stimulate the use of smell and taste input.

1. Take the child to various rooms in the house so he can experience the difference. The kitchen, bathroom, and porch have distinctive odors.
2. Put "good smelling" things on him, such as lotion and bath powder. Let him help you rub it on.

3. Rub his skin with something warm, cool, or stimulating that has a distinct odor. Try witch hazel, warm baby oil, alcohol, and the like. Be careful to discontinue any skin irritant.
4. Occasionally spray the room with a room deodorizer or disinfectant. Let him see or feel the can so he will know more about what is happening. Let him "help."
5. He can help you bring fragrant flowers inside. Let him see, touch, smell, and feel them. Place the flowers in the room he is in most often.
6. Play smell games with small jars filled with pickle juice, cough syrup, menthol, turpentine, paste, alcohol, and spices. You can have your own set of herb bottles. Let him explore and examine the bottles.
7. Be sure he is outside when there is a strong odor, such as barbecue, freshly mowed grass, or smoke. Freshly turned earth has a good smell, too.
8. Try different food textures. This may be difficult at first, as some children are very discriminating about certain types of food and are more aware of texture than others. Think of the difference in grits and boiled okra or the difference in creamed corn and fresh lettuce. He may reject the food because of texture rather than taste.
9. Touch his lips with different tastes—lemon, salt, vinegar, and mouthwash. Try to do this as the occasion or situation presents the opportunity, but do not overdo it. Talk to him about it. These experiences are more meaningful if they occur in the appropriate place at the appropriate time.
10. Strike a match. Let him see and feel its heat if he is interested. The odor of sulfur is strong when the match is blown out. Let him see or feel the match when someone strikes one near him (when smoking or lighting a fire). He will learn to associate the odor with something meaningful. Activities involving fire and heat should be conducted with extreme care and should be avoided with children who are difficult to control.
11. Let him see and feel a pipe or cigar as it is lit. Help him see and smell the smoke.
12. Take him to the grocery store as often as possible.
13. Be sure he is in the kitchen when preparing a dish with a distinctive odor (fish, shrimp, chili, chocolate cake, etc.). Make a safe place for him near the kitchen. Let him feel, see, taste, and smell what is cooking. This is easier at home than in a school, but it is adaptable to each at some time or another.

14. Let him help put perfume on someone. Put some on him, too.
15. Get him to "help" peel an onion. Be sure he tastes it.
16. Take him into a room that is being painted. Put a little paint on his hand. Perhaps he can help paint something.
17. Give the child the experience of starting with a food in its most original state (in a garden if possible or maybe a grocery store) and move through each step in preparing the food. A whole banana can be peeled, sliced, and mixed with pudding, put in a pie shell, and then served as a piece of pie. Prepare foods in a variety of ways. Many foods can be prepared in a classroom.
18. Let the child help and encourage him to taste the ingredients along the way (raw, in combination with other ingredients, and fully prepared).
19. He can help mix cake batter, feeling and tasting ingredients as they are added. Try other foods he can "help" prepare. A "popcorn" party is fun. Also try making pizza, popcorn balls, cinnamon toast, and other good-smelling fun foods. In this way you are making him more aware and having fun at the same time.
20. He can also "help" around the house. Let him mop the floor or clean the windows with a solution that has a unique odor.
21. Be aware of ways to help him become more familiar with things that have distinctive tastes and odors, but do not bombard him with meaningless things. These activities are meant to be done occasionally and preferably at an appropriate time.
22. Your first goal should be awareness, then tolerance. Later, recognition will bring association with meaningful objects and events.

Increased olfactory and gustatory experiences that cause the child to become more aware of isolated or intense odors and tastes will lead toward integration of experiences in other sensory areas. He will look, feel, and then taste his food or touch and then smell his fingers when he sees something interesting. By doing this, he will be receiving information related to his stimuli through several sensory areas. This checking and information receiving will become increasingly important as he becomes more discriminatory.

VISUAL STIMULATION AND TRAINING

Learning to See

Children learn to see, and this learning not only depends on the actual process of increasing the use of this sensory mode (vision) but also is greatly influenced by the experiences and learning opportunities to which the child is exposed. As the child matures, the sense organs normally become more efficient; however, this is not always the case. Learning to see is a two-way process, and the extent to which the child's vision develops to its maximum potential has much to do with the amount of environmental visual stimulation the child receives.

The infant responds to visual stimulation such as a bright light, but the light means nothing to him. His response is more of a reflex, as when the pupil contracts, and requires no conscious effort on his part. Later, one observes that the child responds by blinking when an object approaches his eye. All of this happens many times before the child begins to attach meaning to the stimulation he is receiving. If the child's vision is stimulated by something he sees and if this is a rewarding experience, he then makes more efforts to see. Because he is learning to use his eyes to a fuller extent, he sees more. It is relatively easy for the child with normal vision to go through the developmental stages that occur as he learns to see. He involuntarily reacts to light and then later learns to fixate on the light source. With exposure and practice, he learns to look at one thing, maybe his hand, and then another with fair accuracy. Both eyes may now be moving together in contrast to the previously uncoordinated muscular control observed in the infant trying to focus. Next the baby will begin to track (follow) moving objects, usually horizontally at first and later vertically. These tracking movements will probably not be smooth in the beginning but will gradually become more so as the child matures, provided he has ample opportunity to continue developing his use of vision. As the developmental process continues and new experiences provide visual stimulation, the child will begin to attach more and more meaning to the things he is seeing. As he perceives stimuli and attaches meaning to his perceptions, he forms concepts or mental images that he will store for future use. This "storehouse of knowledge," the concepts he is forming, will provide much of the material needed to develop an understanding of himself and his environment. Self-understanding and an awareness of his surroundings precede other intellectual processes such as language development and communication.

Some severely and profoundly handicapped children are also labeled blind. The very definition of blindness itself can be confusing. A person is considered legally blind when his vision is 20/200 or less in the best eye with correction (glasses) or if there is a restriction in the field of vision so that the widest point in his field of vision subtends an arc of no more than 20 degrees. This is sometimes called "tunnel" vision. In other words, a person with 20/200 vision would see an object 20 feet away with about the same clarity as someone with normal vision would see it at 200 feet away. The field may be so narrow or the acuity so weak that we may not recognize its value without further experience or analysis, but it is sight, and educably valuable vision.

Visual developmental training is important for all severely and profoundly handicapped children who make limited use of all sensory information. If there is any vision, then it is worth developing. Planning for the child must include ample opportunities to experience and learn to interpret visual stimuli. It is important to remember that his use of vision will be largely dependent on two factors: how much actual sight he has and the extent to which it is developed. Over the last few years there have been important findings concerned with use and development of vision in the blind child. One of the most important is that "blind" children with residual vision who have had no training in "learning to see" can, with proper instruction, learn to see better. How much the child will finally learn may depend to a large extent on motivation, which is our problem. Some suggestions as to how we go about developing residual vision will be included in this section.

First, a few problems that confront us in working with the visually impaired child will be mentioned, with the recognition that similar conditions may exist in any severely and profoundly handicapped child. Concern as to *how* the child looks at something, is not necessary; the point is that he does look. Some children may see best when turning their heads at an angle that seems peculiar and unnatural. Others see best to one side. One little boy could obviously see best when he held his hands over his better eye and peeped through a tiny crack. In this way he was screening out too much light or things that were confusing and narrowing his field of vision down to the one thing he wanted to see. It worked for him and that is the important thing. He did not, however, use this technique when coloring, looking at books, or other close-up work, only when trying to see far away. He was looking, and every time he looked he was developing his use of vision.

It is good to see an individual demonstrating this motivation to see and improvising. When a person looks through a tiny slit or a pinhole in a piece of paper, he is telling us he can see better this way. This may be related to an action similar to that which occurs when the lens opening on a camera is decreased. The depth of focus is increased, resulting in a clearer picture. Then, too, the camera and lens also have aberrations that distort the image as it goes to the film. When the band of light entering the eye is narrowed, then less distortion can occur. Children determine these things by trial and error. We can help them to use their senses better by knowledge of the way this sense functions. We can also help by careful observation and by giving the child stimulating situations and opportunities to try their own ways to see best.

Rewarding His Efforts

The child's efforts to see must be rewarding if we expect him to continue trying. We must use every opportunity to help him see and be rewarded by his success. In this way he builds his own confidence—"I did it by myself"—and will continue to make more and more effort. If he tries and fails, he will eventually stop trying and find other ways to entertain or stimulate himself.

Observe carefully and draw the line between helping too much and not enough. Tasks must eventually become more difficult for him as he is required to use his vision to a greater extent, but this increasing difficulty should be gradual and only increased as he experiences some success on simpler tasks. For example, if a child is looking for a cookie on the table, knowing it is there, he will be rewarded when he finally discovers it. However, if the cookie is in a far corner and the child appears to be giving up, as he has not yet developed the persistence needed to continue searching, then he may need help. The cookie could be moved more within his visual range this time for encouragement. Next time it can be put further away.

Wearing Glasses

Another problem we often confront is the child's refusal to wear glasses. This is a common problem and one that can be overcome. Observation is needed to answer several questions concerning the child's rejection of glasses. Do they fit? Is he afraid of them? If so, why is he afraid? Does he reject the glasses because they prevent his eye poking? Remember, although "eye poking" is more often a blindism (self-stimulation habit), it can also be an indication of pain. He may be trying to relieve pressure. An ophthalmologist can be helpful here. Sometimes the child objects to glasses because they are improperly introduced (forced), and he quickly develops an intolerance. Other times, the child may use this as a way to express himself: "I'm not going to do this and you can't make me."

It is best to overcome this problem as soon as possible. If the child needs the glasses to see better, he needs them now. There is no time to be lost since he has much "catching up" to do as it is. The earlier his visual loss is diagnosed and treated, the better chance he has to develop to his maximum potential.

The teacher can begin by requiring the child to wear the glasses for short periods, for a purpose, and making these periods as enjoyable as possible. For example, if the child likes to listen to music or have tea parties, these are good times to begin wearing glasses. If he likes to be carried around the house or cuddled close, use this reinforcing activity for the introduction of glasses. The situation should be structured for maximum enjoyment before he is forced to wear glasses he already dislikes. It is better to introduce them under the best possible circumstances than to remediate later, but if the initial introduction has occurred, then some of the impressions he has developed can be corrected. It is best for the adult to maintain a calm and confident attitude once the decision to wear glasses has been made so that the child will have maximum confidence. Then once the glasses are on, make certain they stay there for a few minutes; one or two minutes will do at first. When this has been accomplished successfully, remove the glasses and say "Fine, we'll put the glasses on again later." Gradually, after the initial distasteful period, the time span can be lengthened. Remember, you are "boss," and he must develop confidence in you and your ability to make a decision and stick with it. This approach will be best for the child.

Some words of caution should be given, however, regarding the necessity for wearing glasses, especially those used with children having severe visual disorders. We have stressed the need for visual stimulation and its effect upon visual efficiency. Our main concern is that the child should use his sight whenever possible and in as meaningful a manner as can be brought about.

Corrective prescription of lenses is not as exact a science as one might expect. While good refraction may be obtained even under anesthetic, it is still advisable for the patient to be able to communicate with the eye specialist about what he is able to see while different tests are being made. The children in our group seldom fall into this category when lenses are first prescribed. This means that the correction may not be exactly what is needed, and at least some of the time the image will be blurred. With high degrees of correction, it is also easy for the focal point to shift so that when the glasses are not exactly situated where they are intended, they may be blurred.

With high magnification, there is also an extreme restriction of peripheral vision, since only the exact center of the lenses has the prescribed correction. This leads to frustration when the child is trying to be mobile. He knows that when his glasses are not worn, he can move about more efficiently.

It is also possible that the child does not need the fine discriminative ability provided, since conceptually he is not ready to see what his glasses allow. This is similar to the amateur bird-watcher using high-powered binoculars to identify a bird when little magnification is needed. With a high-powered lens he can see small details, but because the fields are so restricted, he cannot find the bird to identify. When he learns to use the binoculars for the correct situation and needs to see finer details, he can identify more birds, but this takes much learning. Our children are the same. They need to use their eyes under all conditions. Sometimes they can see certain things better without the lenses. It is our task to recognize these varying conditions and allow for any factors that might influence resultant visual efficiency. A delicate balance must be maintained with some children to determine as well as possible which ones are motivated to see and need flexibility to make the best use of vision, and which are presenting similar behavior patterns to avoid using their sight in a productive and positive manner.

Encouraging Independent Travel

Moving about is an extension of reaching out. Therefore, before we can expect the child to be motivated to move his whole body toward something, he will need to have had many opportunities to reach for objects, and these experiences must be rewarding. Such experiences will help him develop the desire to move further than his arms will reach to grasp objects that are appealing. If he cannot see and yet has had these rewarding experiences, then he will eventually develop the curiosity to investigate his surroundings and reach out further. This subject is considered further in our discussion on Movement in Space.

It is up to the teacher to introduce the severe and profoundly handicapped child to his environment. One goal is to develop motivation to move within the environment and the motor skills necessary to do so. This is an important development and will require knowledge, effort, and a combination of determination and patience. To develop curiosity requires that the child have experiences to stimulate this curiosity. He must understand his body and his immediate surroundings before he will want to investigate larger areas. The child develops many concepts about his environment through constant efforts to expose him to varied stimuli. He also needs the necessary muscular skills before he will be prepared for independent mobility. Upright mobility is not necessary, but some means of independent travel is. This is another example of the necessity to consider the interdependence of several developmental areas. Some suggestions that may be helpful in establishing the child's muscular and motor developmental needs can be found in the section on Movement in Space. Also, the ideas presented in the section on Body Image and Experiencing with Objects should be helpful.

Checking with Vision

Begin where the child is and help him form concepts, mental images, or pictures about himself and his world. Sometimes it is best even to begin below the child's present functioning levels. This creates a more encouraging introduction. The severely and profoundly handicapped child cannot rely solely on visual images to form concepts. Neither can he rely solely on verbal descriptions. Therefore, continue to talk, as he may hear better than you think, and encourage the child to use his vision. Also be sure that the child develops use of other senses as a way to investigate, check, and gain new knowledge.

The importance of teaching the child to "check" by using his vision as a secondary sense cannot be overemphasized. For example, if the child hears or feels something and then uses his eyes to check further, he is in one more way gaining useful information. In addition, each time he tries to see, he learns a little more about how to see, and he also learns to appreciate the value of his vision as a means of increasing his knowledge.

Using Visual Clues

Problem solving is also important in developing the use of vision. While working on increasing the child's use of vision, we continually present the child with visual discrimination problems. For example, a closer look may be necessary to recognize the facial features that supply the child with the needed information when trying to identify a person. At another time, the child must look carefully for a desired object or to find the toy he has dropped on the floor. The reward for the increasing use of vision will be supplied when the child finds what he is seeking.

Encourage the child to look at things as he tactilely examines them. Begin with gross light, then smaller lights (penlights), and then large objects in trying to develop vision. Observe carefully. If the child has learned to rely on other senses (listening, touching, smelling, tasting) to stimulate himself or to gain information, it has not been necessary for him to use his vision as a primary or secondary source of input. If this is the case, the use of vision can be improved, and we must see that it is developed to the fullest extent.

As the child learns to understand himself and his environment, he also needs to realize his position in space, that is, where he is in relation to other things. Later, he can be given more assistance in understanding his environment. For him to understand himself, he must investigate his body and learn that it is the same as others but separate from them. Some of the ideas presented in the section on Body Image Development may be helpful.

The child who is primarily tactilely oriented is limited to the space immediately around him. When a child begins to use his visual ability, knowledge of space and his relationship to it is infinitely increased. If he is to understand his position in space, he has to be constantly exposed to and made aware of environmental clues. He needs to know where he is at all times, and this will be gradually learned as he is helped to investigate his surroundings tactilely. Talk to him about where he is, help him learn to use visual clues and develop a system that will assist him in associating his new experiences with old ones. He must not feel that his only connection with his environment is what someone does *to* or *for* him and that his role is to receive rather than to give and to interact. With help he will learn to anticipate and interpret environmental clues to give him information about what is and will be happening.

Developing Concepts

Visual concept formation depends to an extent on how thoroughly a child is interested in learning all there is to know about a certain object or experience. Some part, at least, is dependent on his ability to use knowledge gained from other sensory areas and merge these together so that a total concept is formed, which is then useful for application to other areas. The concept of roundness, for instance, may be related to tactile experiences of balls, plates, and coins. When visual identification has been joined to the others, then even more use can be made. Round things may then be seen, which would not otherwise have been perceived as round, on the basis of a purely tactile referent system. Eventually, of course, even more use can be made of such knowledge. It forms the basis for many studies and for a knowledge of many other applications that can be made.

Exploring

As early as possible, begin encouraging the child to explore. Give him something to explore. Help him learn that there are things "out there" to discover and examine. When he is in bed, give him objects to touch. Toys with an interesting texture or those that make noise are good starters, but remember, what appeals to one child may repel another. Later, with help, he will learn to use his vision to search for the objects, but first he must be made aware of the fact that they exist. As he develops and other areas of the home are made familiar to him, every opportunity to make him aware of things within his environment should be used. Take him to things in the environment. Call his attention to objects while he is in the infant seat, playpen, baby swing, high chair, or on the floor. Bring objects to him. Do not expect him to develop meaningful concepts and understandings without this effort.

Develop the child's curiosity. If he does not see and hear well and has not learned that there are undiscovered objects to feel, then he will not be motivated to "check around." This also is up to the teacher. He will not investigate unless he is made aware of the unlimited things that can be enjoyed.

Vision makes exploring much easier. An object can be identified and a beginning inspection made even before extra effort is expended in moving to it. Then once the child is at the object, he can use his vision again to gain more information than can be provided by tactile and other sensory cues. Finding ways to motivate the child is part of the challenge, since what motivates one child may not motivate another. The child must realize the necessity of learning to see, and when he does make the effort to see, it must be a satisfying experience. With concentrated efforts, it is easy to find a way to capture the child's interest.

Perceiving

The child should perceive visually the same things that other children are perceiving, even though his vision is limited. Perception (visually perceiving) requires experience. Perception occurs when the child is exposed to stimulation and begins to make meaning from the sensations he receives. As he learns to recognize and then associate the experience with previously acquired knowledge, he begins to form concepts of his world. Thus, constant exposure to varied stimuli is necessary for the child to grow intellectually. Perception is then on a continuum. The child experiences, associates, learns, and is then more prepared for the next experience. The child's first perceptions are then used and changed as he is given more and more opportunities to experience and increase his knowledge. Therefore, what was sensation and perception becomes recognition and the beginning of concept formation. For a child to form concepts, he must be exposed to many and varied stimuli repeatedly and frequently.

Therein lies the problem. A child who is perceptually handicapped, one who is sensorially deprived in one or more ways, will have to rely on outside help if he is to have these needed experiences. A child who is deprived of one or more major means of sensory input receives less stimulation. This means that he begins to look more and more abnormal, and because he looks different, he is treated differently. Therefore, he receives less stimulation and reacts by finding new ways to stimulate himself. This learning pattern is the reverse of what is needed. He becomes different and withdrawn, and he fails to develop the necessary confidence, independence and curiosity. Once this "reversal" begins, the effort it will take to turn the child around is multiplied.

Sequencing Development of Vision

We began this section by pointing out that seeing is a learned skill. For the severely and profoundly handicapped, this skill must be taught. No attempt will be made to pinpoint each specific skill leading toward the ability to see; however, some of the major steps in the sequence are mentioned as examples of perceptual development. The child may be an infant so far as seeing is concerned. If so, then we want to help him move forward, teaching him to get maximum use from his residual vision. This requires some knowledge of the sequence. Always concentrate on the vision he does have, not on what he does not have.

First, capture the child's attention and make him realize something exists in the visual field, that there is something to see. Tactile and auditory stimulation may help here. Touch him with an object, put his hand on it, with your hand over his, and help him contact the object. Auditory toys such as music boxes, jack-in-the-boxes, bells, and noisy objects may capture his attention. A lighted candle with an odor may appeal to the child. (Be safety conscious, though.) Moving objects sometimes attract attention. A bright light is almost always noticed; however, what is used depends partly on the child and what motivates him and partly on the amount of residual vision or his particular combination of disorders.

We have found it helpful, and incidentally interesting, to play "look at what I have" in a dark room or closet. Here we can control what the child is trying to see and have fun at the same time. If we present different stimulating objects to him rapidly, he will probably forget about the dark. He does not have an opportunity to be afraid because we move quickly and with enthusiasm. We have tried several "games" in the dark room. Turn on a bright flashlight for a few seconds, then turn it off for a few seconds. "Where is it?" "Here it is!" This should attract his attention. Shine the light on something bright, such as a bicycle reflector or a ball covered with tinfoil and suspended from a string. Focus the light on noisy toys, those that vibrate and make noise, or those that do both. You will think of other interesting ideas after you begin.

Once the child has learned to fixate on an object, such as the light or other bright objects, move to more complicated skills. Although he may have been aware of the light as it was moved in front of him, perhaps he had difficulty following the object. Begin to work on this skill. Move the light back and forth (horizontally first, then vertically) so he can learn to follow a moving object. Do not shine a bright light directly in his eyes. Watch his eyes and help him follow the movement of the light. This is visual tracking. It is important that the child learn to track moving objects. This activity can begin in a dark room; however, as he progresses it will not always be necessary to work in an artificial situation. As much of his work as possible should be conducted in a normal setting. Hopefully, he is enjoying his experiences, but do not drag any activity out too long; stop before he becomes bored.

When these stages have been passed, it is time to concentrate more heavily on seeing *objects*. This too is learned. Encourage the child to examine objects visually—large ones at first. They should be meaningful (real) objects, not copies; a ball, a box, a block, or a brick are real; a stuffed dog is not. By now, he should be beginning to realize that objects have size and shape.

The child now needs more and more experience opportunities, which requires greater effort on the part of the teacher. However, his successes provide the motivation to continue these efforts. If the child is beginning to realize that objects have visual pattern, this can be useful information to him as he becomes more mobile. He may see the table, chair, or door, which will be helpful as he learns to orient and move himself within the room. It may be said that he now has "object perception," that is he perceives not only light but also objects within his environment.

Using Daily Experiences

Make use of all daily experiences that can be shared with the child. These experiences are valuable for visual stimulation as well for normal child growth. Let him help dust, mop, or wax. He may love to spray the window cleaner, help stir the batter, scrape the bowl, and decorate the cookies. He can recover the dropped pan or find a spoon. If everything spills on the floor, realistic visual stimulation will certainly be provided. Turn on the oven light and peep in. "What do I see?'' Show him. There is no end to the things that can be done together to stimulate use of vision. They are only limited by your awareness of all opportunities.

Begin to assist the child in learning to see objects more clearly, learning to see smaller objects, and learning to see objects in more detail. Later he can be introduced to dark shapes drawn on posterboard that can be matched or outlined with his finger. Much later, interest can be stimulated in pictures.

The more the child uses his vision, the better he will see. He will not "use up" his vision and the best way to "save sight" is by learning to use it more efficiently. Actually the less he uses his eyes, the less he will see. If he is looking, he is doing what you want, even if it is difficult for him. Vision will improve with use.

"Use it or lose it" may be an appropriate old saying. Remember, although he should not rely on verbal descriptions alone, you must still constantly describe what he is seeing as he sees it. Always show the child that you have the utmost confidence in him and that you know he can "do it." A positive attitude is valuable. All blind children with some residual vision that we have seen, have learned to use their vision to a more useful extent following structured educational programming. The same has been true with children who are so severely retarded that they were not making use of visual cues. It required a great deal of effort; however, every one benefited from this effort. Determination helps. We let the child prove to us that he cannot see what we expect him to while giving him ample time to prove it, as we keep trying.

Other Suggestions

The following suggestions include some things we have found helpful in working with visually impaired children. Many have also been applied to children who are not visually impaired but who need to be helped to see.

1. Seeing games like "where is it?" are fun. Hide a toy within his visual range, such as in front of him or on a table or tray, and help him discover it.
2. Footprints taped to the floor can be fun to walk on and often create interest. In the same way, strips of tape or drawn lines can be used. Get down there and feel them with the child.
3. Trace around a black circle or square drawn on white cardboard with his finger. Feel, look, and see.
4. A string of small Christmas lights high along a strip of the wall will

almost always catch his eye. Later, move them or replace them with something more appropriate.

5. Brightly colored shapes, cut from oil cloth, sandpaper, or foil and other shiny materials and pasted on poster board allow the child many opportunities for discovery.

6. Place colorful strips of tape at eye level around the room.

7. Try penlight flashlights with colored cellophane fastened over the light with a rubber band. These are good for awareness, tracking, and focus.

8. Make homemade books by pasting pictures, textures, drawings, or colors on sheets of heavy paper and binding them together. Choose things that are meaningful to the child. Books should be fun—make them so.

9. Arrange an obstacle course on the floor to walk around or through. The objects used can be large or small. Motivate the child so he will want to go through the course. A flashlight to "lead" him or perhaps a reward at the end may help.

10. Label things around the room. If he pulls the tags off, he is looking and seeing; this is a demonstration of his visual awareness.

11. The children will usually attend to fireworks, sparkles, flames, or hurricane lamps.

12. Decorate the room. Fasten paper chains across the ceiling. Balloons tied to strings and discarded food posters from the grocery store are great. The child's own handiwork can be used at different times and in different places. Sometimes churches dispose of posters that are useful.

13. Make your own mobile with strings and cardboard, paper snowflakes, Christmas decorations, or circles of construction paper. Clothes hangers or soda straws suspended vertically by strings can provide the frame.

14. Corrugated paper can be cut into interesting shapes and hung around the room at eye level. Texture and color offer unlimited possibilities.

15. Puzzles are fun. Make your own. Cut large squares, circles, and stars into two or three pieces and put them together.

16. Color black stars, circles, triangles, or squares on white poster board squares, then cut out shapes of the same size from black construction paper. Now match them, "Where does the star go?" "Can you put it in the right place?" Later try forms of animals, people, objects, and colors.

17. Encourage him in every way to reach out. Put an elastic string

across the playpen with many suspended cheerful toys. Touch his hand to the objects. Noisy toys help.

18. Buy or borrow a light that blinks on and off with noise intensity.

19. Use sticks, strings, strips of cardboard, shapes, kitchen utensils, silverware, and more to teach sameness and imitation.

20. Coffee cans for colors are easy to make. Have a different can for each group of objects of the same color. He will have to look to see which can to put the object in. Separate all the small objects you can find around the house into colors. Try poker chips, colored cardboard discs, marbles, small toys, and jewelry.

21. Sort small articles like seeds, rocks, beans, popcorn, nails, screws, and buttons. Also try shapes and sizes. Encourage him to *look* at what he is doing as he separates them into like groups. Start with two groups mixed together; later, the problem can become more difficult.

22. We enjoy several commercial toys. Using *real* objects is recommended, but toys occasionally add variety.

23. Finger paint is great. Some children prefer not to be messy, but we paint anyway—one way or another.

24. Make a face with a paper plate and pieces of colored construction paper. Touch his hand to your eye, his eye, and where the eye on the plate will be. Help him paste it on the plate. Try the same with other facial features.

25. Let him complete a picture. Draw a round face with eyes, nose, and mouth. Now draw another one and draw the eyes and nose, letting him finish it by drawing the mouth. Gradually let him move toward putting in all of the features. Do the same with stick figures.

26. Draw a picture with a mistake, something wrong or missing. He will enjoy this as he progresses.

27. Have three or four boxes of different kinds of objects that go together. In one box have a cup, glass, mug, paper cup, tea set cup, and other such items; in another box have different balls; another could have different kinds of grooming items.

28. Inexpensive felt board sets often have geometric shapes that are fun to match. You can make your own.

29. Sequence stories requiring the child to put story cards in order can be either made or bought. Playing cards can also be sequenced and grouped for similarity and difference.

30. Block design cards used with 1-inch blocks are good for matching eye-hand coordination, and visual perception.

31. Gather objects in a box that can be matched to pictures you have collected.
32. Paper dolls are good to use on posters. Put the boy doll and a variety of boy clothes on one, then do the same for the other dolls. Make a "family" poster. We also use paper dolls to call attention to different weather conditions and reinforce appropriate dress.
33. Paste some envelopes to a poster board, open side out. Color them and let the children put the correct pieces of colored construction paper in the matching slot. The same can be done with clothes, shapes, and numbers.
34. Make a necklace from colorful drinking straws.
35. Don't forget pipe cleaners. The colored ones can be used in a variety of ways.
36. Several companies have available good audio tapes with pictures to match the sounds. You may enjoy devising your own tape and picture sets.
37. Marble games are fun. Look for them, pick them up, count them, and put them in a bottle.
38. Play "follow the leader" with the child, or a modification of the game that will encourage him to track you or objects.
39. Make a geo-board. An 8 by 8-inch board with small nails arranged in equal rows is good for tying strings or using rubber bands to make geometric shapes. Also by placing beads on the nails, you can make numerous designs or teach beginning number concepts.
40. Cut squares, circles, and triangles from cardboard and cover them with cotton flannel. This gives it texture. Now match the colors and shapes. Later try it with numbers.

Perhaps the most outstanding characteristic of these children is that most do have considerable visual ability. This is used in a variety of ways and unfortunately may sometimes be used to avoid social interaction with adults. They also use vision to structure their world and limit their interaction with the environment to a few well-defined nonthreatening experiences. Visual ability can therefore be a strong positive force for the child to gain new experiences and aid his development; or it can be negative and serve to maintain him at a low functioning level, devoid of most social and learning experiences.

Our task is to make the use of vision highly rewarding. We must challenge the child to use his sight to extend his knowledge of the world. New concepts formed by the information gained in this way will be used many times a day; with each bit of information gained visually, there will be many new connections with concepts developed in other sensory areas which in the past were not understandable. Thus, with each more correct and complete concept gained, the child also gains a better chance of becoming a more "normal" and more accepted member of society.

AUDITORY STIMULATION AND TRAINING

Need for Auditory Training

Sensory input comes from all directions and in many fashions. A child may be crying on one side, the television blaring on the other, someone drops a pan, the odor of bacon fills the room, someone steps on a sore toe, and there is much to see. For many children, learning to screen out and separate sensory input while making meaning of individual sensory stimulation is a task that is easily accomplished with time and experience. Other children have difficulty singling out and attaching learning to each or any of these sensations. Still others have limited input in a major sensory area, as with the hearing-impaired child. These children need help in learning to recognize and respond to various stimuli; by helping them learn to understand environmental sounds, we are moving toward accomplishing this goal.

Auditory training includes helping the child learn to recognize and understand oral language (speech). However, our main concern here is to emphasize the importance of helping the child learn to make use of auditory cues within the environment. We know that every severely and profoundly handicapped child will not learn to communicate orally, but he can benefit from auditory training. The deaf–blind child must learn to make use of any remaining vision and hearing, the deaf child stands to gain much from auditory training, and the severely retarded child will need all the help he can get if he is to make any meaning from the sounds around him.

Any degree of hearing is valuable and worth developing, and this should be done as soon as possible. Hearing and associating sounds with situations is a learning task. There are several ways a child can be helped to use his hearing, and for many severely handicapped children this skill must be taught. A positive attitude is important if the child is to learn. A diagnosis of little or no hearing or the fact that the child does not respond to loud noises is no reason to deprive him of the opportunity to learn to use his hearing.

We know that some children who are diagnosed as hearing impaired do not have a real hearing loss or have one so slight that it is a minor handicap. Some of these children have problems that make it difficult for them to interpret or understand what they hear. There may be nothing physically wrong with the hearing mechanism, but they respond much like a deaf child. Auditory training is needed. Other children who are brain injured or mentally retarded need help in learning to use the information that is received through the ears.

Care must be taken not to bombard a child with extremely loud sounds or those that might be unpleasant. It is not always known to what extent a young child's hearing is actually damaged or how much of this lack of response is due to other factors. This bombardment can be frightening and painful.

Prior experiences can also affect the child's ability and desire to hear. If, for example, the child has been frightened or hurt by intense sound, he will reject attempts to introduce amplification or even avoid attempts to introduce noisemakers.

Although some children do have a real hearing loss, most have some degree of residual hearing. Many have enough residual hearing to learn to recognize and respond to environmental sounds. Some even have enough hearing that, when developed, it can be a major means of gaining information about their surroundings.

Learning to Wear an Aid

Young, school age, deaf children have, within a period of several weeks of auditory training, learned to recognize and localize some environmental sounds. It is good that the children learned more awareness, but it would have been much better if they had learned earlier.

Normally, an infant will entertain himself by listening to doors opening and closing, footsteps, voice sounds, and water running. As he hears the sound, he gradually learns to solve the mysteries of associating them with some person, object, or event. The deaf child misses many of these and will not suddenly hear them. Someone must call his attention to the sounds and help him learn to use his hearing to understand environmental noises. Severely and profoundly handicapped children do not gain this information naturally either, and help is required if sounds are ever to become meaningful. When a child is hearing impaired and a hearing aid has been recommended, the introduction of this amplification should be gradual. Introducing an aid to a child who has learned to enjoy and appreciate auditory stimulation presents little problem, but the one who is given an aid with no preparation will not be interested and may be afraid.

Many forms of amplification are found in schools and homes and can be used to create interest. Also, many of these are multisensory, as other senses are also stimulated. The television can be used as a sound awareness tool while also stimulating vision. Vary the volume. A radio or record player can provide stimulating auditory as well as valuable vibration experiences. We have used an old-fashioned ear horn to amplify voice sounds. By holding the small funnel near the child's ear and speaking into the large end, we increase amplification. The same goal can be accomplished by making a funnel from paper or using a cheerleader's megaphone. The child can be encouraged to examine and try the headset to a record player or a tape deck. Individual earphones, which often come as a radio or tape deck accessory, can also provide many opportunities for fun experiences. Other similar experiences can be devised to help prepare the child for the introduction of a headset or hearing aid. Through introduction and exposure, the opportunities to observe readiness for other forms of amplification are provided. Then when the child is ready for the hearing aid or headset, it can be tried.

A headset can often be introduced with more ease than a hearing aid. The set is easier to manipulate, may stay in place longer, and is easier to fit on the child's head. Initial introduction to a headset should be done in much the same way as introduction of a hearing aid.

It is good to recognize the value of using a headset or earphones with children who do not have major auditory receptive problems. When we can encourage a severely and profoundly handicapped child to wear earphones with a record player or tape recorder, much can be accomplished. By using earphones, we are providing purer auditory stimulation, in that many other sounds are screened out. This technique can later be developed for increased listening skills. A simple story told on tape can provide the child with opportunities to work independently for short periods. Also, when the story is told by the teacher in simple language, the child can be taught to listen and turn the pages of the book as the tape dictates. Although this may seem like a distant goal the beginning steps, such as introduction of the headset, may be immediate goals.

If the need for a hearing aid has been established and the prescribed aid has been fitted and purchased, other adjustments will be necessary. Not all children express excitement and wonder over a new hearing aid. In fact, many children initially reject an aid. For the child to benefit from the aid, he must wear it; therefore someone will need to assist him with this adjustment.

Select a time when the child is relaxed and create an enjoyable atmosphere; then begin with small approximations toward the eventual goal of having him wear the aid. Help him gradually become familiar with it. Encourage him to examine the earmold and receiver, the cord and the unit. Be sure he sees others wearing an aid. *You* wear the aid and let him touch and see the earmold in your ear. Hold the earmold close to his ear on several occasions. Gradually move toward fitting the earmold into his ear. The first time this is done, it should be left in his ear only a short period of time (two or three minutes), then removed; that is, unless he insists on wearing it. A casual attitude helps. If you are overanxious, this reaction will be recognized and cause apprehension in the child.

If a child persists in refusing to cooperate, insist. Demonstrate confidence and then demand small steps toward the goal. Say, "I'm going to hold the mold in your ear for a few seconds." If he objects, follow through anyway. One day soon he will decide to cooperate. When insisting, the aid should be turned off or very low so he will not have evidence to justify his fears. Later, the volume can be gradually increased. This same kind of orientation can apply when introducing a headset.

Careful observation is important as children do not always have the specifically diagnosed hearing loss, and loud noise can be extremely painful or damaging to the hearing mechanism. Also when the volume is on, avoid exposing the child to gross sounds such as slamming doors or a car horn. Control the sounds to which he is initially exposed by selecting an area that allows for noise control during the beginning orientation period. A quiet room will do.

Awareness of Sound

One of the first steps in auditory training is awareness, but before we can help a child become aware of sounds in the environment *we* must be aware of them and how they can be used. Many sounds constantly occur around us. Stop and listen. A door slams, someone sneezes, the refrigerator door shuts, a pan drops on the floor, the toilet flushes, the tea kettle squeals, and the alarm clock rings. These sounds may be unnoticed to the child if he does not hear them clearly and if he does he may not understand them. Many severely and profoundly handicapped children lack the motivation and curiosity to seek the source of these sounds and need our help. Others are frightened by them and may even learn to tune out any auditory stimuli. These and other daily occurring sounds can be used to stimulate the child's interest in his surroundings and help him attach more meaning to normal auditory cues.

We use a similar approach as would be normal for any child, but with more emphasis and enthusiasm than would have been necessary with the normal child. For example, if a dog barks outside the window we may calmly remark to a normal child that we wish the dog would stop barking. To the unmotivated or unaware child we say, "What do I hear?" "I hear a dog," or "Let's find the dog." Then we look out the window to see what was making the noise, or we go closer to the dog or even touch him to extend the experience. This visual or tactile association with the sound source is important as it calls attention to the sound and where it originates, which will help the child learn to attach more meaning to what he has heard.

When the child reacts to the sound with pleasure, we have made a giant step forward. This reaction could be indicated by a smile, an interested expression, or the fact that he stops crying and appears to be listening. He is beginning to realize the difference between sound and silence. He is discriminating and this is good. Curiosity about the sound and the localization of the sound source will come later as we continue to help him develop more sound awareness.

Sound Games to Try

At times we control and emphasize certain sounds by playing games with noisemakers. This is a good way to play with the child for a few short minutes, and his attention can sometimes be easily captured. Gestures and pantomime are good here. We find that many severely and profoundly handicapped children will respond to gesture long before there is any indication of meaningful connection between our verbal labels and the object. So, say it and also pantomime it for emphasis. A case in point is the fact that it may be more than chance that most children learn to recognize and say "Bye-bye" very early in their language development years. The fact that the word is associated with a gesture could contribute to the success.

Begin the game by introducing a sound maker, perhaps a cow bell. Do this in a fairly quiet atmosphere. Manipulate the bell so that it makes a noise. Encourage the child to feel, smell, and even taste the bell. Name it for him and pantomime ringing a bell. If it accidentally rings, that is fine. If the child is holding it upside down, or holding it in some way so that it does not ring, show him how to hold and manipulate the bell so that it makes noise. Move slowly; this should be fun. It may require several sessions before the child "knows" the toy so that he can manipulate it by himself. After having introduced three or more sounds in this way, over a period of time, it is time to extend the activity. We put three noisemakers in a box or bag and periodically play with the sound toys together. A cow bell, a toy horn, a pair of cymbals, a xylophone, a whistle, or a large rattle work well. Also a noisy ice tray, a can filled with dried peas, a plastic jar half full of pebbles, or a pan with a spoon are just as useful.

Any variety of household items can be used to make fun noise-makers. The tool chest provides several. A long bolt or nail tied to a string and tapped with a spoon makes a nice noise; a juice can with a few peas inside is a good rattler, and shakers can be made by flattening several bottle tops and nailing them loosely to the end of a flat stick so that they clink together. Likewise, washers on a string rattle or two other pieces of metal will clink together to make sound. Any three noise-makers will do, but three that make quite different sounds are best. It is fun to make a secret out of which is going to be selected by looking excited, rattling them around in the box, and then slowly pulling one out. Next make noise with it and once again let him hold, feel, smell, taste, and otherwise investigate with the object. The same can then be done with the other two objects in the box.

This game can progressively become more difficult as the child matures. We add one or two more objects when it becomes "old hat" or we vary the game. One variation we enjoy, once the child is responding to sounds, is to make the activity into a guessing game. We hold a piece of poster board in front of the box and make a noise behind the screen with one of the toys, then replace the toy and remove the screen. Then we see if the child can select the correct instrument from the box. At first we "help" by placing the child's hand on the object and encouraging him to pick it up. Then we clap and praise him. Soon he learns to select the correct object by himself.

Another listening game we enjoy is fun and also helps prepare the child for a more accurate hearing test. The benefit of this activity is not limited to hearing-impaired children. We help the child place a block in a container (or put a ring on a stick or a peg in a board) each time he hears a sound, such as a drum beat, a piano, or a record player. We enjoy varying the activity by using a record player, but we are careful that he does not always see us manipulate the record player or hit the drum. The purpose is to listen. We say, "Listen, do you hear any-thing?" and capture his attention. Then when the sound occurs, we help him place his block in the box and say "Good boy" or in some way show him we are pleased.

The child is given help as he needs it, then later we begin delaying our "help" so he will have an opportunity to do it by himself. This too requires time and much repetition.

Also we use one activity at a time, such as putting pegs in a pegboard and then vary the activity later by putting rings on a stick; the child does not tire as easily as he learns to respond consistently to sound. Consistency may be best in the beginning, then variations may be added.

Another way this activity can be varied is by having the child raise his hand when he hears the music. One adult stands behind a group of six or seven children to help them get their hands up, another stands in front of the group and responds correctly for those who can watch; for this size group, a third person is needed to manipulate the record player. The enthusiasm exhibited by the adults is important and, in the beginning, may be the only enthusiasm seen. The children sit and look disinterested, flick fingers in front of their eyes, or try to escape. We do not let that deter our enthusiasm. If we allowed them to make all the decisions, we would probably all end up with our backs to the floor making shadows with our fingers, rocking, or just staring into space. Listening to all the noise coming from the room, one would think that it was a wonderful successful experience. Later in the year, the children each start responding appropriately. When they do respond, we clap and jump about, showing them off and constantly talking about our smart children. Before the year is over, we can even play musical chairs by marching around the chairs and sitting down quickly when the music stops. The philosophy "they'll get it" works well, since they usually do.

Sound has rhythm and intensity, and this must be remembered as we play games or help the child learn to connect a sound he hears to an experience. Bells of different sizes and noise intensities are good. Some are loud, others soft, harsh, or sharp. Some make low tone sounds, others make high tones. The child may not be able to discriminate between the bells, but he can enjoy ringing them. If he is receiving an auditory sensation, we have helped him move one more step in the direction of learning to understand sounds. Other variations of intensity can be tried.

Rhythm games are fun. The clapping, stomping, and marching games work well. It is fun to march or walk to music or a drum beat. We enjoy playing "can you do this" by tapping a stick against the table. We tap two times, then we take the child's hand and tap his stick two times and so on. Finally he may learn to listen and imitate the rhythm he hears, even when the pattern is complicated. This is excellent for auditory memory. Placing his free hand on the table is helpful. In feeling the vibration on the table, he connects the tactile experience with the sound he hears.

To assist the child in becoming more aware of sound, it is also fun to let him place his hand on the piano, guitar, radio, television, or record player and feel the vibration while the music is playing. This is also a good way to help him realize presence and absence of sound. As he feels the vibration, we make an exciting experience of the fact that there is sound. Then we stop the sound and act as if a catastrophy has occurred (i.e., "Where is it?" "I don't hear anything." "What happened?"). We call attention to sounds by pointing to our ear before it is heard, then when we hear it, we cup our ear and touch his as we say "Listen." Eventually he realizes what we have been talking about.

It is important to realize in all sensory experience that other senses may be used to enhance a sensation. Thus, a child feeling the vibrations of a drum or the speaker of an electric organ may enhance his awareness of the auditory sensation. Eventually, the auditory can be a single sensation, but it will be skipping many steps if we try to enforce this too early.

For the child who has developed an acute awareness to sound, we sometimes play "hide and seek." The point is to find the noise. This is a good group activity and is appropriate for children with varying sensory impairments. We get under the table or desk, behind the door, or even in the closet and call to the child. If he fails to respond or does not seem to hear, we make the noise louder, open the door a little, or in some other way try to help him find the source. Whenever possible, we help him succeed, even if we have to "cheat a little" at first. When he does respond correctly, we make it a big experience, and the child is pleased with himself. This makes it easier for next time. This does not mean that he will always succeed in everything he does. Tasks gradually become more difficult, and he will occasionally fail. This way he learns persistance and we keep a balance between challenging him and requiring a task that is too difficult for the moment.

Motivating the Child

Experiences should be special, and some way should be devised to make them enjoyable to the child. If the child is disinterested our challenge is to discover a way to capture his interest. This is sometimes difficult. He may insist on flicking the bell against his teeth, throwing the horn down, or pushing the cymbal away, so we continue with our plans and insist that he is "introduced" to each instrument. We let him see how much fun we are having listening to the sounds and talk constantly about what we are doing. If we must insist on his presence, we are careful not to let the activity take long, perhaps two or three minutes. Then we say "All finished," with a pleasant smile and let him up. Frequent, short periods of exposure are much better than long, tedious ones. Another approach is to let him see that as soon as the game is over we are going to do something he likes (i.e., place cookies and punch in sight for a tea party). When this is too distracting, we wait until later to present the refreshments.

Sometimes a child refuses to attend or tolerate almost anything; still he must learn somehow. Patience is good but we cannot always wait until the child is ready. It is sometimes better to insist that the child experience some activities, even when he objects. Some prefer to ignore this behavior and wait for the child to develop interest. Occasionally this works. However, the child's progress will be much more rapid if we do impose on him to some degree. We discover ways to make the activity interesting and move with confidence. The child will eventually begin to rely more on our judgment. A relationship that is mutually beneficial is being established; therefore the approach must be based on trial and error, the particular situation, and the individuals involved.

Sounds are important and we must provide many opportunities to develop his sense of hearing and to understand what he is hearing. Encourage him to play with noisy toys (objects) and develop an interest in them. Take him to the kitchen and call attention to the many sounds that occur, such as the disposal, blender, stove fan, and mixer. Likewise, take him to the laundry room, bathroom and other noisy areas in the house or school. Do not allow him to stay in bed for long periods during the day. If he is immobile and stays prone much of the time, put a pad on the floor in the room where there is activity. The overuse of one type of auditory stimulation to the exclusion of others is to be avoided. Record players are fine for perhaps 15 minutes a day, but he should have other sound experiences too. Music can be soothing and interesting to the child who is initially becoming aware of sounds, nevertheless, it should not be used solely to keep the child entertained for long periods or for avoidance.

Voice Awareness

The hearing-impaired child needs to become aware of voice sounds. Other severely handicapped children have difficulty attaching meaning to the sounds we make and words we use. It is possible that some may never actually hear or attach much meaning to voice sounds, but they will all benefit from this exposure and emphasis, even if it is only to realize that some people communicate by talking. Exposure comes before awareness and we cannot expect the child to realize that people talk, unless there is talking going on around him. We talk constantly, usually in short sentences, in a normal voice, and down on his level. If he has a hearing aid, we talk close to it; if not, we talk near his ear. This not only helps amplify the sound but also helps screen out or cover up other noises in the environment. For some this is important, as learning to pick out one sound from many can be a difficult task. If we occasionally hold his hand or hands to our mouth, he may begin recognizing the source of the sound. Put his hand on your throat or chest so he can feel the vibration while you talk. Talk about what is happening. Talk about the sounds and smells in the air. Call attention to something that can be seen or touched. Constantly label objects and experiences for him. Talk about the here and now.

If the child does become aware of voice sounds, a big goal has been accomplished. He may never talk, but he will learn many things from listening. It might be helpful to review the section on speech training and oral language development. Some ideas presented there could be beneficial. Continue talking and encourage others to do so. Visitors may say "I don't know why I keep talking—he can't hear me!" Help them learn to understand. Say "I don't know how much he can hear, but I'm going to give him every opportunity to learn to use his hearing and then he can prove to himself whether he can hear or not or whether he can learn to understand."

Understanding of sound moves from exposure to awareness to acceptance to recognition to localization and then to discrimination. First the child is exposed to the sound, then he becomes aware of it, and later learns to accept the sound. Some refuse to accept the sound and scream or even pretend not to hear. The child needs help in recognizing voice sounds and where they originate so that they will become meaningful and useful to him.

Play little games. Call out to him before coming to him, so that he can learn to recognize, anticipate, and localize voice sounds. This can be useful information. Modify this into a "peek-a-boo" game. Use a particular sound many times for various occasions during the week and see if any results can be recognized. Pick a sound he makes most often; one of the vowel sounds he makes will be fine. Then say it when you put him in the bath, when you rub him dry, and when you give him a hug. Imitate his other sounds often. The goal here is for him to learn to hear and later learn to imitate, but it will first require a great deal of exposure.

He will eventually learn to discriminate between two sounds you have been emphasizing. The final goal, of course, is for him to attach meaning to the discriminated sounds that have developed into words, as this is the beginning of receptive oral language.

It is difficult for some mothers or teachers to talk constantly to a child who does not respond. After trying for a few days with no response, it is easy to become discouraged. Encouragement is important to us all and with a child who appears completely unresponsive, a first reaction may be "What's the use, he can't hear me." Another common reaction is to stop talking, being completely unaware of having done so. In this case, the child has partially changed our way of thinking and behaving. He ignored our attempts and we stopped trying. These children, so incapable in some ways, are frequently perfectly capable of managing adults.

A Personal Experience

One teacher recounts a particularly interesting experience with a child: "One day I was almost at my wit's end with a six-year-old. She had outfoxed me in every way, responded to nothing, and, to top it all off, she then had an 'accident' (on purpose) in her pants. I took her over to the dormitory and made her clean herself, at least she thought she was cleaning herself. Then I pointed her toward the bed. This child was a real "character," with little obvious language awareness and recognizable visual limitations. She sat on the bed looking at me, and I sat next to her. I really gave her a tongue lashing. I shook my finger at her and with a cross expression told her that I was tired of the way she had been behaving. Everyone else seemed ready to give up on her, and I almost was, too. I told her that I might be her last hope and that she had better shape up soon. Because of her behavior up to this point, I often felt that I wasn't succeeding with her and I doubted that anyone else would try. My tirade went on and on. I told her I was tired of being pinched, ignored, turned off, stepped on, pushed down, messed up, and run from and that my back hurt. I also told her that I was a teacher, but that lately I had not felt or looked like one.

"The child cried and put her arms around my neck. This was a real shock to me as she had never reacted normally. She usually laughed when it was appropriate to cry and vice versa. I sat there and looked at her for a minute or two, then hugged her, told her I loved her, and that I hoped tomorrow would be better. I waved and said goodbye. She watched me leave and was clearly sad that I was going—but I left. The lecture I gave her was good therapy for me, as I was ready to explode, and it obviously worked for the child. Maybe she was unaccustomed to being reasoned with, as sometimes the tendency with a nonverbal child may be to pull him around or correct him by physical reprimand. This child was understanding much more than we knew. She may not have known the meaning of all my words, but she understood.

"The next day she came to school laughing and running, and she was a little more grown-up—no miracles, but better. This was the last time I felt she soiled her pants to get even with me. She and I now have a healthy relationship; it was difficult to establish, but very much worth the effort it required."

This recollection is meant to be encouraging. Many days all seems hopeless, and sometimes there are no positive reactions from our efforts and it is easy to give up. If this does happen and we do give up, then we are joining the group who said it could not be done, and it will be harder than ever for the child to progress. Say some choice words, walk off for a few minutes, or in some way vent your emotion appropriately, but do not give up.

Praising the Child

Anytime the child does something that makes us proud, we let him know, even if it is only one tiny move in the right direction. A child loves praise and if he does not at first, he soon will. Sometimes we have to really concentrate to find something good; other times it is easy. We say "That's good" more times than we say "No, that's not right," and if this seems impossible, we are expecting too much from him too soon. If the child continues to be seemingly unimpressed with verbal praise, we teach him that this is a compliment, a good experience, or a reward. This can be done by giving him something he likes, candy, a cookie, or water, along with the praise. He will eventually make the association and learn to respond. We must constantly show him we accept him as he is and that what he is doing is wonderful. Then we continually reevaluate our present goals for the child. Requiring too much will be frustrating to everyone.

Patience combined with determination works well. It is usually difficult to determine the line between expecting too much and not expecting enough. With practice, this will become clearer. Many times a child will take a big step forward and learn something that seemed impossible. Then if we become overanxious and lose touch with reality we may skip several steps toward our goal and demand that the child perform a task he is not ready for, something too difficult. As we constantly reevaluate *our* performance and goals, these times become recognizable to us. In these cases, we back up a little and start again a little slower. These things happen to us all.

When having difficulty breaking through to the child, we let him know we like him and that we know he can succeed. Then we reevaluate, back up if necessary, and try again. We do not expect too much in one day, for although we may think he did not learn anything today, we cannot be too sure. It may show up tomorrow or next week.

We are trying to develop concepts in a meaningful manner and develop in the child the ability to discriminate. The only way this can be done is through practice and experience. By learning to use all senses more acutely, he will become better acquainted with his environment and challenged by having additional ways to gain information.

MOVEMENT IN SPACE

Training in Independence

A little boy is sitting calmly on the floor near a toy box examining a large top and suddenly spies a big red balloon across the room. He drops the top and hurriedly makes his way over to the balloon. As he reaches for and bumps the balloon, it bounces away. For a few moments, the child plays chase with the balloon, until finally he traps it against the wall. Now he can examine the object carefully—seeing, tasting, feeling, and even hearing the sound his fingers make as they rub against the peculiar surface. He is curious and interested. He is utilizing the information received through his senses. He is learning. He is interacting with his environment.

What this child is doing represents months and perhaps years of learning. This learning may have come easily and normally for many children, while others require a much longer time to learn even one small part of one task.

Another little boy is brought in and placed on the floor beside the toy chest. He stretches out on his back, turns his face toward the window, and flicks his fingers rapidly in front of his eyes. When the top is presented, he grasps it and hurriedly passes it between the light and his eyes several times. He then discards it and continues with his hand–light play. Later, the child pays little attention to the balloon, even when it is rolled directly to him. He then spies a small toy soldier on the floor near him and quickly reaches for it. This encouraging move attracts everyone's attention. The little boy now stretches back out on the floor and begins flicking the toy rapidly in front of his eyes, content to stimulate himself with the object. What he is learning is not useful information. He appears content to stimulate himself in this way for an indefinite period of time. This child is not motivated to move about and interact appropriately with his environment.

The difference between the two children is remarkable. A short period of observation will quickly establish the fact that the first child is developmentally several steps further along than the second child. Information received from the parents and from early professional evaluations indicates that the difference between the two children has been increasing over recent months. According to the reports, a year ago both of the children described were involved in eye–hand self-stimulation; neither manipulated toys appropriately and neither moved independently about in their environment, other than occasionally to satisfy certain basic body needs. What then has made the difference during the last year? We are told that the first child, the one who appears to be developmentally progressing at a more rapid rate, has been in a structured program designed to develop independent skills. He has been required gradually to develop more self-reliance, he has been motivated to begin solving his own problems whenever possible, and he has learned that he must depend upon himself to move within his environment.

The uncountable hours spent helping the child learn to identify objects and sounds has been time well spent. However, what the child sees and hears will mean little to him if he cannot reach out and interact. The visually impaired child is deprived of the integrating experience of connecting a sound with an action or object, unless someone intervenes. This same lack of association is sometimes seen in other children who cannot or have not learned to integrate sensory information. For example, a child does not always know that a certain sound means water is running unless someone helps him identify that particular sound with the actual experience of seeing and feeling the water. Someone will need to take him through the whole process of associating the sound with the actual experience several times. Once the association is made and the sound of running water represents a real and meaningful experience, some progress has been made. This information will, however, be of little use to the child if he does not eventually learn the independent skills necessary to reach the water when he wants a drink. He must also be taught to use other sensory cues in a similar manner. Development of skills leading toward the independent movement within his environment should be a primary goal in planning a program. If he remains immobile, he may begin finding more and more ways to use his energy for self-stimulation with less energy used for interacting appropriately with his environment. The problem is finding ways to motivate the child to begin developing independent behaviors.

Mobility

For the purpose of this discussion, we use the term "mobility" to refer to the child's ability to move from one place to another. He must not only be *capable* of moving around but he must also *want* to move. Motivation, then, is important. The child must feel comfortable and confident in the physical environment. For him to develop and maintain this attitude, some planning is required. He will need to be taught to investigate his surroundings and each attempt to do so should be as pleasant an experience as possible. When he reaches out in his environment, he must be rewarded by the experience. When he does attempt to move forward, we must assist him in reaching his goal. This will encourage further attempts. Constant frustration and failure will bring negative results, as will too much help.

In order for him to be efficient in mobility he may also need help to compensate for handicaps resulting from his disability. If the handicaps are based primarily on auditory problems, then the modifications necessary may be few and primarily related to safety. For example, when crossing a street, it will be necessary to teach the child to look carefully, as he usually cannot rely on street noises to warn of approaching traffic.

Visual disabilities are of greater concern. The problems arising depend not only on the nature of the disabilities but also on the motivation of the child, the environment he is in, and any past experiences he has had or problems he has solved.

He can learn to modify his behavior in several ways to accommodate for the visual or auditory restrictions. When other sensory problems accompany this, then still further adaptations must be made. The teacher will need to be aware of the individual child's unique problems and plan accordingly. It is important, though, for the child to be rewarded by movement and have many chances to practice, as well as having a high ratio of successful experiences.

Orientation

The term "orientation" is used to describe the child's awareness and understanding of his surroundings. This can be orientation within *part* of a room (i.e., the bed) and eventually orientation within the whole room, the house, the school, and the community. The process of becoming oriented will be a continuing one, as there will always be new places to go and new things to learn. The child should begin the process of orientation within his environment as an infant and continue to add to this knowledge throughout his life. He first learns about those areas closest to him. As he develops confidence, he must begin familiarizing himself with areas that are further removed. In this way, he gradually gains the knowledge necessary to move about in larger spaces.

For the child to develop the necessary understanding of the space around him, he must have many sensory experiences. Those designed to teach him to use environmental cues are most important. Much can be gained by the knowledge that certain olfactory, visual, or auditory cues are associated with particular places and experiences. The knowledge that his room has a distinctive odor or that the clock chimes in the dining room will be filed in his memory. Later he will use this knowledge to help locate himself within his environment.

The child will need many experiences if he is to develop an ability to move about with confidence. Children who have been confined to a playpen or bed and protected from anything that might be ''dangerous'' frequently are less active and more withdrawn than the ones who have had more freedom. It is more desirable for a child to enter a program as ''too active'' than to be a real problem to motivate. For the child to move, we must learn to recognize his wants. These can then be used to motivate him.

An Experience

Little Susan, with a brace on her leg, wanted to be in the station wagon. She waited patiently for the other children to climb in, then looked at her teacher. ''Now put me in,'' her sideways glance was saying. We all waited, pointed to the car, put her hand on the tailgate nudged her leg, and continued our waiting. Susan persisted in her patience. ''They'll get me in a minute and I won't have to do this all by myself'' she seemed to be thinking. Not so. This little one had been showing us in many ways that she was very capable of manipulating herself within the environment, brace and all. The teacher kept talking and Susan turned on her tears. This had often worked for her. One teacher climbed into the car and started the motor. We all waved ''Bye-bye''. Now what? Susan began to make the necessary effort to climb into the car and with a little help from her teacher, accomplished the feat and received a big kiss and many cheers. The child's expression was a priceless combination of bewilderment and pride. She knew what she had done. After a big ice cream, we gave her the opportunity to try again; this time it was a little easier. Soon she found that she could do many things ''all by herself.'' We had to help her learn to live

with the things we could not change for her. Some tasks would be difficult, but with our help she could learn to do them. Besides she was
already a little different from many children. For everyone else to be
independent while Susan waited to have things done for her would not
develop the confidence or the self-image she needed.

Another teacher insisted that a child with cerebral palsy slide on
his stomach to reach the water fountain. He could not walk, but he
could get there and he could sit up. He could also turn on the water.
This was not being cruel. Think of the satisfaction the child derived
from being able to get to the water when he wanted a drink. If he had to
depend on someone to get it for him, he would probably often be
thirsty. Such fostered dependency *is* cruel.

When possible, let the child get what he wants independently. Do
not bring him all he desires. If he likes what he struggles to get and succeeds, he will be rewarded. Encourage him. Give him less and less assistance each time, until he reaches the goal independently. When the
task is difficult for the child, it is usually best to begin decreasing assistance toward the end of the task. For example, if the child wants a
cookie he has dropped, give him less help just before he reaches the
cookie. If he finds he can move the last step (wriggle or crawl) alone
and is rewarded by getting the cookie, then he will want to try again.
Next time let up on the assistance a little earlier, requiring more and
more effort on his part. He will continue to progress if he is motivated.

Stimulating Reflex Movement

When working with a child, no matter how young, there is much
that can be done to assist him in progressing through the stages of
physical growth that lead toward independent movement. The specific
tasks chosen will depend on the level of major functioning the child has
reached.

For the very young or inactive child, stimulating the reflexes is
one way to encourage movement. Move his arms and legs in a walking
pattern several times a day, while he is stretched out on the changing
table or bed. Raise one leg and then the other. Stretch his arms and
legs. Gently play little tactile motor games like "goosie, goosie," "I'm
gonna get you" or "here comes a little man walking on two fingers."

Tickle the palm of his hand and the bottom of his foot to encourage
reflex movements. If he likes to curl up in a knot, unfold him and let
him recoil. This is reflex movement for our purposes. Touch the side of
his cheek or lip to stimulate the searching movement that comes when
the child is seeking the bottle or other food. This movement will be

rewarded when he finds the desired object. Stimulating other senses may result in movement. For example, if the child learns to localize sound, he will be looking for the source; if a bright light is shined to the side of his face, he may turn and search; if touched by something unfamiliar, he may quickly move back.

Tickling is not recommended for the child with cerebral palsy who is already in a condition of muscular tension. This would only stimulate uncontrollable muscular movements. As with any suggestion presented here, analysis and adaptation is required when dealing with individual cases. For the child with cerebral palsy, gentle movements and massage are best. Forcing muscular movement is not useful. When we force the child's arm to extend or attempt to uncurl his body by force, we only cause him to become more tense and actually strengthen the muscles working against normal movement.

Massage works well here. If we can gently massage the wrist so that the hand opens, then much can be accomplished toward our goals. Likewise, by extending the child over a giant ball, face down, we can gently massage his back and increase relaxation and extension. Then he can stretch his arms and reach toward the floor to manipulate objects. He can also learn to raise his head, as the infant does when he begins to strengthen his neck muscles. This is one step toward independent movement.

Also, with the child who has severe motor involvement, we must realize that by applying pressure opposite to the motion we want to stimulate, we can usually get results. When we want the child to open his mouth, we can better accomplish this by pressing gently under the chin than we can by trying to pry the mouth open. Likewise, if we want him to close his mouth so the drooling will decrease, our goal may better be reached if we push gently down on the chin. Then if he does respond correctly, we let him know. The more he correctly uses his voluntary muscles, the more normal growth and development patterns we will see. But the movement must be voluntary, not forced, for this to happen. Forcing will build his flexors (drawing in) and voluntary actions will build the extensors (stretching). This is why we must be careful not to force or frighten the child who has severe motor problems.

Balance can also be used to stimulate reflexes. The child who leans far over the edge of the bed or feels someone put him down too quickly may tighten his muscles in a reflex action. Care should be taken not to frighten the child continually; however, if startling him is one of the few ways to get a response, you may want to use this technique occasionally. Learning to balance is important, and comes only after ample experiences, some of which may be unpleasant. Also, by gently placing the child in an unbalanced position, he will not be too frightened and will still have to change position to maintain his balance.

These activities should be fun and can be enjoyable games for both child and adult. Laugh. While playing, talk about what you are doing (i.e., "up goes a leg, down goes a leg"). Occasionally play with him on the floor. By imitating his movements, his awareness may be increased. He will have an opportunity to learn imitation, which is very important in developing motor patterns. Also play in front of a mirror, even if the child appears not to notice.

It may be necessary to teach the child to reach out. This is a prerequisite to moving out, and for some children comes very slowly. The earlier this begins, the better for the child. We cannot expect the unaware or unmotivated child to begin reaching for things without encouragement. Tempt him with an object he seems to want. Hold something close and let him smell, touch, or see; then move it a little further back and encourage him to reach out. If he wants it (food, flashlight, or toy), he will be rewarded when he succeeds. Encourage exploration. Take his hand and show him how to reach. It may help to touch or nudge him gently with the object, so he will know it is there. If he is more hearing oriented, try a noisy object. Always talk about what you are doing. Say "I've got something pretty," "Smell it," "Try to find it." Then, whenever possible, extend the goal beyond his reach so he will have to move his whole body and even use all modalities to maintain sensory contact. He will then be stimulated to reestablish physical contact and will move toward the object. This seemingly simple goal-shifting act is the basis for maintaining motivation in many areas and can become extremely complex.

Moving Forward

No child should be on his back all day long. He cannot learn mobility in that position, and orientation will be confined to the bed. Also, if he stays on his back a great length of time, we can expect him to develop self-stimulating activities, such as eye–hand light play. Put him on the floor on his stomach, or if he is developmentally ready, put him in a crawling position. He may be ready to sit up in a chair, if so get him into an appropriate chair. The tilted infant seats designed to prevent the child from falling forward are good for short periods.

Awareness of the child's needs is necessary for planning and prevention of wrong behaviors such as sitting slumped, staying in bed too long, or constantly entertaining himself with self-stimulating behaviors. The child may feel more secure on a stable base, such as the floor, and rebel against sitting, standing, or in any other way losing this stability. Others are "confused" about the normal body orientation of head up and feet down. Children who do not see well or who have not had the body contact necessary for this understanding, sometimes create their own way of positioning themselves in space (upside down, bent over, or other peculiar body positions). Some children even learn to stimulate themselves by assuming abnormal positions in bed, as when the child hangs his head off the side of the bed for sensation. Our job is to help the child develop so that he will eventually accept the normal upright position. Activities suggested in the section on Body Image may be helpful.

When trying to motivate the child to move forward (creep, crawl, or walk), think of something he likes and use it to tempt him. Many children love light, so flashlights often work well. A child who appears "helpless" may be motivated to crawl across the room and around several objects to reach a small, lighted flashlight. The same objects, the ones he likes, can be used to encourage him to reach out or up. Let him see, smell, and feel what you have; then play, "can you get it?" Perhaps he likes a certain noisemaker, maybe a drum or bell. If so, beat the drum or ring the bell and talk about it: "Come and get it." Do not demand too much in the beginning. Often the child has only made a small move in the direction of the desired object when he is given what he wants. Next time, it may be further away. Remember, also, he may lose interest in one particular object. Today he may want the bell badly and be willing to work for it, but tomorrow, when trying to entice him with it, he may turn off completely. You want to help *him* become aware, but it is also important for you to be constantly aware of what he is saying and why.

Some ideas we have tried may prove helpful when teaching a child to walk. Let him walk by standing on your feet, facing forward, several times a day as you walk. In this way, he will learn the rhythm and the posture of walking, and he can see where he is going. He will be moving, and he will be close to you. By leaning over and holding the child's hands out to the side as you back up and "walk him" toward you, you limit his chances to learn to balance, which is an important part of walking. As he develops and learns to support himself, "walk" behind him, holding under his arms or around his waist, not by the hands—he needs them for balance. If he is ready, stand him up and let him walk the two or three steps toward you by himself. Catch him and stand him up again. Brag, laugh, talk, and have fun. Have a big celebration if he does anything at all. If a tangible reward such as candy or a sip of juice increases motivation, then use this as a reward for his attempts. Also, it will help if you relax. This can be repeated several times a day. He may need the confidence of something in his hand when he tries to walk. If he does hold your hand (not high up or straight out to the side in an awkward position), let him do the grasping. In time, his grasp will become more relaxed and can be gradually replaced with something other than your hand. If you find it necessary to hold his hand, then gradually give him more grasp and less support as a firm hand clasp may provide the needed confidence. At any rate, if you continually support him, he will not develop the necessary balance. Let him do as much of the "work" as possible.

Be sure the walking space is large enough. An uncluttered room with a sofa or strong chair for him to hold can be ideal. No sharp edged tables for now. Many children feel more secure when holding something. Try "sharing a toy" with him. Hold one end or side of a toy as he holds the other. Tie a rope to two stationary objects for him to hold as he walks across the room. The idea works well outside too, as does a low fence.

Wherever possible, use the same approach to a particular place within the house or outside area. For example, take him to the bathroom by the same route each time, and help him see, hear, and touch the same reference points. Develop a patterned routine and repeat it each time he goes to the bathroom. Soon he will begin to realize what is happening and where he is going.

Remember that auditory and olfactory cues can be helpful to him in localizing himself within his environment. The record player, the television, or the crackling fireplace will give him useful information, as will the kitchen and bathroom odors. These, too, can serve as reference points. You might enjoy making a little sidewalk with tape or rope for him to walk on when he crosses the room.

If there are no signs of awareness, reevaluate and try again. Visible signs indicating that he knows what is happening may come much later than the actual knowledge.

Developing Confidence

A child will not be motivated if his experiences are not rewarding. If you want a child to develop mobility, a reward should be offered as motivation. The kitchen or table might be a good goal. If he is motivated to get his supper and is rewarded by what is there, he will be willing to repeat this on other occasions, which will lead toward independent mobility. The energy required will be well worth the effort.

Help the child develop security and self-confidence. He must not be treated as if he will break. He needs enough help to build his confidence but independence should also be encouraged. Do not overprotect him. His attempts should be rewarding and satisfying, but a few bumps and falls must also be experienced. Some objects may create unnecessary problems. These should be removed. Unstable objects often confuse the child; stationary ones serve as reference points to learn where he is in the room. These will be important. As his ability to move about improves and he gains confidence, these obstacles can be replaced. He must one day learn to manipulate himself around them. You do want him to be motivated to walk, therefore the beginning must not be too difficult. Also, if he prefers a stable base, he will remain flat on the floor in preference to depending on objects that may move when he holds to them or applies pressure. As he begins to move about, you must be sure he continues to gain security, but at the same time he will need to have some of the normal experiences that are not always pleasant. These experiences are necessary for normal development. Your attitude is important. If you make a big scene when he falls, he will make a worse one. He will learn from his mistakes. Sometimes we allow the child to "almost" get hurt, and then show him what would have happened (i.e., hot stove, stairs, open window, hot water). He must not, though, be allowed to make so many mistakes that he wants to give up.

Tasks that are too difficult or even impossible for us or for the child are delayed. These experiences lead to failure and will be introduced as he matures. If we insist he walk before he has developed a readiness, the experience will be frustrating and cause the child to pull away from the very activity we are trying to move him into. Also when the tasks we require are impossible, the children often resort to self-stimulation or some other withdrawal behavior that is more satisfying. Think of the normal sequence of development through which all children pass and help this child pass through most of these same stages. He must develop several reflex patterns before he can walk. If he does not have adequate ability, then he must develop accommodative patterns. Some of this will take much time and depend on his individual characteristics.

Encourage tactile exploration with his feet, body, legs, head, hands, or other methods he may invent. When he reaches out with his foot or touches something with his head, this is an important part of orientation. One little girl loved to touch the edge of the record player with her chin. This was a big step forward for her. As long as the activity does not become passive stimulation, then it is still exploration.

However, if the child persists on holding his body against a brick wall or sitting with his forehead resting on the grill around the fan for a long period, he is not exploring. Determine the sensory input he is using in his behavior and plan constructive learning around it. For example, if he seems drawn to vibrating objects, vary his experiences in this area so he can become more aware of the piano, drum, record player, guitar, or homemade rhythm instrument. If the child is flicking objects constantly in front of his eyes, then he is using vision. This can then be developed and used in productive ways. He has also developed some fine motor skills. Well-developed coordination is required for some of the complicated motor patterns we see, so our goal is to find a way to use these skills for manipulation of objects.

Coordination

The child must learn to coordinate the use of his hands and eyes. Such tasks as picking up toys or stacking wood may not be interesting to the child, but are worth a try. Smaller objects can be scattered on the desk or floor for him to gather and put in a can. He will need help and encouragement. Roll a flashlight to him—if he picks it up, then he is coordinating his hands and his eyes. Put little cookies, pieces of candy, or other desirable foods on a tray or on the floor in front of him. He may be interested in shiny keys, pieces of foil, cellophane, marbles, clips, pins, or something fuzzy. If nothing else works, do something he does not like. Any reaction is better than none at all. One little boy objected when we put a toy car in a small plastic bag. Each time he grabbed the bag and took the car out, he was accomplishing our goals. He was looking, reaching, developing better eye–hand coordination, and we were playing. At first it did not seem like such fun, but it soon developed into a useful and productive game.

Eye–foot coordination is also important. As the child becomes more mobile, obstacles may be placed on the floor. He then learns to move his feet in the direction his eyes tell him is best. This takes practice. The same is true about going up steps. We often play by stepping up and down with a brick, piece of wood, or foot stool. He soon learns it is easier when he uses his eyes. A few stumbles may make the need to look more realistic. As he develops proficiency, he can also be encouraged to practice going under, over, and between objects.

Some children have difficulty crossing the midlines of their body. This is not usually a severe problem, but one that can easily be corrected. The child's movements will be somewhat restricted and sometimes awkward if this behavior persists. This difficulty might be exhibited when something is handed to him on the right side of his body and he grasps it with his right hand, yet if the same thing is extended to the child on the left side he reaches with his left hand. He should be encouraged to reach across his body to grasp a desired object. One way to correct this is to hold something directly in front of him, then repeat the activity by holding it a little to the side opposite the hand he is using. If he switches hands, you do, too. He will soon be reaching across his body with ease, which can be important in performing some skills he will be learning.

Varied Experiences

The severely and profoundly handicapped child needs many of the same experiences that other children have to help them develop. He needs to kick, slide, skip, jump, run, fall, trip, and wrestle. The roughness, the experience of being tossed up in the air, and the scramble on the floor with others are also important to him. Some of these activities will need to be introduced slowly if he is defensive or frightened, but they can gradually develop into fun activities. We have seen many severely and profoundly handicapped children who were afraid of a swing, slide, wagon, or tricycle later learn to enjoy them so much that a substantial amount of playground time was spent comforting them when they had to wait their turn.

There is a fine line between making activities fun, so that the child will be motivated, and forcing him to do what he must. We cannot wait for him to want to do everything, but we make experiences pleasant whenever possible. We usually make our forceful requests short experiences and then immediately switch to something we know he does enjoy, later repeating the procedure.

Teaching the child to imitate is a continuous goal. It is especially important in the motor development area. We want him to learn to imitate our movements and those of others, both gross and fine. Large body movement is usually best in the beginning and this gross imitation may be difficult for the child. Many of our children exhibit complicated fine motor skills with their hands in front of their eyes and yet cannot clap, stomp, march, jump, or even raise their arms when we demand this kind of imitation. Sometimes it seems that the motor development is more normal in the area of fine movement than in gross movement. For example, many children who demonstrate these fine motor patterns with their hands and fingers have an awkward, clumsy gait. Perhaps this is due to the lack of demands made on a child to become more independent. It could be a lack of body image understanding necessary before development of imitative behaviors. It could also be his method of adapting to an odd combination of sensory disorders.

We create interest by imitating the child's movements. In this way he learns to "see himself." His *sounds* can be imitated too. Later, he will learn to imitate us. Roll like a log and then help him roll. Occasionally imitate him when he crawls or falls. Later, introduce animal imitations; you pretending to be a monkey, elephant, dog, seal, or duck. Play "follow the leader" around the house; play "horsie" by having turns sitting on each other's back; or vary the game "Simon says" to suit the situation. Time required to teach imitation of body movement, will be time well spent.

Another important area to remember while considering mobility and orientation is problem solving. This will be an excellent time to develop the ability to work things out independently. The box in the middle of the room may be in the way, and the child will have to devise a way to get around it. The door must be opened—how is this done? The candy is in the dish on the table and must be reached. Things that motivate the child to move can be used to create little movement problems he must solve. Do not solve the problem for him but do encourage and accept his first attempt. This way he will become more confident in his own ability.

Orientation to many surroundings can be promoted by providing these problems. It is also valuable over a period of time. When the original problem is finally solved, then repeated successes in the same place will provide increased learning. If the problem is repeated the next day, and the child remembers nearly every step, then considerable progress has undoubtedly been made. Transfer of this learning can also be seen when similar problem-solving behavior is noted in a different location but for a similar task. For example, if there is an object in the child's path, and he must move around it, then on another occasion he may use this learning to help him solve a more complicated but similar problem.

Constant awareness of the child's use of free time is necessary. Knowing how he entertains himself when no demands are being made gives us valuable information. He may stare at the light or twirl things in front of his eyes. Patterns such as these will tell us something about the child. If he moves about in his environment with curiosity and interest, we will also have important information. Watch closely. These observable behaviors help us make plans for the child.

Children with sensory handicaps need to develop in other areas to help compensate for the sensory loss before they can begin to understand the nature of the space around them. The development of motor skills combined with memory allows for this. The nonhandicapped person sees a mountain and goes toward it. He can then begin to comprehend distance, size, and height. The child whose vision is restricted must be "shown" many things by moving close and then using other senses—touch, taste, tactile, and olfactory—to gain further knowledge. In the same way, a large lawn may be investigated through a multitude of sensory experiences. The shape, texture, size, and slope can be discovered if the child feels free to move about. His freedom to do this, combined with his memory, allows him to reproduce the information he receives into a composite sensory pattern. Repetition strengthens this memory. Constant experiences of this sort encourage the mind to sort and classify so that the concepts may be developed.

In addition to this learning of space, other feelings are also experienced and may be used. Going up a hill and climbing a ladder are experiences of different slopes. The time it takes to walk the length of a block is built into a combined motor and memory to create a temporal (time) factor.

Other Suggestions

Several other suggestions that may be helpful are listed below. Some may require adaptation, others may not apply for certain situations. Also check the sections on Infant Learning and Body Image Development for ideas.

1. Put pieces of paper on the floor for him to step on.
2. Make lines on the floor from brightly colored masking tape.
3. Play singing games with motor movement: "Hokie Pokie," "Little Boy Blue," "This Is the Way We Wash Our Hands," "Eensie Weensie Spider," and "If You're Happy and You Know It Clap Your Hands," are good starters.
4. Make a "doorknob box." The child can open small boxes with knobs, nailed to a large board, and find something interesting. Use the same idea with latches or locks and keys.
5. Encourage development of rhythm. Clap, tap, stomp, or click things. This can be good imitation as he develops. Rhythm is important for learning a well-coordinated walk.
6. Walk to rhythm. Beat a drum, play a piano slow and fast, play a record, or sing.
7. Put stars on the floor in important places to step or stand (in front of the sink or commode or on the steps).
8. Use the mirror when working on imitation and body image development.

9.   Do not continue the same activity for long periods of time. Ten minutes is long enough for most, and two or three minutes may do well in the beginning.

10. Roll down a hill with him.

11. Swimming is excellent. Water play in the bath is a good time for fun things together. Get in with him or sit on the side of the tub with your feet in.

12. Trampolines are great. So are mattresses on the floor or bed springs covered with plywood. Walk through a ladder that is lying flat on the floor. Step through a bunch of old spare tires thrown out on the ground.

13. Balls are fun. They roll from you to the child, and they roll away and have to be chased. Large ones are best. Texture balls work well inside, are easy to grasp, and also feel good. Balloons are great.

14. Steps offer all kinds of challenges. The ones you buy that can be climbed up, over and down are fun but often expensive. Try real ones.

15. Make a balance board. It takes a couple of bricks and a strong 2 foot × 4 foot board. Try walking on railroad tracks or low brick border walls.

16. We like the wagon and wheel barrow. Discarded strollers are also fun. The children have turns pushing each other.

17. Place something on the floor to jump over. A rope, straw, or stick will do at first. Later, try a box.

18. Loose clothing helps. If he feels all tied up in tight clothes, he is not going to move freely.

19. Let others help. Big or little brothers and sisters are great, if you help them develop the proper spirit. Neighbors can also be good. Young people who have free time can prove to be excellent with their energy and enthusiasm.

20. Be sure he goes barefoot sometimes.

21. Talk to him about what you are doing. This talking will help him understand the what and why of the activity; it also helps you relax.

22. Be consistent as far as possible.

23. Chronological age (his actual age) is not as important as developmental age (what he is doing that is normal for a certain age).

24. Do not expend much effort comparing him with others; compare him with himself—what he is doing now as compared to what he was doing last month or even last year.

25. Hold him up high or push him down low so that he can discover things he would have missed.

26. Let him lead or pull you around. This should not continue indefinitely, but it is a start. Later, you will want him to point or communicate to you about his wants.
27. Call him to come to you. Touch him. This can develop into a little "hide and seek" game between you later.
28. Reward his attempts. Rewards can be an important way to establish that beginning relationship. A reward can be a hug, a piece of candy, "Good boy," a pat on the knee, or anything else that he likes.
29. Watch for actions that indicate poor motor use or other bad habits that may be developing. There may be a physiological reason.
30. Get a jump rope. It can be used to pull on, jump over, or even make a pretend clothesline for wet clothes.
31. Make some bean bags. Put them in containers, throw them at a clown face made from cardboard, and even throw them at each other. They are fun to feel. Play "go get it." Giant bean bags can be climbed on, jumped on, and sat on.
32. A ball on a rope or a balloon on a string is fun. Hang it from the ceiling within his reach so he will be interested.
33. Sponges of all sizes and shapes make fun toys to throw or squeeze.
34. Putting clothespins in a bottle is fun and inexpensive.
35. The lines you draw on the floor can also be jumped over, stood on, and crawled on.
36. We enjoyed a big cloth tunnel and everyone crawled through.
37. The large hopping balls are good. A giant ball can be used for him to roll over with your help. This is also for balance and stretching. The child with cerebral palsy can often relax when held in this inverted position over a ball. Also extension is easier in this position.
38. An inexpensive, inflatable punch bag provides some motivation for pushing and hitting.
39. A sand box, scoop, and two or three cans or pans provide many opportunities for fine motor skills (dip, pour, dig). Try sand tracing with your finger and then his while you are playing in the sand. This is sometimes fun to do with simple designs.
40. Pegboards have many uses and are good for eye–hand coordination. They are also good for tactile work.
41. We have fun with a magnet. Big ones are best.
42. Do not forget the seesaw. You can make your own.
43. Blocks and beads should be large at first. Real blocks, boxes, pieces of wood, or bricks are best. Sealed and painted shoe boxes stack well and are safe.

44. Get three colored light bulbs, red, yellow, and blue, and place them in sockets wired to a board. Have long pull cords for the lights. Fasten this to the wall. The child will enjoy reaching up to pull the cord and causing the light to go on.
45. Place a row of folding chairs, back to back, with enough space between for the child to "practice" walking sideways. He can edge his way down the little alley while playing "follow the leader" or to reach a goal such as a beautiful red light (your bait).
46. Try crawling *under* the same row of chairs. Small bodies can go in small places, and this is a good activity for the "moving all around set."
47. Sit on the floor with your legs apart and place the child in front of you. Now "scoot" forward toward some goal (light, toy, water fountain). If he does not walk or crawl yet but can learn to scoot, he may learn to move around independently in this way.
48. Use different motor patterns for moving from place to place: crawling, rolling, hopping, and skipping.

The importance of developing a child's ability to move about cannot be overemphasized. Physically, it develops his body and gives him the strength to find new worlds and gain new experiences. These new experiences further mental growth by placing the child in position to develop new concepts. Motor ability allows for manipulation of materials for both production and learning. Finally, the ability to move about in space makes it possible to go to and from places where people are. Without this, the person is at the mercy of chance social experiences, or he must face the restriction, isolation, and delay that comes from having to ask others for help.

SELF-CARE SKILLS

Need for Self-Sufficiency

Someone says, "Hold up your foot" and the foot that needs a sock is extended; a spoon held by an adult touches the lip and the child opens his mouth for a bite; a wet rag is brought to the desk and someone cleans red paint off busy hands; the child with wet pants is put on the bed or cot to be cleaned and dressed in fresh clothes. This is not what we want.

All children need to learn to dress, bathe, feed, and go to the bathroom by themselves independently, and the severely and profoundly handicapped child is no exception. There is actually little reason to concentrate on teaching a child to work puzzles, match pictures to objects, or count to five if he cannot take care of his bodily needs. So many times we have seen a six-year-old child who has learned skills that enable him to sit at a desk and perform tasks, but who has little awareness and possibly little confidence in his ability to care for himself. Skills that lead toward normal living are the most important ones for him to learn. Emphasis placed on learning unnecessary skills while neglecting more important learning is discouraging. In this case, the child is forming a dependent, helpless image of himself—one we do not want him to form. Also, if he can learn more complicated tasks, he can learn skills needed to function independently in the normal activities of daily living, which is necessary for acceptance and adjustment in society. And, finally, it would be much better for all who work with him, particularly his family, if he could become self-sufficient to some degree.

There are times when the child trains the adult so he will not need to be self-sufficient. If he continues to receive "excellent service" there is little reason or motivation to learn the self-care skills necessary for independent functioning. The child is always learning, although he may not learn the correct behaviors. Perhaps he is learning that someone will find food and feed him when it is time or that pants should be wet because the reward is a pleasant experience on the cot with a warm washcloth and baby powder. He may be learning, "I am different from other children I see and people do things *for* me." These learned attitudes must be changed before he can progress. Remediating is time-consuming when the child needs to be going forward as fast as possible.

Self-care skills have a special importance to parents and those who have responsibility for the child during his first three to four years of life. If certain things are not accomplished during this time, then the mother frequently sees it as failure on her part. Eating and toilet training are significant examples of these concerns.

In addition to the fact that a child who is not toilet trained is a burden, most parents have considerable pressure on them to accomplish this in their child. Lack of toilet training to many people is a sure sign of mental slowness. At best, it indicates that a mother is inadequate or that perhaps the child is emotionally disturbed. Few people consider the fact that possibly the child has been conditioned to enjoy the extra attention or that the mother's anxiety is transmitted to him during this period, which makes communication of needs even more difficult and less consistent. Sometimes it can even be that the child knows he is bothering the parent and he chooses to do so.

Eating is also an important concern. Many parents feel that if the child cannot or does not eat, he will starve, so they feed him. Give him anything he wants so long as he eats is then the adopted philosophy. Often the type of food he likes is more deterimental than if he had not eaten. Foods with high sugar content are favorites. These harm teeth and are not nutritionally beneficial.

When these concerns exist and affect the child's development, they should be recognized. Positive changes can come about much easier with recognition. Goals can then be set up and appropriate reinforcers prescribed. Frequently these areas are the most important considerations when a child first enters a formal program.

It is no wonder that entering a school program requires such an adjustment to many of the children we see. The bottle is put away and the child must learn to drink from a cup. Training pants replace the diapers as he must learn acceptable toilet habits. The child is put on a schedule—he will eat, sleep, rest, and play at the same times as other children. He is now expected to be one of a group. All of that "good service" he may have known, is gone. What a shock! Most of this should not have been necessary. Early intervention with those who will be working with the child in the home and an early effort toward coordinating the prospective school with the home could have prepared the child for this big step in his life: entering school. Having so many efforts directed toward helping the child without establishing future goals and defining a preparatory program often develops into a situation similar to this.

When to Begin Teaching

Do not wait until the child is "ready" to learn independent self-care skills, such as toilet habits, feeding, dressing, or bathing, or until there is *time* to attack this problem. Begin early. Start watching and planning and begin trying to reach small goals that will eventually lead toward bigger ones. The child is developmentally very young, and he needs encouragement to begin helping; then as he helps more, we can gradually demand more. Eventually our assistance will fade, and he will be completing these tasks alone. For example, we may assist him in learning to dress himself by beginning with a first goal such as *cooperation*. Gradually, he learns to straighten his arm into the undershirt sleeve. Later, he may help by pulling the shirt down over his head. By being aware of the steps he is going through in learning to put on the shirt and also being aware of what he must do next, we help him move forward. In this way, we are planning very early some goals for him to accomplish. If someone continually rolls the shirt, pulls it down over his head, lifts each arm to push it into the sleeve, and asks for no help, not even a flexed muscle, then there will be no progress. It is not cruel to teach the child to care for himself; it is teaching and it can be fun—for everyone. This learning experience can be made into a game. Also if the child knows we expect something from him, he will learn much quicker.

Be prepared. Each of the messy tricks all children seem to know and demonstrate as they learn self-care skills will also be tried by this child. They all seem to know how to spit the food back out faster than we can get it in or how to spill the milk and knock the plate on the floor when we are gone for a second to turn off the stove. They know the most inconvenient time to soil themselves, and they recognize our fatigue and know when we prefer to be left alone. These children are as fast as any when it comes to discovering our weak points. It seems almost impossible to teach some new skill, yet they quickly learn that if there is no other way to get our attention or to escape from an activity we have planned, wet pants may do the trick. By looking at them, we may think they are completely unaware of what has happened, except we know that these accidents happen too frequently when we know they want to escape or when we have gotten them all settled and have work to do. It is important to recognize the occurrence and consistency of these times. They help us to predict many things about the child's readiness and his ability to analyze situations.

If this child is to learn these and other self-care skills, he must go through most of the stages all children experience in developing independence. Someone may have to insist very strongly or even demand that he do certain things; things that may seem more trouble than they are worth at the time. We all know how much easier it is to do for a child rather than struggle through all that it may take if we expect him to help. We also know, though, that these struggles will eventually have to occur if the child is to progress. The kitchen floor may be a wreck after a little "learning experience" during lunch, and this would not have been the case if he had been fed and nothing demanded of him. However, no progress would have been made. Eventually the floor will be messy a few times if he learns to feed himself. However he needs all experiences possible and much help to move through some of the stages we will be discussing on the next few pages. He will finally discover what you have in mind if you exhibit determination. He is going to grow up soon, and he will need as many grown-up behaviors as possible. He will be more socially acceptable to outsiders, and he will fit into the home and community more comfortably when he has learned to care for himself.

Toilet Training

The severely and profoundly handicapped child can learn to conform to most socially acceptable standards of toilet behavior. But before he learns, there will be many trying experiences; some will be funny and some will not, at least at the time they occur. Few, if any, children learn that pants are not to be wet and soiled without someone going through some messy procedures for and with them. Also one cannot expect him to be trained at the same age as some other child. Comparing his progress to another child is useless. Start with what he *can* do and move forward in steps that are appropriate for him. If he has developed very slowly in other areas, he will probably be slow learning this behavior. If other learning has come fairly easily, then this may too. This depends on many factors.

You cannot always wait until you are "ready" to initiate toilet training, as there will always be several convenient reasons to delay beginning the training program. You cannot wait until he can "understand" either; teach him to understand as you work on the skill. The proper attitude will be helpful. Learning will take time, patience, and planning. It must be done when the child is developmentally ready. How do you know when he is ready? If he is capable of certain physical skills, such as sitting on a toilet or potty seat, he may be ready. A lengthening of the time interval between wettings may be the sign. You may just *know* that it is time for toilet training. The skill must be taught.

Readiness for training does not often occur with severely and profoundly handicapped children at the chronological age considered normal for most children. Certain behaviors and experiences must be accomplished before a child is prepared for a toilet training program. If he has been deprived of sensory experiences that help develop this readiness, then he will not respond to toilet training regardless of his age. This deprivation of sensory experiences includes lack of a visual model to imitate, disorientation within his environment, lack of body image understanding, and physical unreadiness. When the child has enough of the necessary experiences, he will be ready. Another reason for his unreadiness may be that he has not been expected to care for himself or made aware of the need for independent toilet habits. Therefore, when we speak of toilet training the severely and profoundly handicapped child, we may be referring to a child who is five, six, or seven years old, yet developmentally is functioning at or below the two-year level.

By observing the child and charting frequency patterns, we may be able to predict fairly accurately the child's readiness. He may be urinating so frequently that it is obvious he is not yet ready to go further. Make a chart and put it in a convenient place so his bladder and bowel patterns can be recorded. This chart can be a simple check sheet for recording his daily behavior and can be devised by anyone. One way we have done this is to make a chart indicating check periods such as upon rising, after breakfast, before recess, before and after lunch, and so on. Then on the chart we record our findings at those times. After a few days of charting this behavior, there will be more evidence.

If the child can be "caught" before he wets, we reward his success and communicate to him our pleasure. Chances for repeating such behavior will then be improved. To find the first opportunity to say "Good boy" (success) will probably require some detective work. After weeks of charting and predicting by taking him to the bathroom, there should be less frequent urination patterns and other signs that he is developing more control. This gradual lengthening of time between wetting, which indicates progress, may cover a period of months. These small steps forward are important. Eventually, more satisfying goals may be reached.

Toilet training does not actually "begin" at a certain *point*. Perhaps the toilet training will begin when you start calling more attention to accidents or when the child shows distaste in wearing soiled pants. Maybe he shows interest in others when going to the toilet or tries to remove his wet pants. As his interest and awareness increases, respond by calling more attention to what is happening and expect more. Increased emphasis and gradual goal adjustment results in a full-fledged program of toilet training.

Sometimes it helps to exaggerate a reaction when a seven-year-old child, who can do better, puts a puddle in his chair. Look at the puddle, say "No!" or "What happened?", feel the wet pants, and point back at the puddle. Then have him help clean it up. These may not be much help, but at least the child is becoming more aware of what has happened. Next, go to the toilet and take as long as needed for the child to remove his wet clothes and put on dry ones, with minimal help from you. Always talk, sign, feel, and talk some more. Say "It's hard to get those shoes back on, but *you* wet the pants." Then the accident is forgotten. Hopefully he is beginning to store this information and will soon remember what he is to do. It is over now, and perhaps next time will be better. Very often we have to suppress a desire to laugh at the child's struggles, and it is usually hard to keep from helping. We often say "the bigger the experience the more they get from it," and that is true. He will not learn as fast in the long run if we take too many short-cuts, and do the work for him.

Ideas to Try

We have tried all sorts of things. What works with one child may not with another. Perhaps there is a suggestion here that will be helpful.

1. If he dislikes or is afraid of the bathroom, make it more fun. Decorate it. Try small Christmas lights on the wall, mobiles from the ceiling, or music.
2. He may cooperate better if you stay with him. If so, stay, particularly at first.
3. Give him a favorite toy as he sits there. Play with him. Tie his toy to the seat. Your purpose is for him to like the potty and the bathroom. Later, as he progresses, you will not want to confuse the issue with so much distraction. The point is to perform, not just play.
4. If you are using a potty chair, it should be kept in an appropriate place such as the bathroom and not be moved all over the house.
5. You may not have access to a convenient bathroom. Then use the potty chair in the classroom, but keep it in one area. If you are having difficulty keeping him on the chair, try turning the chair toward the window, for now.
6. Keep a chart. This may help you know what to expect and when.
7. Try to "catch" him before he has an accident, then you can be there to brag. The success helps us show him what we want. For a short period, try to catch him about once each hour. When you do finally catch him, be sure he knows how thrilled you are. Clap, hug him, talk about it, or sign, and give him a reward.
8. Consistently use words and with the language-impaired child also use signs or gestures as a signal, before and during the situation. The signal we usually use is to make the manual sign for "T" with the child's hand each time we toilet him. Someday he will give the signal when he needs to go.
9. Let the child see you go to the toilet. Take him with you often. Boys need to see fathers, too.
10. Five to ten minutes is long enough to sit on the toilet in the beginning. You can lengthen it gradually, but do not go overboard. For some, who do not like the idea, one minute may even be a first goal, particularly if *his* goal is to be uncooperative. Also, if he thinks he is going to fall in, you cannot expect much cooperation. A foot rest or stool may be helpful.

11. Try a potty seat that will fit over the regular commode. This is more like Mommy and Daddy. The small potty chair will be different from what he sees others using.

12. Soiled pants should be removed as soon as possible. Your purpose is not to condition him to wearing soiled clothes. If he prefers clean clothes, he may be easier to train, so help him become accustomed to the clean ones.

13. Be sure he wears training pants and clothing that is easily removed. Diapers are not for training. If the weather is too cool for training pants and bare feet, try long pants with an elastic waist. Occasionally, let him run around undressed for a short period. This may make him more aware.

14. Have him dress and undress in the bathroom if possible. You may need to help. This way he will learn to associate wet pants with the toilet room more quickly.

15. If he uses a potty chair, then take or send it when he visits Grandmother for the weekend or spends the day in his teacher's home.

16. Do not delay starting this learning activity just because he objects. There are many things he will need to learn, and he cannot make all the final decisions.

17. If he refuses to sit on the seat, hold him there firmly for a minute or until he relaxes enough so you can say "Good boy, you sat on the seat, now you can get up." Do not let him up while he is screaming and pinching, as this will strengthen the screaming behavior, and it will continue longer next time.

18. Observe! Watch for signs that mean he will soon soil or wet his pants.

19. Try pouring a little warm water on him or giving him a drink to encourage urination. Once he succeeds, you may be able to communicate with him better.

20. Some people say you should begin with bowel control. This is not true for all children. Catch what you can and begin with what seems best.

21. Let him help pull up his pants. Place your hands on top of his and hook his thumb or finger under the pants, then pull.

22. Help him learn where the toilet paper is kept. It should always be in the same place. This will be helpful in developing memory.

23. He needs to learn to tear it, even if this does mean some of it will be wasted. Once he finds it rolls, he may do as many children and see if there is an end. This is learning too.

24. Do not forget to wash up.

Eating

Teaching a child to eat properly can be rewarding to both child and teacher. It can also be frustrating and will be very messy at times. Many children who are severely and profoundly handicapped eventually learn to feed themselves independently with little outside help or instruction. Some may even learn this skill fairly close to the age normally expected; they may just be a bit messier. Others require extensive assistance and may even need encouragement in learning to chew or swallow. Possibly some who enter school with a bottle and are unable to handle solid foods in their mouth could have made more progress if the adults working with them had been aware of the usual steps necessary for learning to eat independently. Others, however, may have problems, such as the spastic tendencies of some severely handicapped children that complicate this learning process. Nevertheless, it does appear that many of the children we see could have made more progress in this area.

Eating is a necessary function and to many children it is self-rewarding. Every bite of food that goes in the mouth is a reward in itself, at least the more desirable foods are, and will often motivate the child to repeat the process. This behavior should be one of the easier independent self-care skills to teach. Also the muscles used for eating are the same ones that will be used for speech. As the child develops in his ability to handle food in his mouth, he will also be developing speech muscles.

It is necessary for the child to move forward gradually toward eating solids as his development dictates. We must see at what level the child is functioning before we can decide what must be done first. If he has learned to chew and swallow food that is put in his mouth, then perhaps we will want to work on independent finger feeding. If he cannot handle solids, we may want to concentrate on learning to swallow semisolids. The child may be able to eat finger foods but unable to handle a spoon. Therefore, our goal may be for him to eat with a spoon.

There are many separate skills necessary if the child is to learn to eat at a table, with a spoon, independently. Starting with the beginning of the task, we can recognize some of the separate skills. The child must sit in a chair, reach out and pick up a spoon, bring it to his mouth, open his mouth at the appropriate time, chew and swallow the food, then repeat. This is no small task. It may be difficult for him to grasp the spoon or he may not want to try. Getting food on the spoon without pushing the bowl on the floor can be a real challenge. If he has no usable vision, there will be certain problems, and if he is spastic, there will be others. Then, if he does get it into his mouth and does not like it, out it comes. Now he is not motivated to try again. This will be our problem since we *do* want to try again.

Some children seem to have an extreme sensitivity in and around the mouth. This sensitivity is indicated by complete rejection of any attempt to touch either the tongue with an eating utensil or place unfamiliar or unusual food textures in the child's mouth. If the oral area can be desensitized by gradually introducing sensory experiences, there will be improvement.

The usefulness of this method will depend on the individual child; therefore, we must first observe the child and analyze what he is doing. Is his tongue round and smooth? Has it been doing its share of work? Do his lips have any vertical lines? Does he ever purse or wrinkle them? How do his lips and tongue compare to another child's? Does his tongue hang down over his lower lip? What does he do when you touch a spoon handle to his tongue? How does he swallow? Drooling can be an indication of this sensitivity; if he cannot purse his lips or control his tongue, then he will not swallow. He may even reverse swallow. We may not be able to *teach* him to swallow, but if we can develop a tolerance for variety and thus cause the child to use his tongue and mouth in a normal way, then he will *learn* to swallow.

If it is evident that his mouth is especially sensitive or that his lips and tongue suffer from lack of use, there are several things that can be tried. Stroke the child around his mouth by circling the oral cavity, outside of the lip line. Go around several times, then reverse. You may notice that he pulls his lips in a little as if almost to purse them. This is good. Some try this by using a small, pencil type of vibrator. One or two minutes at a time three or four times a day is good in the beginning; then further analysis can determine the need to lengthen or shorten the intervals. Take care not to overdo.

The tongue can sometimes be desensitized by using a spoon handle or tongue depresser. Ease the instrument into the mouth and touch the tip of the tongue. Rub by gently pushing or forward stroking the tip. Gradually move a little further inside, using the same motion. Keep easing back. When the instrument has reached the farthest point, the child may gag slightly. Pat him on the back, give him time to relax, and begin again. By desensitizing the tongue and stimulating the gag reflex, you are helping the child learn to swallow. This takes time but is often well worth the effort.

There is no need to make a problem of eating when no problem exists. But remember that the longer someone feeds him, the harder it will be for him to learn that he can be independent. If he is developing at a rate that seems acceptable and is making progress, then gradually keep expecting more from him as the weeks go by.

Conflict between the parents and the child over eating can set the stage for some trying times. Many of the children we see have learned to hate or fear mealtime. The child begins to cry or fuss the moment he is placed at the table. He knows what is going to happen. Possibly he has experienced numerous occasions that have stimulated this response. A feeling of concern on the part of the parents can develop into an uncomfortable atmosphere for the child. Continuous forcing and nagging will cause what may not have been a problem to develop into one. Eating should be a pleasant experience.

Some people have a tendency to give the child a bite of food and then start massaging his jaws so that he will chew. When something new is tried, a reaction can be expected. He may spit out his first few bites of solid food. Continually evaluate what you are doing. Should you give him something softer or more palatable? Is he ready for solids? Is there some better way the food could be presented? Remember, what does not work may be your fault and not the child's. If you give him a bite and start immediately holding his mouth shut or rubbing his jaws, you can be sure that he will not like it. He needs a chance. Later you may find it necessary to resort to firmer ways of approaching the situation, such as insisting on a tiny bit of cooperation or help before he gets that food or drink he wants so badly.

Steps Toward Independence

There is no age that is ideal to teach this child to feed himself properly. Progress may come slowly, or he may move rapidly through each stage as he learns to feed himself independently.

It is helpful to recognize some of the skills the child learns as he progresses toward independence. His first eating experience may be breast-feeding and then a bottle. Later, he may be given a small amount of cereal in his bottle with the milk. As he matures, activity will increase, and he will require more solids. Then he is introduced to spoon-feeding. He learns to keep a small amount of food in his mouth and swallow it. Next he will probably begin learning to chew foods that are placed in his mouth. These foods are sometimes pieces of baby crackers, cookies, buttered bits of bread with sugar on top, soft toast broken into bite-size pieces, and regular baby foods.

About this same time, he may begin to enjoy holding finger foods. Soon he may start hand-to-mouth eating. This should be encouraged, even if he is trying to pick up something that should be handled with a spoon. He must learn to put things in his mouth, and he cannot do so if we are always concerned with the mess he is making, so we help him wipe his face and go on. Now we can probably begin helping him hold the spoon with our hand over his (if this has not already been done). If he tries to take the spoon out of our hand, we let him. His every attempt at independence is encouraged. He then begins learning to dip the food and bring it to his mouth.

Gradually we give him less and less assistance and keep telling him what a "big boy" he is, several thousand times. Here again it works best to start withdrawing assistance by having the child complete the last part of the task. This way he is more likely to succeed. We help him until the bite is almost in his mouth, then encourage him to make the final move. He will probably need help to hold the spoon at first, since the natural tendency may be to drop the spoon when it is emptied. If it does drop, we let him help find it. He needs to learn that spoons do not drop and then suddenly reappear. As he begins to develop more independence, we continue to let him do more and more. Eventually the only assistance he needs will be scooping the food on the spoon. Without going through the hand-to-mouth feeding and other stages, it will be difficult, if not impossible, for him to ever learn to eat with a spoon.

If he has passed through all these stages, he is well on his way toward independent feeding. Teaching him to scoop a bite of food on a spoon and put it in his mouth will best be accomplished by using foods he likes and those that are the best consistency for scooping. Ice cream in a cup often works well. Remember, he must be hungry for the food. Sometimes when we know a child is capable of a task and he refuses, we let him leave the table. At the next meal, he usually does much better. Remember, no snacks in between meals at those times.

When the child reaches this point, we gradually help him move on to new goals. Once he learns a new skill, we expect him to repeat it regularly. Move forward and build his confidence. As he learns new skills, weak areas that may need strengthening can be observed. For example, it may be difficult for him to get certain foods on his spoon and keep them there until the spoon reaches his mouth. It may be difficult for him to chew some foods, or he may stuff his mouth too full. These and other skills can be strengthened and corrected with consistent efforts. Other appropriate skills can be developed and perfected as the child progresses. Every goal will depend on this individual child and what he needs, so it is always necessary for us to observe his behavior and development carefully so we can set appropriate goals.

Evaluate, observe, and plan. Attempt tasks that seem possible—success experiences are important to us all. When there is a problem, try different ways of approaching the child or other goals. We all make mistakes, but planning will prevent many. Decide what small step forward should be next and present it when you feel it is time. Attempting to get the child to perform tasks that are three steps away will be discouraging.

Some children exhibit strong willpower in their determination not to cooperate. One five-year-old boy liked baby food and refused all table foods with the exception of bread, cereal, and sweets. A specialist advised us to let Joe eat the table food or do without. We were somewhat apprehensive but felt it was time for him to learn to eat, so we set that goal. Almost three days later, Joe still had not eaten, and we were not enjoying our meals very much either. He had, however, lost 5 or 6 of his 30 pounds. This time we backed down. Some children have a strong resistence and will hold out so long that we must begin reevaluating our goals or techniques. In this case, the possibilities of harm coming to the child outweighed the usefulness of continuing.

Some Suggestions

The suggestions listed here have all been tried and found useful in at least some cases. Perhaps these ideas might prove helpful when concentrating on helping a child learn to feed himself independently. No one thing works for all children, since so much depends on the individual child and the teacher. Check these suggestions and begin. We must all understand that the longer the child depends on us to do for him, the more dependent he will be.

1. Encourage the child each time there is a sign that he is trying to help.
2. Occasionally, his hand can be placed on the face of the person feeding him to feel a chewing movement.
3. Encourage him to feed someone or put a bite in your mouth. This can become a game.
4. Put food in his mouth and do not be upset if he spits it out. For him to allow it to be put there may be progress.
5. When he indicates interest in your face, try moving your jaw with his hand on it, then placing his hand on his own jaw. Gently help him move his jaw, but do not force him. Sometimes the opposite action stimulates the response you want best. If you want him to

open his mouth, press gently *under* his chin. Encourage imitation whenever possible; it does not have to be at the table.

6. Mixing foods he likes with foods he does not like may or may not work. Some children decide not to eat any of it; others may eat it all. We do not, however, want to turn him against all table foods.

7. The same may be true with mixing baby food and regular table foods to encourage him to eat the solids.

8. Try requiring him to eat one tiny bit of the new or undesired food before he can have his very favorite food.

9. Do the little things that are very important to him. For example, when we are trying to get a child to feed himself and he seems to want someone to stay there beside him, we stay. It is fine to give in on some of the "other things" as long as we are aware of our real goal.

10. If it appears that a child will eat better while sitting in someone's lap and we are having difficulty with the eating, then we hold him while he eats. After he has made some progress, he will gradually learn to eat sitting in a chair. Once we decide which step should come first, we move forward with confidence.

11. Talk to him about what he is doing and remember to sign "eat" consistently in meaningful situations. (The signing is not, of course, necessary for all children, but it is mentioned to remind those who are working with children with hearing handicaps or others who cannot speak.) He will learn to anticipate mealtime if you continually give him the language needed to associate with the experience. Later he will learn to tell you when he wants to eat.

12. He must realize that you are proud of him, so continually show him.

13. Consistency helps. You cannot expect him to be independent today and then tomorrow, when you are in a hurry, give in and feed him.

14. Encourage him to feel his food. He needs to know what it is, how it feels, how much is there, and when it is gone.

15. It is fine to allow him to taste food with his fingers, if this is appropriate to his development level. However, once he has passed the finger-feeding stage and is beginning to learn to eat with a spoon, he should be allowed to investigate, but not eat, the beef stew with his fingers.

16. A bowl may work best when beginning spoon-feeding. It is often difficult to corner those peas on a flat plate.

17. Help him learn to hold one hand on the bowl and the other on the spoon.
18. We work behind the child often. In this way our arms are coming from the same direction as his, which helps control and guide his arms.
19. A little ridge on the edge of the table helps keep the bowl from landing on his lap every time. This is the reason high chair trays are made with a rim; it is especially useful for the child with cerebral palsy.
20. If he only uses his tongue for spitting the food out, try peanut butter. It requires much more tongue gymnastics to get all of that out, especially if a little is smeared on the roof of his mouth with a tongue depressor or a dull table knife.
21. He is not going to do anything for or with you if he does not like and respect you. Exhibit love and affection, along with pride, but also show him that you know what is best.
22. Refusing to eat is one way the child can get even with you or demonstrate his general unhappiness. Look at the total child. Perhaps he is telling you something else when he refuses to eat.
23. When learning to eat solids, find something he likes; this may be difficult for some. We have had success with sweetened dry cereal, potato chips or sticks, cooked macaroni, bananas, animal crackers, cookies, graham crackers, saltine crackers, or small, bite-sized squares of bread with butter and sugar on top.
24. Sometimes ice cream or Jello is an excellent starter.
25. Pickles and other sour tastes appeal to some children, but be sure he is ready to handle it in his mouth, as he might swallow it whole and choke.
26. Dip half of a cookie or cracker in milk and offer him the "soggy" half. Perhaps after eating through the soft part he will eat the solid half.

Dressing

One can easily become frustrated when analyzing all the different skills a child needs before he can dress himself. He will eventually need to know how to button, tie bows, pull a shirt over his head, snap and buckle pants, loosen shoelaces, find the front and back, distinguish the left from the right shoe, put a belt in loops, get the sock right side up, work a zipper, hook pants, and much more. It seems impossible. We need not, then, look at the entire task now, but rather begin thinking about what comes first or where to begin. In the case of toilet training, for example, the child will need to be able to put on and take off his pants, which could be a natural skill to begin developing. Also he will be wearing a shirt daily, so we can begin gradually to work on letting him help with this task as he dresses.

It makes little difference where he starts if he has a fair chance of success. Begin with something that seems possible. Opportunities to help him develop independence in dressing will occur daily.

At first, a little assistance from the child is reason for celebration. When he first straightens his arms into the sleeve you are holding, he is learning. When he takes off his shoes, even at some inappropriate time, he is learning. When he extends his foot for the first time, he is learning. Be aware of small changes. The way his body feels as you help him provides many clues. If he is floppy and limp, you know he is not helping; if he stiffens a little, he is progressing; if his fingers mold under yours a tiny bit as you help him pull up his pants, he is making progress. Look for steps forward.

Pushing too hard, when he is not developmentally ready, can cause more harm than good. He will know he cannot do it and perhaps build himself a little world that is more comfortable for escape or avoidance purposes. Insist on tiny steps, and do not look for miracles.

Provide the child with a model. Many children learn to dress themselves by "outdoing" others. If he can see, be sure that he has the opportunity to watch others dress. If he cannot, find some way to make him more aware of normal dressing behaviors. It will take a little longer than seems necessary. He will learn what is to be done if he goes through the process daily. This requires special help and attention and can be easily overlooked. We volunteered to work with 8 four-year-olds for a year, and each one needed to learn independent self-care skills. This can seem like more feet, legs, arms, teeth, hair, shoelaces, and soiled pants than can be handled. They taught us a lot, but we did manage to teach them also. Anyone who is motivated can do the same.

Suggestions

There are several things we found helpful. Some ideas we developed, some we heard from other teachers, and some we just stumbled upon. They are all included here.

1. Keep the child's clothes in a place that is convenient to him. Be sure they are always there.

2. Let him know where his clothes are and help get them. Eventually he will get them by himself, if we are consistent.
3. We often work from behind with our arms coming around the child, so that he can follow our movements. We stand to help with pants or sit to help with shoes and socks, but we are usually behind him.
4. Always talk about what is happening in short, meaningful phrases: "Get the sock," "Where is the sock?" "Pull the sock," or "Look, the sock is on."
5. Clothing that is easier for him to manipulate is best. Overalls are not ideal.
6. For the child with auditory receptive language problems, use a signal before dressing. Develop one that can be used consistently while saying "Let's go dress" or "Where are your clothes?" We sometimes pat the child's body to indicate that we need clothes "right here."
7. Guide the child's hand while zipping, buttoning, snapping, or buckling.
8. We gradually withdraw our assistance as he becomes more helpful.
9. We always make sure he knows he is great and that we are pleased when he does something, no matter how small the accomplishment may seem. We let him see us smile or we nod "yes." We clap and nod our head.
10. Many children begin independent dressing by *undressing*. If they do, be sure they do so at the appropriate times so they can be encouraged. However, do not be surprised if a child undresses immediately after he has helped dress himself. This may be a big step forward. Possibly he is confused. He may need and want attention or he may be practicing. Decide why he is doing this before reacting.
11. Let him remove your shoes, fasten your laces, or unbutton your shirt. If you discourage him because you feel his behavior is unnecessary, it may take longer than ever to teach him in exactly the way you had planned.
12. Try to dress him in approximately the same order each time. If you prefer to start with underpants, then pants, then shirt and then shoes, try to do so each time. He will learn to anticipate.
13. Name the articles of clothing as he is helped to dress. Talk to him, even if he does not seem to hear. This helps you treat him more normally.

14. When teaching him to pull on his pants, start with small steps and begin at the end of the task. That is, when the pants are almost pulled, let him complete the task. It will probably be easier for him to perform this part first, and he will feel successful by completing the task. Then as he progresses, gradually work through the task by letting him accept more and more responsibility. He learns to pull the pants up over his hips and then from his knees up. The last step or goal would be to hold the pants and step in them, independently.

15. When teaching him to button, buckle, tie, zip, and snap, it may be helpful to make models for him to use for practice. An interesting pillow can be made from a scrap of material or part of a blue jean leg and covered with tasks to practice such as buttoning, snapping and zipping. Large buttons are easier at first.

16. When teaching fine motor skills, accept small approximations and keep motivation high. If he does not want to button, he probably will not do so.

17. It may work well to practice pushing unconnected buttons through a hole cut in cardboard. If this is too difficult, then work on pushing large things into openings. Pushing bean bags in the mouth of a wooden clown face may be a small step forward.

18. Tack a zipper to a strip of wood. He can learn to open and close it this way and later move to the real pants zipper, which requires many more skills.

19. Teaching him to get into a pullover shirt is much easier when you begin at the end. Help him until he gets that last arm halfway in, then encourage him to take over. Hopefully he will straighten his arm into the sleeve. Then cheer and shout (naturally).

20. If, after all this effort, the shirt is on backwards or the shoes he worked so hard to put on are on the wrong feet, let him wear them anyway. We can help him change them later, but if we immediately take them off, he is going to feel like a failure. Brag on his best efforts.

21. Begin at the end with the socks, too. Help him get the sock up over the heel, then when he pulls at the top a little, up it comes. Success. Gradually expect more, working from the end to the beginning of the task.

22. Use tangible rewards if useful. Any way you can get the point across to the child that you are proud of his accomplishment is acceptable.

23. When working on tying shoes, start at the beginning. If he can

tighten the strings that is a good start. Later, he will learn to tie the knot, and finally he will learn to make a bow.

24.   Continue to show him how to distinguish the front from the back of clothing. He will get it one day. Pin a tag with his name on it to the front of his shirt. This will help him make the distinction. Textured tags work well for the visually impaired child.

Grooming

The activities of daily living require that the child have many separate abilities before he can independently perform a particular skill. We will discuss briefly some of those that pertain to social acceptance. The child should enjoy being clean and well groomed as often as possible, particularly on special occasions. Because of his handicap, it will be more difficult to teach him these skills, but unless he is taught, he will be unaware of the need to be neat and clean. However, because of his problems, he may appear somewhat different from other children and may attract more attention. We want people to react positively to him, and few people are excited when approached by a child who has food all over his face, is drooling, and has on dirty clothes. The child will pick up negative reactions; he may even become accustomed to these reactions. This is not what we want. He will realize others do not hug him and do not want his kiss. He will recognize this when people draw back as he reaches for them or move away as he comes close. Keeping him clean and helping him learn the importance of cleanliness will help prevent these reactions.

The child must have a positive feeling about himself. When he is approached as if he is wanted and loved, he will feel more accepted. He will develop the wrong self-image if he is approached in a negative way. One of our challenges may be to educate the child's public. It may be necessary for us to show everyone how proud we are of his accomplishments, how cute he is and how much we love him, before he can be accepted. People are sometimes cruel without meaning to be. They say things without thinking. They stare. Faces sometimes register disgust. It is well to prepare for these reactions in advance.

We often take a trip to town on Friday morning. The day begins with grooming; hair, nails, face, and clothes. We look in the mirror and we talk about how pretty the children are and how proud we are of one another. We talk about our trip to town in language appropriate to the group. If possible, we look at pictures of some things we plan to see or do. Then we go to our goal, proudly, with our clever children. Very soon we will meet our "public." A well-meaning lady may say, "Poor little thing." How could anyone pity little Marie, who needs love and acceptance so badly. We all begin talking about how much Marie has learned and how proud we all are of her progress. We also mention that she is very pleased with her new dress. Then one of us straightens her hair and gives her a sip of a Coke (she has already spilled hers). Our observer may say "Don't you get depressed working with these children all day?" We all look cheery, and another teacher goes into her tirade about the fun we have and how excited we all are each time one of the children learns something new. Then we go merrily on our way. Getting the desired reaction can be difficult; however, it is much easier if the child is well groomed.

One of our goals is for the children to become a part of the community. We want them to be citizens of the town and to understand that the world is not a school with a few buildings and children with similar problems. We also want other people to get to know the children. This is a two-way learning experience, and everyone stands to gain. After several trips, we begin to notice that there is a difference in the reactions of salesladies, waitresses, policemen, and others we frequently see. Someone may take a child by the hand and show him the three-way mirror, hold a child high so the balloon will be easier to see, ask what one of the children is trying to communicate, or an interested gentleman may pick up the tab for 11 banana splits and remark "I'm so glad to see those children having fun." And we do have fun.

Several grooming behaviors the child will need to develop as he becomes more independent and socially acceptable must be considered here.

WASHING

This is perhaps the most important grooming skill. For the child to learn to wash his hands, he will be required to know and perform several separate, smaller skills. Because of this and the fact that the skills must be performed in order, this activity may be difficult to learn. Washing may begin best with water play. Most children love to sit on the floor and splash their hands in a bucket of water or play splashing games in the bath. Washing is best, though, in a setting similar to the sink, as we eventually want him to associate the sink with the task of hand washing. On the other hand, they may learn the necessary skills fairly quickly. If we think of the task as a sequence, we are more aware of the skills that will be needed. He must find the sink and faucet, then turn the faucet on, find the water, wet his hands, locate the soap, rub the soap between his hands, replace the soap, rinse his hands as he wrings them, find the faucet again, turn it off, find the towel, dry his hands, replace the towel on the rack, and leave.

Most children learn all these steps in order, simply by observing others. The severely and profoundly handicapped child must also observe in one way or another. He needs to experience washing many times before he will understand the sequence. As the activity is repeated and he begins to respond, we gradually decrease our help. Probably the best place to let up on assistance is during the "hands under the faucet" stage, particularly if he likes the way water feels. He will soon learn to rub his hands together or at least move his fingers some under the running water. He may even want to stay there until he fills the sink. Then as he shows more interest, more can be expected, in gradual steps.

SUGGESTIONS

1. Try to perform the hand-washing task in approximately the same order each time. Habit and anticipation will speed up the learning process.
2. We often help him from behind, with our hands on his when needed.
3. Teach him how to locate the faucet by beginning with his hands at the front of the sink and moving them slowly around the sides until he finds it.
4. As one hand turns on the water, be sure the other hand is under the faucet to feel the water as it begins to come out.
5. As always, talk about what is happening. Use key words frequently such as "off," "on," and "water."
6. Before going to wash up, say and, if appropriate, gesture or sign, "Wash your hands." We usually wring our hands together to signal this activity. When using visible signals, we must be as consistent as we are with auditory signals.
7. To encourage him to rub his hands together, try using liquids. We put lotion on his hands during group play and encourage the rubbing motion; when he is trying to rub it off, we go to the bathroom and see if he will rub under the water. Liquid soap works well, too, in the beginning.
8. Real towels are much easier to handle than paper ones, as there are several other skills connected to getting paper towels out of the dispensers. Also, paper towels go in the trash and real ones do not. What will he do with his towel at home? Do not just teach him to manipulate things that are used only at school. Later he may

need to learn both ways, as most community buildings do use paper towels.

9. Encourage him to rub his wet hands on his face to "bathe."
10. If he is performing one of the separate skills and does not move on to the next one, try giving him a little nudge. For example, if he has wet his hands and has not reached for the soap, say, "Where is the soap?" If there is still no response, help one hand locate the soap; he will finally get the message, with a little guidance.
11. Be patient. By hurrying, you do too much of the work.
12. Keep telling and showing him how well he is doing. There is always some part of the child's efforts worth bragging about; if you cannot see anything positive, then you probably are not looking hard enough.
13. Do not expect too much too soon, and do not teach what will have to be untaught.

NOSE BLOWING

We mention this as a reminder that mastery of this skill will need to be encouraged. He needs to learn to associate the tissue held to his nose with the need to blow. Watch for signs of small approximations toward learning so the child can be rewarded and encouraged. When encouraging the child to blow from his mouth, he may spontaneously blow his nose (by accident). Be prepared to reinforce this when it happens, as he needs to learn. By "catching" him, you can better communicate to him what you want. Grab a tissue. If he does not learn this skill easily, it will probably be best to start at the beginning and work forward. The first step may be for the child merely to allow someone to wipe his nose. Later he may learn to help, in small steps.

BRUSHING TEETH

This task is sometimes difficult, but if we get off to a good start we have won half of the battle. By beginning slowly and calmly, without forcing the child, we can prevent him from developing a fear or distaste for brushing teeth. He must eventually need to learn to complete complicated skills such as opening the toothpaste, squeezing it, and putting a little bit on the toothbrush. These fine motor skills will be difficult and will come later. First we want him to learn to clean his teeth, so we are not too concerned if he seems a long way from performing the other necessary skills. Continually let him help while going through the tooth-brushing sequence. By using the same sequence each time, we make quicker progress. He will need clean teeth and fresh breath, so this is important and worthy of our attention.

SUGGESTIONS

1. Accept very small approximations. If he lets you put the tooth-brush in his mouth, this may be progress.
2. We work with our hands on his, usually standing behind the child.
3. If he objects, put a little sugar or peppermint on the toothbrush. Make it as pleasant as possible, so his motivation will increase.
4. If it seems unlikely that his teeth can be cleaned with a brush at this time, try wiping his teeth with a wash cloth or towel.
5. Breath mints or spray mouthwash can be helpful if his breath has an unpleasant odor. Speech work and other close contact work will not be pleasant with bad breath.
6. If he refuses to open his mouth, start with small approximations. Try a taste of honey, syrup, or mint on your finger.
7. A mirror might help. Emphasizing imitation during *other* activities and working toward getting him to imitate mouth and tongue gymnastics sometimes works with the child who refuses to open his mouth.
8. Play "spitting out water" when doing other things (swimming). This is a good imitation activity, and perhaps he will eventually learn to rinse his mouth rather than swallow the toothpaste.
9. Have a definite place for his toothbrush and cup.
10. With the hearing-impaired child, always signal before tooth-brushing time. We usually rub the index finger on our teeth and help the child do the same, then find the toothbrush. Of course, appropriate words are always used. Severely involved cerebral palsy children can usually learn to communicate their needs by using signals long before they can say the word clearly enough to be understood.
11. Look in the mirror after brushing. Let him see his pretty teeth!
12. Allow him to brush your teeth, if he wants, with your toothbrush, of course.
13. He will benefit from watching others brush their teeth. Let him watch someone else brush his teeth; perhaps Daddy will help here. He will want to do it more if he knows it is something that everyone does.

COMBING HAIR

This should be fun. We usually use the comb as one of our first meaningful language associations, as it is something the child has seen and felt many times. Many children like to comb. When one of our children reaches the point of understanding that a comb is put to your hair, we are thrilled. He knows its purpose. Later when he sees a comb, he may learn to respond by rubbing or touching his hair, long before he learns to say the word. He is associating the object with its purpose, and this is inner language. By all means, let him help comb his hair. Encourage him, even if the comb is upside down. He will improve with help. Try anything possible that might help him learn to appreciate the fact that hair is more acceptable when it is well groomed.

SUGGESTIONS
1. Let him comb your hair, encourage him to do so.
2. Use the mirror to work on grooming the hair. Talk about how handsome he looks. Your expression may tell him more than you know.
3. "Comb" the doll's hair with his help.
4. Always groom his hair before going on any outing. He will learn to associate this experience with something important.
5. Use a large comb, one he can handle easily.

NAIL CARE AND MAKEUP

Good grooming experiences can develop into enjoyable interpersonal activities and can be an excellent way to relate to the child. Let the child watch the finger and toenails of another person being clipped, and then groom his nails. Play "let's paint your fingernails." This can be fun and is terrific for body image development. Probably the child will learn to enjoy having his nails painted bright red.

Makeup play can also develop into a fun time. The child needs to learn how nice it is to smell and look good. Everyone can have fun with makeup. Paint the boys, too; we always do. Little Jim will become more aware of his body appearance when he sees his colored lips in the mirrow or feels the lipstick glide over his lips. Besides, it tastes good! Rouge and eye shadow are also great. All experiences can be beneficial and by sharing with the child some of the normal daily grooming activities, much can be accomplished.

Care of Possessions

To live in society, we must learn to take care of ourselves. Learning responsibility for one's own possessions is a part of this. It is important for a child to know that certain articles are his. This helps establish identity and provides us with some measure of security. "My coat," "my shoes," "my mama," and "my bed" are all part of the child's picture of himself.

Every child should own something and, with guidance, learn to care for it. His possessions can be as limited as a toothbrush, a bed, and his clothing, or as inclusive as those that would fill many boxes and drawers. Whatever they are, if they are his, he must learn to care for them.

Possessions have a place to be kept and knowing this helps the child understand the specific function of the object as well as accepting responsibility for its preservation. Then he knows not only where it must be kept but where to find it when needed. Shoes belong on the closet floor, the coat hangs on a hook, glasses are kept on the bedside table, and dirty clothes must be put in the clothes bin. Other things are shared by all and also have a special place to stay. The soap is kept on the disk, a glass belongs in the kitchen, and the towel hangs on a rack. These, too, are lessons worth teaching. As the child gains this knowledge, he gathers confidence in himself, is relieved of the frustration of wanting without knowing where to find, and begins to be a helpful addition to the home and school.

Problem Solving and Self-Care

Daily occurrences provide an excellent opportunity to work on solving simple problems. Discontinue doing too much for the child or helping too often; he needs to work out problems whenever possible. Encourage him. Talk about what is happening. It may be necessary to provide a little assistance at first, but you want him eventually to learn to solve problems alone. If he has reached the point where he can put on his pants fairly independently and he still often gets two legs in one opening, give him an opportunity to solve the problem. Or when he is chasing peas around on his plate with a spoon, see if he can discover that this skill will probably require two hands: one hand as a pusher, such as with a piece of bread to hold the peas still, and another with a spoon. If he still needs help, give him as little as possible. Try putting his other hand on the plate or in some other way showing him that it will take two hands. If that does not work, try helping a little more. You must give him a chance, as he will merely wait for you to work it out for him if he sees the opportunity. Another opportunity to work on problem solving might occur when he loses the soap in his bath. Do not recover it for him; talk about what has happened and encourage him to look for it. There are many similar ways to assist him in independently finding solutions to daily living problems.

We enjoy these times. When children are motivated to complete a task and suddenly confront a problem, they can usually find a solution, although sometimes it is not the one we were expecting. The dressing room at a pool is a good place for some children to learn to put on pants. If they like to swim or play in the water, they will be eager to devise a way to get into that bathing suit. If a child is thirsty, he may learn how to make the water come out of a cooler by pushing the button. If there is a "surprise" partially exposed in a difficult place to reach, a child may discover a way to get it down. This can be amusing. Usually the child tries a "you do it for me" approach, then he may fuss or cry. However, if we feel he can solve the problem with little or no help, we let him. Sometimes one should feign ignorance. When the child tries to drag you across the room to do something for him, pretend to fall, as if he pulled you down. Other times offer a limp hand or arm that will not function. Still other times pretend you cannot reach the object. It is funny when the child starts communicating his method of solving a problem. If you pretend you cannot reach it, he may push you closer so you can get it. *Now* he is thinking, and if he can do that much thinking, he can do the rest.

This kind of problem solving works well in group work, as children can watch and learn from each other. Remember to have a celebration when the child does work it out himself. He will probably be rewarded by the fact that he has what he wanted, but we let him know we are pleased, too. Patience helps. Children are good at manipulating others to solve their problem or do things for them. They have often practiced long and hard at this skill. We assist the child in developing more self-confidence in his own problem-solving ability by presenting him with small problems we know he can solve; then as he progresses, more and more is required of him.

COMMUNICATION

Finding a Method

Smoke signals will not do. Neither will drum beats. You can, however, find a method of communication that is best for a particular child. Finding the system of communication most appropriate for a severely and profoundly handicapped child may take some time, and it will require some planning, some successes and failures, and many varied experiences.

Any time an idea, feeling, or thought is transferred from one person to another, we say that communication has taken place. The communication need not be verbal; it can be signed, gestured, or pantomimed; it may even occur through facial expression and body posture. Any method of communication capable of transferring information from one person to another is acceptable if it works and is practical. What method then will we select for this child and how will we go about it?

Ultimately, the child makes the decision. As we are constantly giving him every opportunity to develop, we begin to notice certain things about the way he is responding. For example, the child may not respond orally and yet we notice that he is beginning to copy simple motions. This may be a signal that he will soon be gesturing and pointing to indicate his needs. It may also indicate that he could learn a few signs even before vocal expression begins. Another child may respond to verbalizations such as "No," "Eat," or "Stop," yet have problems in the motor area that prevent development in the use of his body. Perhaps he will learn oral language easier and quicker than he could learn signs. Still others seem to develop in a way that makes it difficult to decide on the best method for communication, as progress, which is exceedingly slow, seems to be about the same in every area.

When the child is not communicating and should be, doubts about what method is best can be resolved by using a simultaneous method—gesture or sign and talk at the same time. You cannot go far wrong with this technique, and we have found it works well. Develop several appropriate signals and use them consistently with the matching words. If this seems helpful, learn a few manual signs to use. This is discussed further in the following section.

The severely and profoundly handicapped child may have difficulty learning any method of communication. Since it is important for him to learn to express his needs and desires, look for the best method or methods for him. Observe carefully. Continue to talk and watch for behavior indicating the method of communication that will be best for him. This evidence may occur when he begins manipulating people, responds to gestures, indicates an understanding of routines and situations, or seems to know some of what you are saying—yet does not try to communicate. Do not stop talking and encouraging vocalizations, but also do not impose your method on him. Many language-impaired children learn to communicate by using gestures and signs and then later learn to speak. When the child can communicate, he feels a part of the world and wants to learn to do everything we do. If the child knows what a word means, learning to express it will be easier. Therefore, *communication* is the important goal.

One four-year-old girl refused to vocalize and easily became frustrated when we worked on speech. After several months of work, she began to express her needs by pulling the adult toward what she wanted. This manipulation is an important step toward communication. She knew what she wanted and had an image in her mind; she only needed to communicate. Soon she began pointing and responding to gestures and signs. Within a few weeks, she was using our homemade signs for a few meaningful situations, such as, eat, toilet, bye-bye, and sit down. From the first day the child began to express herself, we saw positive changes in her behavior. Along with an emphasis on signs and gestures, speech work also continued. This child even now uses only a few oral words meaningfully, but she is learning them faster. Language development is remarkable. The fact that she (now seven years old) expresses her needs by use of manual signs in the form of short sentences, not single words, is to us and to her parents wonderful. Although her mother and father did not know any signs at first, they are now learning along *with* their daughter.

Using Unacceptable Communication

There may be evidence of a level of communication that is unacceptable. Some will be mentioned and are usually recognized when observing how the child uses his free time. This is not to say that you must stop this communication, but it should be recognized for what it is. As the child progresses to more acceptable communication, this undesirable behavior will gradually disappear.

Many children who have developed slowly learn to communicate with themselves. At these times we see self-stimulating activities, such as when the child flicks fingers in front of his eyes, hits himself, grits his teeth, makes gross sounds, or masturbates. Others may communicate with objects, such as rubbing a spot on the floor, tapping a toy against his teeth, or playing with objects that make reflections on the wall. This is not the level of communication we want for the future. The child will remain withdrawn or draw further into his own world if this continues indefinitely. The distance between this child and what we expect of a normal child then becomes greater.

If the child does begin to communicate with objects and himself, do not punish him. Find ways to change this behavior into a positive activity whenever possible. This may require creativity, but we know that if the child can think up so many ways to withdraw through unacceptable behavior, we can think of as many ways to make it more acceptable. For example, if the child continually stares at his hand, we put a ring on his finger or paint flowers on his hand and talk about what we see. Or we tie colored ribbons on the child's fingers, paint finger-nails, put a colorful mitten on the hand, or give him something to hold.

For another child who is obsessed with light and wants to stare at it constantly, the light can be used as a reward. He can have a flashlight for a moment or two when he does something great. Or if he likes to lie on the floor and stare up at the ceiling light, that light can be turned off and table lamps used. It is all right occasionally to rearrange the environment to suit our needs, but we cannot allow the child to take over completely. Then we spend all of our time arranging things, while he merely shifts. If rearranging the environment does work, do not do it. He must learn to live there—*everything* cannot change because of him.

Perhaps it would be easier to readjust a few things and then get him into the real environment in small steps. If he sits on the floor and rocks to stimulate himself, encourage him to rock in a chair—more "acceptable" rocking. Eventually, this behavior will be replaced with a higher level activity. Talk to him, teach him new skills, and help him become more aware of himself and his environment. He will be grow-ing developmentally, and eventually these more primitive types of communication will begin to disappear. Show him that he is loved, and do not punish him for mannerisms that are irritating. Gradually teach him alternative behaviors.

Learning Manual Signs

Unfortunately, adults often want the child to learn their way of communication. It is easy to say "I don't know signs" when con-fronted with a child who needs them. We all had to learn sign language at first. Many knew speech development and the importance of lan-guage development, but no signs. When we realized the need for com-munication other than oral, we felt as confused as anyone. In order to be able to help the child learn to express his needs, we developed some meaningful gestures that would work for the time being and could be understood by anyone. This can easily be done. The real manual signs should be learned if needed, but the goal for severely and profoundly handicapped children is communication. Examples of some gestures we devised and used as signs are: comb, expressed by running your fingers through your hair; toothbrush, gestured by rubbing your teeth; ball, expressed by pantomimed bouncing; telephone, by holding one balled-up fist to your ear and the other to your mouth; and glasses, by drawing circles around your eyes. Many language concepts can be in-troduced by pointing, such as, nose, eyes, ears, up, and coat. Others can be expressed by pantomiming. "Pour" by turning your wrist over as if pouring; "jump" can be acted out; and "angry" can be communicated by expression.

When a situation presents itself and the manual label for the concept is not known, devise a gesture. For example, if someone brings a real rabbit to school and we do not know the manual sign for rabbit, we create a reasonable sign substitute. We do not want to miss this opportunity to begin developing a new concept, so we say "rabbit," and pantomime long ears on our head. The next time we are prepared with the real sign. Then if the signing seems to be developing into a child's major means of communication, he will need to be provided with more universal signs. Gestures are used in beginning communication and may be used for the purpose of stimulating language, but the child needs to move to higher levels.

It should be remembered that children do have a need to communicate. If they are in a group situation and are involved, then one way or another most will make their wants known. Varied experiences, then, are important factors in helping the child to recognize the need for communication.

Constant Input

As we work on developing communication with the severely and profoundly handicapped, we often feel as if we are the only ones communicating; however, if we express ourselves and the child gets a clue from what we do and say, then we have communicated. We hope the child will begin to express himself, but we cannot expect it immediately. Say the same things over and over at appropriate times and he will learn to understand. Words, signals, or signs used consistently will give him a clue as to what is going to happen. If we splash a few drops of water in his hand each day before bath time, he will learn to anticipate his bath. Then, at a higher level we consistently use phrases such as "Let's eat," "Time for bed," "Time for bath," "Let's go," "Time to get up," and "Time to play." As we make these statements, we use a key signal, such as, "bed," "go," "play," and "wash." It is easier to start with four or five phrases that can be remembered and used regularly.

Probably one of the first indications that the child is understanding what we are saying will appear when a meaningful command is given, such as "eat," and he responds. We constantly observe so that plans can be made for the next steps. First we want him to be aware of communication and realize a need for it; then we hope to begin seeing indications that he is understanding some of what we say or do. Also, we look for signs that he is understanding himself and his environment. If we see all or most of this, then we will begin looking for and expecting some gesturing, pointing, or other symbolic communication. Later, we will probably see more expressive communication. Expressive communication may never occur, however, unless we push him through the stages necessary before learning to communicate. He will not be ready to express himself until he has had many language experiences. Be aware of what he is doing and what is needed next, but do not skip several steps and expect too much too soon.

Here is an example of how one teacher taught a new concept, in this case "candy," to a deaf-blind child (with residual vision) who seemed ready to express himself. Each time she held up the candy, she would make the sign and say the word perhaps three times. The candy was held near her mouth. In this way he would be more likely to see her mouth move as she said the word. The child was encouraged to make the sign and rewarded for any response by getting the candy he wanted. Any attempts toward vocalization were also encouraged. If he made a noise, she said "That's right, candy," and gave it to him. If a child wants the reward, then one day he will respond. When he begins making attempts to communicate, we can start demanding more perfection. He is then required to vocalize or sign more accurately. At some later date, when he is ready, he can be required to express himself without the adult doing it first. For example, in the beginning, when we hold the candy and he attempts to say "candy" in any way, he gets it. Much later he will begin asking for what he wants without any clue from us. It may be necessary to force this recall. He may understand the meaning of the word or remember the correct sign, but fail to respond unless he finds it necessary.

Make language building activities fun and make them big; then insist on getting as much communication from the child as possible. A trip to the store is fun. The child can help find a carrot in the store. Buy it. Wash, peel, scrape, cut, and eat it together; or you may want him to help cook and butter the carrot, then eat it and clean up. Talk constantly and sign, if needed. Ironically, the less the child communicates, the less others talk to him, which is the opposite of what he needs. With activities such as this, select two or three main concepts to emphasize, such as carrot, eat and wash, cook, or clean.

We enjoy trips to the zoo and always present the essential vocabulary before we go, then use the concepts again repeatedly as the child participates. Later, we find someone to listen as the child "tells" about his experience. This activity could be prefaced by showing film strips, looking at pictures, talking about animals, and even acting out the animals' walks. Then go to the zoo and take the pictures used earlier and compare them to the real animals. Later, the child will enjoy the pictures, and the trip will mean more.

One experience that allows for many types of communication is the weather. We talk about it, look out of the window, and walk outside to look at what is happening. Some teachers make an ugly face and act as if a great catastrophe had occurred when the weather is dreary, clap and point to the sun when it is pretty, or pretend to be cross when the rain wets the sidewalk where we walk. These same teachers follow up by helping the children dress paper dolls in proper clothes for the weather and put them on a weather bulletin board. Next they complete the board by adding sun, clouds, or rain to the picture. After this, the group may sit down and make a picture of rain or clouds. Last, the children who are more mature can write sentences or phrases to describe the weather, such as ''Where is the sun?'' ''The sun is in the clouds,'' ''No rain,'' or ''Ugly today.'' The adults' enthusiasm is usually contagious. The activity may be repeated the following day if there is a noticeable change in the weather.

Taking the child on trips is enjoyable. This often stimulates the need for communication. There are many places he will enjoy going, and in many ways it is more important for him to adjust to going out in the community than to learn to perform school tasks. We often confront people who do not understand our little one, but the experience will be good for all concerned. We particularly enjoy taking our students to the local ice cream parlor as a language experience. To prepare for the trip, we look at pictures of ice cream, make cones from construction paper and cotton, draw pictures, talk, and then go. The initial planning and preparation is necessary. If we do not plan and help them understand what is going to happen, the experience will mean less. Our efforts are often parallel to the child's response to an activity. Less from us—less from him.

Other Suggestions

1. There must be a need for communication. If the child can get everything he wants without communicating, there will be no need to communicate.
2. Before any expressive communication will occur, there will have to be constant language input.
3. Accept small approximations and do not expect perfection.
4. Acknowledge and encourage all attempts to communicate.

5. Set goals that are reachable.

6. Sensory motor communication is often an easier method of expression for severely handicapped children, particularly if the child is hearing impaired, is unable to interpret verbal communication, or has serious motor problems that affect speech production.

7. Concepts such as, "eat," "sit," "stand," "go bye bye," "candy," "toilet," "Coke," "more," and the like will be easiest to teach because they can be made meaningful to the child.

8. Use other people to demonstrate what you want the child to do; he may understand more if he sees others do as you wish him to. Try demonstrating. "Teach" it to another child nearby, then give him another opportunity.

9. Go from real to abstract things. Most of the objects you present to the child should be meaningful to him, not copies. For example, a toy dog is a toy, not a dog, and a stuffed doll is a doll, not a baby.

10. Be constantly alert to ways of motivating the child so that he will want to communicate. Use every opportunity.

11. Meaningful gestures are symbolic and will lead to receptive understanding if repeated often enough. Think of the purpose of objects when making up symbolic gestures. How is a comb used? Gesture combing your hair and this can be the symbol for comb.

12. Always accompany a signal or gesture with the appropriate vocalizations, even though you see no auditory response. Talk constantly.

13. Imitate sounds or signals the child makes. This will help him become more aware of what he is doing.

14. Work in front of the mirror to get feedback. Every kind of feedback and every possibility of receiving the information through another sense is better for the child.

15. Work on communication when the situation occurs, in a variety of places, not just in the classroom. The store, bathroom, kitchen, soda fountain, and car are much better and more meaningful places to teach communication than in school because that is where the need arises. Use the environment.

16. Be sure to praise him for each little thing he does, things you want him to repeat.

17. If the child is showing no response to oral expression yet is responding to gestures, devise a sign for frequent visitors. The sign can be tactile, like a cross on the forehead for Papa and a tap on the wrist for Mama. Sign before and as they come in, so the child will learn to associate the sign with the appropriate person.

18. Make him aware of where he is and where he is going. You can communicate this to him by letting him touch or investigate the bed, chair, or car.
19. Materials need not be elaborate. Use real objects easily found around the school or house: things you eat, play with, work with, or manipulate.
20. Whenever possible, objects should be used for one related purpose. The bed is to sleep on, not for changing clothes; the spoon is for eating, not for playing in water.
21. Remember, if the child gestures or points or motions to you, he is thinking. When this first begins, there is cause for celebration.
22. Communicate meaning before, during, and after each activity. In this way he will learn to anticipate and associate activities.

It may be possible to exist in a solitary, noncommunicating world, but it is improbable that anyone does not communicate in some way within the limits as described here. Our goal for these children must be for them to recognize the importance of communication and to motivate them toward it. Then we must supply them with the skills that make it possible. Body movements, gestures, signs, and vocalizations are only beginnings to the process of expressive communication that allows us to share thoughts and feelings with others. The extent to which our children learn to communicate dictates the extent to which they will be recognized as human beings and allowed to function in society.

LANGUAGE DEVELOPMENT

Language: A Major Goal

If we were without speech, like some stroke victims, we would soon develop a way to communicate with others, such as by blinking our eyes or tapping our fingers. There is an innate desire and need to communicate with others that makes us part of the world. This need to communicate may or may not be evident in the severely and profoundly handicapped child. If he is to live with us, the need must be developed. We do not want him to live in a separate world of his own.

Language development is a major goal and should be incorporated into every activity and experience that confronts a child. Language is the system used to transfer a thought or idea from one person or another. When a child (or adult) is "happy," he can show us this by his facial expression, by signs, by using words, or by some other means of communication that may even be original. If the person transfers the message to another person that he is "happy," then he has communicated. Any of these systems can, for our purposes, be considered language. They are methods of communication.

It is of little importance which system is used first in the development of communication with severely handicapped children. It is important, though, for the child to communicate with someone. The system that is best is the one that works with this child at this time. A goal may be to develop a system that looks most normal. But the immediate goal is communication that is functional. Most of us use more than one system to communicate a single idea—we gesture, smile, and speak at the same time. The severely and profoundly handicapped child must be taught any system that he will use.

Sequencing Development

The child must understand himself before he can be expected to understand his environment. He will be unable to communicate with his environment until he has made this adjustment. The normal child sees and hears other people talking to one another. Communication looks and sounds useful. He sees that he has a body like others but is also separate from them. He learns, without the necessity of teaching, that he has an arm, fingers, and a mouth, the same as others. He also knows, or learns, that he can imitate the actions of others with his body. The severely handicapped child lacks this knowledge. He cannot imitate as easily. If he is visually or auditorily handicapped, he cannot easily see and hear the things he needs to learn. With the deaf–blind child, the problem of finding a model is multiplied. He has no model to copy unless someone helps him. A severely retarded child does not easily understand his body and its capabilities; therefore it is difficult for him to use his body to communicate with others. To compound the problem, he lacks the independent motivation to learn to communicate.

In order to develop language with these children, we must start where the child is and move forward. To do this, it will be necessary to observe the child's language readiness patterns in order to establish his position and set reachable goals. In this way, we avoid demanding communicative behaviors that are beyond the child's present capacity. Many of the children we see are expressing themselves (usually object-centered communication) in a way that indicates a lack of the inner language which is made up of early experiences. If inner language is not developed, the child will not be ready to understand the language he is receiving or to express himself.

Language development should be of primary concern during every interaction we have with the child. It may be helpful to review some of the suggestions in the sections devoted to development of body image and motor development.

The three main levels of language development—inner, receptive, and expressive—must be understood in order to successfully help the child. Development begins with the child's first experiences and continues as he goes through many of the same stages as the normal child, but at a different rate and with more help. By being familiar with language development, we can better establish the child's functioning level and set goals that are appropriate for him. Help and direction will be necessary if he is to develop language.

Inner Language

Receptive and expressive language are terms that may be considered self-explanatory. The ability of a person to receive information from someone else indicates that the person has receptive language. One who is the communicator has expressive language ability. These two areas are usually the basic categories involved in discussions regarding elements of the communication process. There are times, though, when another area is discussed. This has to do with inner language.

The term "inner language" is applied to a developing perception of relationships based on experiences. The person then has this experiential information to aid him in classifying what he receives and in responding to this information in a consistent fashion.

For our purposes, the term "inner language" is similar to the meaningful experiences received through the senses and stored to be remembered. Everything experienced leads a child toward understanding the world around him. Therefore, language is in a process of development as long as meaningful experiences are occurring. Inner language must develop before other language will be evident. He may begin to understand situations or even words and yet in no way show that he has this inner language. For example, he may know that getting all bundled up means he is going somewhere, that the odor in the doctor's office means impending pain, and that angry voices mean something is wrong. He will have learned all of this from many repeated experiences, yet he may not be developmentally ready to show us. Inner language begins to develop very early in life. When the child has had the experiences necessary, he will begin showing us some of the things he has learned. The severely handicapped child will do this slowly. At just what rate he will develop depends on the amount of input and the number of meaningful experiences to which he is exposed.

The child may have more inner language than is evident. Many children with severe problems have inner language but do not express themselves. They will communicate with no one. We can best know that there is inner language by observing receptive and later expressive communication.

Building Inner Language

How, then, can we help the child develop the inner language that leads to receptive and then expressive language? He must have constant input and continuous exposure to the daily experiences all children need for proper growth and development. With this child, though, we must create situations and purposefully expose him to many of the events the normal child experiences with little or no extra effort. To make the problem more difficult, much of this will be done with very little encouragement from the child. He may even reject our efforts.

Because we are all human, we like to be reinforced by outstanding results or at least a little appreciation. We cannot count on this with the severely handicapped. The fact is that much will have to "go in" before anything will "come out." This is true of all children. The big difference is that now more effort will be required. It is easy enough to say that a normal child is not ready to walk or talk, but when we are continuously using our energy to develop these abilities in the severely and profoundly handicapped, it means much more to us.

Need for Varied Experiences

This child, like every child, needs to experience as much variety as possible if he is to understand his environment and develop the necessary concepts that form the basis for language. He needs to know that the faucet turns on the water and the water comes out of the spout; that we eat with a spoon and it has food on it to go in our mouth; and that a chair is to sit on. He needs to know that dishes do not clear themselves after supper but are washed by someone; that a glass of water turned upside down will wet you; and that clothes are washed, put in the dryer, and later taken out all warm and clean. Experiences can be broadened, and he can be exposed to other activities. He will be learning from these experiences and building a foundation for language without obvious signs. As he develops, evidence that he is learning will be provided when he reacts to situational cues or manipulates objects appropriately, as when he takes off his pants and puts them in the hamper.

Effort is required. A visually impaired child who sits down to a meal that has been placed in front of him, eats, and then gets up and leaves the table, does not realize what happens before or after he eats. Perhaps the child thinks the food drops from somewhere above to his table. A curious child looks around and sees where the food is coming from; the blind child needs to be shown if these and other similar experiences are to be realistic and meaningful. Similarly, children with other sensory handicaps need extra help in learning to attach meaning to their experiences.

The child needs to know it is dark when we go to bed, that some things burn, and objects pushed from the table stop (or break) on the floor. He also needs to know people love him and that a loving hug is comfortable. He needs to know he is a person too, with many of the same characteristics as those adults around him, and that people walk on two feet and do not remain on a bed all day.

Many things must be called to his attention and this is not usually an easy task. Remember seeing a child repeatedly throw things on the floor, from his chair, to see what would happen? The handicapped child should have many of the same experiences, only more effort will be needed to make the learning meaningful. In this case, someone must help him down to the floor to find the toy or cup, then back in the chair, and probably repeat the whole process. Otherwise he will not know what happened when he pushed it over the edge. These experiences build understanding and form the basis for inner language development. He must spill the water on himself over and over before he makes the association. He needs to experience hot before he will learn "hot," and he must fall and occasionally be hurt before he will learn to walk independently. It is important, though, to connect the experience with every possible sensory channel. Tactile association makes every experience more meaningful and will be worth the effort.

All children need love, attention, and acceptance. This child also needs to know he is important and others appreciate him. If others love him and show him they do, he will learn to like them, which will increase his interest in communicating. Therefore, pleasant experiences interacting with adults are important. This child needs to know people enjoy playing with him. Experiences will help him understand himself, know that he is a person like others, and feel accepted for himself alone.

Recall the numerous experiences common to most children and be sure to arrange them for the severely handicapped child, too. When developmentally ready, he will move to the next stage, as do all children, but he will need more pushing. Help him participate in activities. It may take several tries before he seems to understand, but it is worth the effort. When he finally develops enough inner language, there will be evidence of receptive language and eventually expressive language. As he moves to higher levels of communication and expresses himself, inner and receptive language will continue to develop; therefore, experiences will always be important.

Receptive Language

Receptive language can be observed by the way the child responds to environmental cues. These cues can be vocalizations, gestures, or many other types. If the child responds correctly when we sign or say "bathroom," then he is understanding the language he is receiving. This is receptive language. If we point to a chair and he sits, he is receiving language and understanding the meaning. When we say "No" and he stops, or when we fuss and he cries, he is receiving and understanding our message. By observing the child's receptive language, we can begin to analyze inner language. We know that he is developing inner language and understanding because of the way he is reacting. He may have more receptive language than we realize. Only careful observation can give clues as to the extent of his receptive language.

When the child begins to respond appropriately to gestures, expressions, vocalizations, and signs, cooperation will be easier to obtain. The child's behavior will improve; he may appear better adjusted and seem to realize he is part of the family or school group. He will begin to notice more what is happening around him and become aware of the need to communicate. He will need much encouragement, and careful analysis of steps forward must be made so that the beginning of expressive communication can be developed. With progress, he will eventually become a communicating member of the family, school, and community, capable of expressing needs, feelings, and ideas.

Building Receptive Language

Since we do not know what sensory modality will serve as the severely and profoundly handicapped child's major receptive system, the beginnings of a signal system should be used while giving the child all possible experiences. By coupling verbal expressions with visual or tactile signals, we provide him with alternatives. Talk to him and say and sign "bath" several times before and during the bath; say "Open your mouth" before a bite of food nears his mouth; pat his diapers when they are wet and say "wet." Before he is to have his hands washed, rub them together; when it is time to eat, touch his mouth; before going to get his glasses or hearing aid, touch his eyes or ears; and when it is time for a ride in the car, say and sign "car." All who work with the child will need to agree on signals. Each time a signal is used, accompany it with appropriate verbal communication. Constantly explain or talk about what is happening, so he can begin to make the association.

Early evidence that the child is associating will be at a low level. A first sign may be when you touch a child's lips and he starts smacking and searching for food. We are constantly looking for behavioral changes that indicate an association between the action that precedes the event and the event itself. If this is seen, then we know he is thinking and remembering. At a much higher level, the child will learn to respond correctly to the verbal or manual command, "Open your mouth." This response is evidence of receptive understanding. In this case, the situation is the same, but the demands made of the child are more difficult. As he progresses, language will be stored and remembered when needed. He may then be able to transfer and recall the needed information, when the situation is different. For example, if in a nonrelated situation we say, "Let's go for a ride," and he finds his jacket and heads for the car, we know he is transferring his learning to other situations.

Once language has begun to develop and the child's learning patterns have been established, other people can be used to reinforce the concepts we know the child understands and also help develop new ones. When we know he understands certain words or phrases that make up verbal commands, then others should be informed, so they can demand the same cooperation. If language cannot become communication and be useful in situations outside the "academic" setting, it is of limited value. This transfer requires cooperation and application by others who know the child. Therefore, if we say "eat" and the child smacks, others can put this learning into use.

Other goals can also be set to move the child forward in language development. He will learn to go to the table when we say "eat," then later learn to wash his hands and go to the kitchen when we say "wash and go eat." At the same time, the child will be learning new concepts that can also be enlarged. The examples mentioned here are auditory receptive; however, the same examples could be used for visual or tactile receptive language.

Success experiences should be particularly enjoyable. For example, if he responds correctly to the signal for "eat," his lunch should be made enjoyable, even if the diet has to be varied a little this time. In every way, encourage him. Those days spent preparing for this success have now paid off. Imagine how the child feels; he is more aware of what is going to happen to him next and can anticipate his daily routine. This knowledge will help relieve some of his isolation, and he will feel more a part of the total situation. Continue gradually to enlarge the child's vocabulary and add more concepts. Meaningful ones and those easy to put into use should be selected.

Encouraging Small Approximations

If the child tries, he needs encouragement. Perfection must not be expected or demanded. If he makes one move in the right direction, encouragement will make him continue to try. If his efforts are ignored, he will give up. For example, if he begins trying to repeat a sign or word, even though it is not exactly correct, we let him know how proud we are and that he is doing well. Guidance toward perfection will come as he develops more confidence. To learn to imitate is a giant step for many children. Later he will begin attaching more meaning to the words he hears or the signs he sees. When learning to communicate, some children learn to imitate a concept before they understand its meaning, while others respond correctly but are incapable of imitating. For the child who has previously neither responded to the concept nor imitated it, either is progress.

Expressive Language

The third level of communication becomes evident when the child begins to express himself. Expressive language is a big step, and the child must have many meaningful experiences before this will occur. Then, as he learns to express himself and continues to be provided with additional experiences, other concepts begin to form as inner language and will also one day be used expressively.

With expressive language the child begins to make his needs known and should be encouraged and rewarded for his attempts. If he says or signs "bathroom" and walks out the door, he has expressive language. He is saying "I need to go to the toilet" and he knows what he means. If we must say it first, and he imitates us and goes to the bathroom, he is still at the receptive stage.

When he babbles "words" or uses his voice for some real communicative purpose, he is expressing himself vocally and communicating. His vocalizations may not be the exact voice sounds or words we use, but if he is saying something and both parties know what he means, he is communicating. If he says "ma ma ma" for Mama or "oh" when he means "no" and is understood, this is communication. These sound patterns will become more refined as he practices oral expressive communication and continues to be rewarded by understanding. Expressive language is a long-term goal and cannot be expected in other than very primitive forms (scream or cry) until the child has gone through many steps. Left alone, the child will never reach this goal.

Building Expressive Language

When the child develops much inner language and has indicated receptive understanding, he will one day surprise everyone by expressing himself and communicating with another person. The normal child usually begins expressive use of language by babbling or using his voice to get an adult's attention. If he eventually gets what he wants, which may be food, dry pants, or to be picked up, he will continue to refine this method of communication.

The severely handicapped child may also learn to cry to get the adult's attention and have his wishes fulfilled. As primitive communication of this type continues, there may be doubt that the child will be orally expressive. If he shows that he is thinking and he knows what he wants, yet has made little progress toward learning to talk, expressive oral communication may not be a realistic goal for now. He may reach a stage that involves manipulation of people to make his needs known. This may be observed when the child pulls the adult or places the adult's hand on the desired object. Here we see a primitive form of tactile expressive language. He is using the adult rather than communicating with him, but it is obvious he is thinking and that can be used to help the child move to higher levels of tactile motor expression. He may later be led to communicate without touching another person, as when he extends one arm toward what he wants instead of using an adult. The beginnings of a person-to-person idea exchange are now seen. Much later, the child will learn to point to a desired object rather than manipulate people. In this case, he is truly expressing a thought or idea to another person (i.e., ''Give me that toy up there''). Other examples of emerging tactile expressive communication are observed if he pats his seat and starts toward the bathroom, touches his mouth and reaches for a piece of candy he wants, or sees the car drive up and pantomimes ''ride.'' Although these signals are accompanied by primitive vocalizations, the message is conveyed by the child's motions.

Creating a Need for Expression

There are countless ways to create a need for using expressive language. For example, if Jill wants a cookie, has vocalized and imitated the sign many times, and is trying to get one, the teacher might sign and say ''cookie'' and then eat the cookie herself. Next, she will tempt Jill with a cookie and give her another chance to ask for it. At another time, Jill may want to ride in the car, a concept that has been presented many times. So she pulls an adult toward the car and waits for the door to be opened. This occasion can also be used to stimulate expressive language. In this case, the teacher might try standing by the car door and feigning ignorance, as Jill may come up with the appropriate language if she really wants to ride. If this does not work, the teacher can pantomime and say ''car,'' then get in the car and shut the door. If she objects, the teacher might get out and give her another try. If she still fails to come up with the right word or sign, it is provided, and the child is encouraged to imitate before getting in the car.

When the child first expresses himself, he is communicating with his environment and the people in it. He is more a part of the total situation. From this point, he can move forward gradually, as we strengthen the newly learned skills and encourage continuous use of expressive language. We begin expecting more from the child in small steps, such as a correct sign or correctly pronounced word. Also we begin demanding that he express his wants more often. If he knows he can tell us what he needs and tries to do so, and if he is rewarded by the response, he will continue to communicate with us and eventually with others.

As the child begins to develop language, the frustrations he has experienced making his wants known will decrease. Also, at this time, more in-depth communication patterns will be formed so that he can learn to describe experiences and ideas that will be the basis for future communication.

SPEECH TRAINING AND ORAL LANGUAGE

Total Communication

If the child has learned the importance of communicating and if he has developed the need to express himself to others, then it will be much easier for him to learn oral language. Therefore, during the early years, language development is of primary importance. As the child becomes more motivated to express himself by using any language appropriate to him, interest in all forms of communication will increase. It may be evident that oral language could be a realistic goal as the child develops. However, if he is unaware of the need to communicate and sees no relationship between what is being said and a particular concept or idea, then this oral expression is not yet communication. Examples of this can be seen when a child is told to repeat a particular sound or even words but has no awareness of the connection that sound has with some meaningful object or situation.

It is our opinion that a system of total communication works best for most children who are deaf in beginning to establish language. This system also often works to advantage with children who are severely and profoundly handicapped. Total communication allows the child to "hear" the word at the same time as he sees the word signed or pantomimed. In addition, he can benefit from lip movements, facial expression, pantomime, tactile symbols and any other additional forms of communication that help make it more meaningful.

One of our severely handicapped cerebral palsy children, now four years old, is using several manual signs to express her needs, yet her vocalizations are still at the vocal play stage. She may later learn to use her voice more meaningfully, but we suspect that she will be using basic signs for functional communication for a long time. Seeing her sign "toilet" to the teacher, touch her mouth when she wants to eat, and wave when she wants to go out is evidence enough that she has benefited from a total communication approach.

At a period early in a child's life, when language development is most important, it is often difficult to determine which method of communication may be most appropriate. Requiring a child to learn language through either the ears or the eyes before any response has indicated his learning patterns can be ineffective and lead to unproductive teaching. The manual sign or a gesture provides the child with a visual form to represent a concept, and it can be presented within the child's visual range. This will become more meaningful with repeated exposure, and skills leading to expressive communication can be developed. At the same time, the appropriate word is used, which gives the child an opportunity to experience oral communication but does not require oral language as the only method.

Many severely and profoundly handicapped children respond well to a visual symbol system. Imposing our ideas and desires too strongly may work to the child's disadvantage. What is best for him psychologically, socially, and intellectually may not be what we wish for him. If we insist that a child with severe hearing problems learn oral language, we may retard development of communication skills. Our attitude toward the child is a great factor for determining future success. This attitude includes acceptance of the child's learning patterns. It is important to remember, though, that oral language can develop even after manual signs have been learned, but during the critical language years, maximum opportunities for developing a useful form of communication must be emphasized. The earlier a versatile language program is begun, the better for all concerned. Communication is the immediate goal though, not oral language.

The amount of time devoted to structured speech training should be carefully controlled. It is easy to overstress the development of oral speech to the detriment of all other areas necessary for the child's growth and adjustment. The development of oral speech can only be accomplished as part of the child's daily life. With these words of caution, the remainder of this section will be devoted to suggesting ways to encourage oral language and techniques useful for stimulating interest in speech.

A Real Experience

When emphasizing the importance of an early beginning to encourage speech, it is easy to recall a variety of teaching experiences in this area. One teacher tells of a little boy who has now completed a three-year program emphasizing early stimulation and language development. This hyperactive four-year-old was successfully capable of manipulating others to "do" for him. He entered the program with no speech, no expressive language, no method of communication, and indicated no awareness of voice sound. He was not interested. The majority of the day he concerned himself with devising ways to get light bulbs—and usually succeeded. Progress seemed slow. After two months of rewarding him with tiny pieces of peppermint candy each time he vocalized, there was a breakthrough. This child suddenly realized that the praise and reward resulted from a simple sound he could make all by himself. The noise he made sounded much like the word "five." After everyone jumped up and down, screamed, and almost cried for joy, they ran up and down the hall demonstrating the boy's new learning. This was mid-November, the teacher recounts, and by Christmas the young man (barely five years old) could say "Mama," "Papa," "Hi" and something that sounded a little like "Bye-bye."

Our involvement with this child has continued, and he is now communicating spontaneously by means of total communication. He uses manual signs and gestures as he speaks and has an oral vocabulary of over 200 words that are understandable to those of us who work with him. It is amazing to recall his behavior when he entered the program, and then listen as he says "I want more candy," "Thank you," "Stop it, Ruby," or "Surprise," appropriately, with no prompting. He is a happy, well-adjusted little boy, and his chances of continuing to progress are good.

When he first came to the program, there were those who doubted that he could ever learn and had even advised his parents to "forget him." Now he reads first-grade material (large print), cares for himself independently, and talks constantly. He had parents and teachers who gave him a chance.

If we are to begin a successful program to stimulate speech, we must first realize that some things we have been told about the child's limitations may be incorrect, as in the case described above. When confronted with a child who is severely and profoundly handicapped, psychologists, doctors, and others are often discouraging. This negativism, along with the trauma the shocked parents have already suffered, is depressing and can lead to complete nondirection and nonfunctioning. The reaction of parents and other important adults will be reflected by the child, as he will be able, very early in life, to discover whether or not he is "acceptable." Therefore, a positive attitude exhibited by parents and teachers who really believe the child can and will learn is especially important.

Teaching and Getting Results

Speech is a living experience and can be shared by everyone. In this respect, nearly anyone can be a speech teacher. This does not mean that we are all speech therapists, but there are things a person familiar with the child can do as well, if not better, than an outsider. The person who is there and has an established relationship with the child will be able to do much toward preparing for speech training at some later date.

Obtaining consistent vocalizations from a child who is severely handicapped is not usually an easy task. It is important to give the child constant input (sounds, noises, talking), so that eventually he will give something back. Sometimes it seems this will never happen. Too often, because of the child's lack of interest in language, parents or teachers have failed to talk normally, so that he is even less likely to learn to speak or notice voice sounds. If there is no input, then obviously the child has no model to copy and will never talk. The child must hear many hours of sounds before he will try to produce any by himself.

Never assume because the child fails to respond to loud noises that he is not hearing. Infant audiological examinations indicating problems in this area may be incorrect. He may not respond at certain frequencies yet respond normally at others. There may be other problems causing the lack of response. We must let the child prove he cannot hear, and give him time to prove it, while giving him every benefit of the doubt in our work with him.

One little girl fooled everybody for almost two years. According to her mother, she responded to her name or a loud noise at home; however we saw no such response. The audiogram indicated a profound loss in both ears, and no voice awareness with amplification. We continued our attempts to elicit response to sound with no reward. Somehow we knew she could hear; it was just a hunch we had. One day, while driving on a short field trip, someone in the car laughed a loud cackle over something that happened and our little one in the back seat mocked the laugh. We were all shocked and set it up for a second try. Sure enough, she mocked the laugh again. She had heard. All the days of speech work had paid off. This child, a year later, could use several words meaningfully; not as many as we had hoped, but she had progressed. Also, we felt she would begin making progress even faster with her newly gained confidence. As she learned to use her hearing to gain information about her environment—and each tiny bit of information is important—this child was making use of environmental sounds long before we could see any response.

When working on speech activities, it is important to avoid tension and help the child feel at ease. The quality of the relationship developed with the child will make a big difference in what can be taught. Developing this relationship is sometimes difficult, particularly when we are anxious for the child to learn. Our determination prevents us from realizing the pressure we are applying. We push, but by pushing too hard, we only make progress slower. We must relax with the child, enjoy each step forward and each experience, and not look for giant strides forward.

Any child may learn to speak by going through the same stages as

other children, but for the severely handicapped more effort will be required from everyone and it will take longer. He will not necessarily
pick up oral language as he hears others talking. With the severely and
profoundly handicapped child, we must direct his attention toward the
source of sound and make him aware of this means of communication.
Children with other problems may also need help in associating vocalizations with communication. The three-month-old child experiments
with babbling sounds. The sounds he uses for early experimentation
are usually the early crying sounds, made up of vowels like "a" as in
"man" or "e" as in "pen." Later these sounds are combined with
consonants "m" and "b," making a blend like "mamama," "me-
meme," or "bababa." Of most importance is what happens when the
child makes these sounds. If the mother makes it a big experience by
talking back to the child, picking him up, or calling someone to come
look, the child soon learns that talking is important and he tries again.
These trial and error experiences will expand, and he will soon be
saying simple, meaningful words.

For some children, being given the opportunity to listen, try, listen
again, and finally pronounce the words with little effort from others is
not enough. To complicate the problem, since he does not respond,
people may talk to him less. He may go through the same stages in
learning to understand and use oral language (experimenting, listening,
and trying again), but he needs help. If he is made aware of oral language, regardless of his problem, the chances of his vocalizing are
greatly improved.

We talk to the child constantly. We may not know the extent of his
hearing or the reason for his lack of response, but the more we talk to
him, the better his chances are. We work on the child's level. If
deafness is suspected, we talk close to his ear in a normal voice. We do
not shout or use baby talk. We also make sure he can see our faces. If
possible, we arrange the light so that it is on our faces. The window
light or lamp should not be shining in his eyes if we expect him to
see us.

Talk about what is happening in natural language. Short sentences
with key words at the end are best, not single words. Say, "You're
wet" or "Why are you *wet?*" He will learn the rhythm of sound as he
listens. By talking in short sentences and emphasizing key words, you
will be saving a space for the words he may add and also teaching him
the rhythm of your language. He may hear only a mumbling and part of
the key word, or he may only relate to the emphasized word, but that is
a good start. The words may be distorted to him. Speak distinctly, but
do not exaggerate the words. Always keep volume within normal
limits; it is not helpful to scream.

Amplification

There are those who can be recognized as deaf. In these cases, amplification may be prescribed. Many things happen when a child first receives a hearing aid. It is good to experience some of the sensations planned for the child. Try on an aid and turn the volume higher. How does it feel? What sounds are heard? People often feel that the louder they speak into the hearing aid, or the louder the volume, the better the child can hear. Therefore, they yell loudly to the child, and the noise is sudden and unexpected, or the child has not become accustomed to the noise; he then screams and rejects the aid. This may be painful and should be avoided. We cannot always be certain a child is deaf. To move from minimal auditory stimulation to too much is a big change and uncomfortable to anyone. Naturally, the child will jerk the mold from his ear or cry from pain. See the section on Auditory Training for suggestions directed toward the introduction of a hearing aid.

Tongue Exercise

Mouth and tongue exercises provide stimulation for muscle development and control and are helpful in making a child more aware of the mouth as a source of sound. Activities such as tongue and mouth gymnastics are excellent for fine motor imitation. These exercises will be difficult for the child who is having trouble understanding his body. For the child with severe motor impairment, such as cerebral palsy, tongue gymnastics will also be difficult, but well worth consideration. Also if he is incapable of imitating gross motor movement (jump, hold arms up, turn around), he will not yet respond to mouth and tongue exercises, but if our attitude is right, he will benefit from the experience. If the only goal reachable for now is mouth awareness, then that is one step forward. Later he can learn to imitate movement (facial) and much later learn to vocalize. As he progresses, some of the suggestions in this section may be more helpful.

The following suggestions for tongue and mouth exercise may prove useful.

1. Work very close to him, facing the child. Try putting him in your lap or on a chair higher than your chair, so your faces will be nearly the same height.
2. While holding his hand on *your* mouth, open and close your mouth, stick out your tongue, blow on his hand, or talk to him. Work on these activities by selecting one to emphasize for several days.

3. Next alternate putting his hand on his mouth and waiting for a response. You are trying to help him understand that the mouth is the source of movement and sound. Repeat this exercise daily for a short period during some time when the child is relaxed. It may be helpful to begin with two hands.

4. Later, when he has become more aware, work on tongue gymnastics. Move your tongue in and out of your mouth, from side to side, outside of your mouth, lips, and the like. Encourage him to imitate. Let him feel your tongue.

5. It is sometimes helpful to work in front of a mirror so he can see what is happening.

6. Encourage him to examine your mouth by touch; let him look in if he is interested. Curiosity, if not satisfied, may not recur.

7. Put some peanut butter in his mouth in different places. He will have to use his tongue to get the peanut butter out or swallow it.

8. Be sure he has enough chewable foods in his diet for proper development of speech muscles. Check suggestions in the self-care section under "Eating."

9. Puff up your cheeks and let him "squoosh" the air out. Make a game of this. Encourage him to imitate you.

10. Hold a hand mirror close to your mouth and say "ah," and let him see the vapor on the mirror. Now see if he would like to try. You never know what activity might provide the needed motivation.

11. For the more mature child, try reversing the teacher-pupil role. He may respond by teaching you. One little girl refused to make sounds for me, but later demonstrated her learning as she played teacher with another child. Many days later, we saw her teaching a large doll.

Blowing

The child should be taught to blow. This can be fun. Sometimes this works best by trying to blow an object such as a feather, a balloon, whistle, party horn, pinwheel, or even a little scrap of toilet tissue. This way the child is rewarded by what he sees, which makes the experience more enjoyable. We have found that a candle or a lighted match works well. Caution is required, however, and if the child is difficult to control, this activity should be postponed. It is necessary to move beyond the natural curiosity of fire, as the child may be content to watch the flickering flame or determined to touch the flame. First we blow out the flame, then relight it and give him an opportunity, and repeat. Any attempt toward reaching this goal is rewarded, such as when he purses his mouth, blows through his nose, or even attends to the activity. The decision as to whether what he is doing is progress can be made by comparing what he is doing now to what he already knew. Encourage him.

Learning to Vocalize

While working on awareness of the source of sound, encourage the child to vocalize. There are several ways this can be done. Call attention to his vocalizations by imitating him when he makes a sound. If he cries, says "mu mu mu"; if he coos, do it, too. It can be a game. We encourage the child to mock us. Point to your ear and say "I hear you." If he makes a sound, pick him up, clap, pat him, or give him a tiny taste of something he likes. These rewards are used each time he does something we want to encourage, even when unplanned. If, for example, while straightening the room, he is heard making a nice sound, go to him and quickly show your delight. Rewarding does, however, need to be immediate, otherwise he may think something else he was doing is important. If we wait and he is quietly sucking his thumb when rewarded, he may think he is being rewarded for that behavior.

The four-year-old boy mentioned earlier was playing with some small pieces of paper near the window when he finally realized his actions were causing the reward. Until then, he had not been aware of the reason for the rewards he was receiving. But when he first realized it was his voice that was so important, he also thought it was because he was looking toward the window. For a few moments he would make a sound similar to the word "five," look toward the window, and then turn toward the teacher for a reward. After the reward, he then turned back to the window and repeated the whole process. Later he learned that where he was when he made his sound was unimportant, just so he made one. We must be aware of every circumstance—the children sometimes misunderstand us.

Beginning "Lessons"

While working on tongue gymnastics and blowing we begin simple speech lessons. The main purpose may be to assist the child further in learning imitative behavior. It is important for him to learn to imitate others in every way possible. Behaviors, motions, and vocalizations can all be imitated, and this is one way we all learn from each other. Finding a beginning point may be difficult. Usually if a child spontaneously makes a certain sound often during the day, it is a good idea to work on getting that same sound back. For example, if he says "ah" during the course of the day more often than any other sound, work with him on imitating that sound on demand. Call attention to his sound, imitate him when he says "ah" and encourage him to imitate your "ah." Since we know he can make this sound, it should be good for a beginning.

When encouraging these or other sounds, connect them with something tangible, such as the vibrations of your throat. It works well to put the child's thumb on your lips and his four fingers on your throat when making the sound. This is part of the vibration method of teaching speech. By assuming this position, he can hear the sound and feel the vibrations at the same time. Later, try putting his other hand (thumb on lips, fingers on throat) on himself. He can then tell whether he is or is not getting the same sensation. This takes time and requires much repetition. At other times, put his one hand on your lips and throat and vocalize several times, then put that same hand on his lips and throat—and wait. It may be easier, though, to begin by holding both his hands on your throat first, then on his, and repeat before going into the position with the thumb on the lips and the fingers on the throat. The position is only important to the extent it works.

Always accept any move in the right direction; for example, if the child grunts, accept that as a start. Little Martha's burp was the first step forward. Burping does cause a vibration, so this was rewarded. As the child begins responding, more difficult feats can be required.

Speech training can also be combined with rhythm and movement. A tap on the table or a clap can accompany a short, sharp sound, such as the sound of the letter "p" or the word "up." A long, gliding movement of the arm or swing of the body can accompany the "wh" sound or the word "go." Motions can be devised for many sounds, words, and even sentences if this seems useful for the child.

Do not expect perfection. Any reasonable move in the right direction should be encouraged. If we insist that the child do *exactly* as we wish, he may become discouraged and withdraw, devising ways to avoid any confrontation with others. Reward him for vocalizing by giving him something or doing something he likes, then he will try more. If we ignore his attempts because what he did was not good enough, we lose. He will stop trying and then we must begin all over again. Watch, listen, and learn to determine quickly whether what the child does is a step forward. Much practice and many mistakes will be experienced before evaluating his responses becomes an easy task.

Early Speech Elements

Learning the elements of speech is only a small part of the total concept we call "speech work." Once the important teacher–child relationship has been established and the child seems ready, some prefer to begin speech lessons by isolating certain elements of sound as used in the English language. The easiest ones with which to begin are blowing (the "wh" sound), humming (the "m" sound), puffing without voice (the "p" sound), "ah," and "b-b-b-b" as in "bubble." (The sound of "b" is similar to the sound made if imitating water bubbling from a small mouth bottle.) However, since the purpose of speech is communication, it would be best for this child if the learning could be made meaningful as soon as possible. The approach that works well for us is to use a sound the child learns to make or makes regularly as a meaningful word that closely approximates the sound. Therefore, if the child says "ah", that becomes "orange"; if he says "b-b-b-b", that becomes "banana"; and if he says "p" that becomes "pear." Likewise "m-m-m-m" becomes "Mama" and "p-p" becomes "Papa." Other sounds the child learns to make spontaneously can be used in the same way. In this fashion, the sounds have meaning and can be used by the child to get results. With encouragement, the sounds can gradually become closer to the correct pronunciation through trial and error. With the opportunity to learn useful sounds, more can be accomplished for the purpose of realistic communication and less time will be wasted.

Attitudes

Teaching speech to children who give very little indication of even being aware of our attempts can be discouraging. Attitude will be of primary importance. On the other hand, there is almost no better way for developing the close relationship needed with the child than speech work. The close, physical contact during this time is valuable. There may be no other activity that draws us to the child in so close a relationship. Though no visible results of our teaching are evident, we cannot discount what this activity may be doing for the child.

Sometimes it helps to think of what we are doing as one of the ways to help the child become more aware of what is going on around him, rather than as teaching speech. He may never talk as we would wish, but this opportunity for learning must be made available to him. We know he will gain something from the experience. Whether or not his learning will be of value to his development depends on our approach and attitude.

One little girl did not like speech work and told us so in every action and response. She jerked away when anyone tried to touch her mouth and was extremely resistant when an attempt was made to put her hand in or on the teacher's mouth. She often refused to vocalize, when we all knew she could. We continued our emphasis in this area, and after several months she was enjoying success in making several consonant and vowel sounds. She learned to tolerate speech work and enjoyed auditory training. This child later lost her vision. Speech training was then one of her favorite activities and a major channel of learning. We are grateful for every moment spent on speech awareness, since without it, her world would be much more isolated.

Another little girl continued to show little vocal response after months of speech work. The only vocalizations she could emit were "ah" and "m," but she did not realize the difference in these sounds. We even had to manipulate her mouth to obtain those responses. However, she so thoroughly enjoyed the special one-to-one attention and the contact that several times during the day she would get a chair, pull it over to the teacher, and hand her a microphone as if to say, "Come on, let's work." She was getting something! Never discount an experience provided for the child just because there is no immediate or obvious measure of progress or response.

A speech program can bring a great deal of frustration to both the child and teacher if the goals are wrong. Throughout emphasis on beginning speech, we must keep in mind that whether or not the child learns to speak is relatively unimportant at the moment. Developing a closer relationship and one conducive to communications with the child, through close body contact and mutual enjoyment of the activities, will be one of the first goals. Getting the child to look at us and show interest may be a major goal. Later, the goal may be to help him understand his body and learn to imitate our movements. Still later, our goal for him may be voice awareness. If he accomplishes the smallest goals, our efforts are justified.

SOCIALIZATION, PLAY, AND
USE OF FREE TIME

Observing Use of Free Time

Free time may best be considered as those periods when a child has only minimal requirements on his performance. The choice during these times is up to him except for certain unacceptable behaviors, such as violence or behaviors that could be labeled as moral infractions. The way the severely and profoundly handicapped child spends his free time is certainly worth observing if we are concerned with his program and progress.

A wide range of choices is open to even the lowest functioning child. Most can make a choice between total withdrawal or self-stimulating activities and some other activity, depending on social skills and academic achievement.

Observations of the child's use of free time can yield much information and allow for comparison of behavior between that situation and other activities during the day. This can also be related to the choices a child has during these free periods. If there is a variety of stimulating materials and a choice of social companions, then it is important to know how these choices are used. Presumably, if stimulating choices are available and recognized, the child will take advantage of them and use his free time productively. Our evaluation then depends on consideration of the choices available and how well the child makes use of them.

At least some of these choices are made when the child interacts with objects or with others in an activity that is obviously enjoyable. We call this behavior play. It seems useful here to separate this behavior from that which is more directed and not left to the choice of the child (work) and that which has no direction or purpose except perhaps simple self-stimulation or withdrawal. Admittedly, this is a simple categorization and does not consider all ramifications. This differentiation, though, has proven to be useful in observing behavior. Anyone who wishes to add other categories may find this a practical place to start. To clarify, then, if the child has free choice of activity, we call it play; if the child does not have free choice or if his choice is directed by an adult, we will not call it play. We are concerned here with helping the child learn acceptable alternatives to inappropriate use of free time.

When the child interacts with adults or other children, even if it is only to play beside them, the beginnings of socialization may be detected. Many of the children in this group are not highly social at any time. They seem especially interested in staying away from any physical contact that might involve a need for communication. As experiences are presented both formally and informally which make interpersonal interaction desirable and rewarding, then the child can be expected to become observably more social. This is an especially important area of concern and one that should be considered in program planning.

Play

Playing with the child is an excellent way to help him acquire new skills, learn to manipulate objects meaningfully, discover ways to amuse himself constructively, and learn numerous other lessons of life. Playtime can be fun, but it is also the child's business. It is during these times that learning occurs easily. ''Play'' can include most activities of childhood, many that are learned quickly and without concern for most normal children. We must recognize the importance of these activities for any child and when necessary insist that they are experienced.

It is easy to encounter communication problems when discussing toys and their use with severely and profoundly handicapped children. Most toys as seen in stores are scaled down models of the life-sized objects they represent. As such, they could be considered one step toward the symbolic representation of the object as it appears in real life. The final step in the process would be a representation of the same object by a word in print.

The children here are far from the stage where they perceive such symbolic items. Therefore, they need items that are life-sized with true-to-life texture. Because of this, we must begin with another type of object when they are ready for this kind of ''play.'' In the beginning, most of these children are not at a stage where they use any objects for their intended purpose. They are adept at using them in some stimulating way, which is not always of a positive nature. Since this is the case, we call most items that the child deals with at this stage of his development objects rather than toys.

We must provide the child with a variety of objects to manipulate and help him learn their real purpose. These need not be expensive. Objects such as a spoon, an egg beater, a spool of thread, a giant rubber band, a plastic egg filled with candy, an old golf ball, and a small hand mirror can all be toys to the child.

If he does not tolerate the objects, we present some daily anyway. If he throws them on the floor, fine. Picking them up and throwing them down is better than no response at all. He will be more aware from having been forced to touch them. If he cries because we are interfering with his world and interrupting his self-stimulation activity, fine! He is communicating, and this is a good sign. Many times we have felt like celebrating when this kind of behavior occurred.

If the child is tactilely defensive and strongly dislikes textures, such as furry or slippery ones, do not give up. Continue giving him various experiences daily and this defensiveness will gradually disappear.

Tolerating Toys

Objectionable objects can often be sandwiched between those he likes. For example, if he likes a light, hold a lighted candle for a few moments for him to watch, then extinguish the candle, and put the soft, fuzzy toy he hates on his lap; he will probably push it off, but by doing so he touches it. Now quickly get out the flashlight. He will probably be interested in the light, so perhaps the fuzzy toy can be presented now. Then return to one he likes. The child can overcome this fear with your help and you do want him gradually to become more accustomed to differences in textures, as this is one way he gains information.

Devise play activities by using household items. Sometimes we gather several objects into an old beach bag, a pocketbook, or a similar container. We include several fun things he likes, or will learn to like, and call this a "surprise bag." Occasionally, we get the bag and encourage the child to play with each object as it is introduced, while talking to him about each one. This activity can be varied by occasionally having a new surprise in the bag (i.e., candy, chocolate cookies) to discover when he is beginning to lose interest. With this activity, awareness will be increased, the child's attention will be directed, and this will be one more meaningful way to relate to the child. Other articles good to include in the "surprise bag" are a zipper, a comb, soap, hand lotion, perfume, a bicycle reflector, a toothbrush, cellophane of several colors, a puppet, a whistle, a jack-in-the-box, a party hat, and a flashlight.

Think of all that can be done. The colored paper can be used over the flashlight or your face and the puppet will be funny with the party hat. The comb, toothbrush, and soap can be used meaningfully in pantomime. Occasionally, several objects that belong in the room or one nearby can be added. When finished exploring, the child can help put the objects away, rather than returning them to the bag. If his attention span is fleeting, quickly present a few things you feel are most interesting, then say, "Okay, that's all for now." Other suggestions in the sections on Sensory Stimulation might prove helpful.

Participation

Stop soon enough and yet not too soon. Some children need a degree of force to attend to an activity. A child can be held in your lap or the chair can be held close to the table; then once a favorite object appears, he will probably forget he was trying to escape. If he does insist on escaping, insist that he stay for a period of two or three minutes or until he relaxes, then say, "Fine, I'm finished, you can get up now and we'll play more later." Be sure to try again later.

The purpose here is to encourage and also insist that the child learn to play. He will find a way to entertain himself during free time and probably what he does will not be constructive. More appropriate play will come with direction and experience. If he only knows to flick the puzzle pieces in front of his eyes, that is what he will do. With help, he will learn other ways to use his free time.

It may be necessary to insist. Eventually, and soon we hope, he will learn to manipulate toys meaningfully. It is thrilling to see a child pick up a ball and throw it, try to cut with the scissors, or undress a doll. This time could have been forever spent in self-stimulation if someone had not intervened and taught him other behaviors. And he must be taught. Do not expect this child to "pick it up"; he needs help. Observe the toys with which he seems obsessed and determine the reason for his interest in the particular toy. He may be stimulating himself in some way. Barbara loved to crawl inside the giant play tunnel and ran to it each time we were in the gym. It drew her like a magnet. When we crawled in and looked, we saw that the porous material allowed light to shine through the tiny spots. Lying on her back in the tunnel, Barbara could roll back and forth slightly and create stimulating light patterns.

Cleaning Up

It is advisable from the beginning to help the child learn where his playthings are kept and to be sure that they are put there consistently. Let him help pick up each time the toys are put away. Begin expecting him to accept some responsibility for his things; he should not think others will do all the work. He can benefit in many ways from the experience of picking up his toys. By helping, he learns to accept responsibility, gets some good exercise, stays busy in a constructive way, relates to someone, becomes more aware of what is expected of him, learns about his environment, and experiences other good lessons. It is also important to realize that putting toys in his special place develops identity. ''This is my place and these are my things.''

Plan for consistency. Do not ask the child to work a pegboard and then, when he has completed his work, say, ''Okay, now put them all back in the box.'' How deflating! He worked hard to create something and now it must be destroyed. Let him put it on the shelf or table as it is for now as a display. Taking all the pegs out again immediately will not be encouraging ''clean-up'' behavior; the completed task is not a ''mess,'' it is his creation.

When purchasing toys for the child, buy sturdy toys, those easily moved from one place to another, and those that can be manipulated. Such toys as puzzles made up of triangles, circles, and squares, balls, plastic pop beads, cones with different sized rings to place on them, a jack-in-the-box, a music box, and a box with different shapes to fit in slots are good starters. Many of these toys can be easily made.

Some conventional toys are good. Clay is fun and good for developing hand strength (squeeze it, pull it, and mold it). Also, a ball can be made from the clay. The child can also be shown a real ball to compare as the difference is explained. This may strengthen a concept introduced in other situations. The clay balls can also be counted, made into different shapes, and grouped according to size, shape, or color. There is no end to what can be done with a simple toy like this. Colored homemade dough also works well.

Finger paint is great. Some children object to the texture and may need encouragement. When the child refuses to put his hand in the paint, try to make it more interesting by putting a little paint on yourself, then on him. Usually *more* on him. This is fun in front of the mirror. The child who seldom looks at anything for long, except perhaps his hand or the light, changes his expression to interest when his hand is suddenly yellow and red. The child who is not interested in his mirror image sometimes looks with curiosity at his blue nose. If he plasters his hand on the mirror in an effort to touch the funny face, that is great! He will see his handprint too. After all, everything will come out in the wash, and his attention has been captured.

We always enjoy painting. Add extra water to the finger paint and try a large bowlful on the floor, then encourage everyone to remove their shoes and step in the paint. It is fun to walk on newspapers with painted feet. If the child demands to wash his feet, let him. The red or blue water in the sink during clean-up time will be fun, too. This activity is good for body image work and tactile-visual stimulation and is an excellent opportunity to work on language and communication development.

Homemade Toys

Make color cans. Gather several coffee cans and cover each with a different color paper. Inside each can put several articles of the same color found around the house. In the yellow can put everything yellow: a crayon, a block, a pencil, a spool of thread, a sock, a bead, and a lemon. The same can be done with two or three other colors. Occasionally empty one can and let him look, feel, and examine each article. Then help him replace them. Eventually, he will realize that the objects have something in common. When he begins to grasp the significance of groupings, try emptying two cans in a pile together and see if he can correctly replace them. Help him if he has difficulty and reward all attempts. Maybe he will soon do it by himself. This same activity could be done with shapes, textures, and sizes.

The toy situation need not involve a large sum of money. Odd-sized pieces of wood make excellent blocks as long as they do not have splinters. An old muffin pan or an egg carton can be used for sorting small objects or for putting one object in each hole. Discarded frozen dinner trays or large pizza pans make good work areas for small objects that might otherwise roll off the table (i.e., pegs, marbles, or small cubes). Coke bottle tops, poker chips, or even small rocks are fun to empty and then replace in a coffee can. Medicine bottles filled with odd-sized nuts and bolts are fun to rattle and also good to manipulate for eye–hand coordination development. Various sized pots and pans can fit inside each other or be stacked in a tower.

There is no limit to what can be done with available objects if we use our ingenuity. We look at the sky and then make clouds by pasting cotton on blue construction paper or make tiny wheelbarrows from a custard cup by using a bent soda straw for handles and a Lifesaver for a wheel. We make long tails from jump ropes for all of us to wear when "playing dog;" fasten long rabbit ears to our heads with hair bands to be a bunny; and play "dress up" in the oddest assortment of clothes imaginable. Fun things can be made from pipe cleaners, cotton, tape, paste, boxes, spools, and slivers of paper. Water play is almost always a good way to have playtime together. The large empty box outside the furniture store will make an excellent play house; the old beads ready for discarding will be fun to restring; empty spools of thread make great stringing beads and are also good for blowing soap bubbles. Upturned empty strawberry baskets can become animal cages; a chair turned upside down over a waste basket will provide the posts for ring toss; and objects placed in small freezer containers and stuffed inside socks can be used for a touch identification game. All of it is just plain fun if the atmosphere is right.

Playing While You Work

Talk to the child while working about the house or school; this is play to the severely and profoundly handicapped. Turn on the light and say "on"; when it is turned off, say "off." Emphasize a concept that seems important and repeat it with enthusiasm. As he helps dust, hold your hand on top of his and say "round and round" while wiping. If something falls or breaks, call attention to it with "Uh oh, something fell," "Where is it?" or "What broke?" If he puts his hand on the hot pan or warm oven door, help him realize what has happened. This can be done by putting the child's hand near the source again, close enough so that he can feel the heat, thus helping him make the association. Every opportunity should be usd to teach the child and make him more aware as daily situations occur. The child needs help to learn to relate to people and his environment, and he must also be involved.

Always make a big experience of anything that happens, otherwise he may not notice. He learns from seeing and doing. If you cut your finger, let him see the wound and then help you wash it or apply alcohol and a bandage. If you have on a wig, allow him to remove it one time and laugh. If your hair is different today, let him investigate it carefully. You can even let him remove your glasses. All these experiences can be fun. We can all become accustomed to small invasions of our privacy. When walking into the classroom with gay new beads, a teacher may say to herself, "I bet Suzy is going to want my beads," and if she is not interested, the teacher will feel disappointed. More than likely, before the hour is over, one of the children will be wearing the new necklace and will have earned it. The beads can be a reward for good work. Who can refuse a child when he does something we have been anxious for him to do? Sometimes we even find ourselves purchasing gaudy jewelry just because we know the child will love it. Besides, it's normal for him to want to play dressing-up like Mama or teacher.

All who have worked with severely and profoundly handicapped children have shared many of their prized possessions with these little friends. When the child who does not communicate shows an interest in something that we have, then we will know he is becoming more aware and this is encouraging. After all, the curiosity and interest is what we want, so we cannot reject it just because it comes unexpectedly at an untimely moment. These experiences will eventually become very pleasant memories.

One of the most enjoyable and challenging things about teaching a severely handicapped child is trying to find a way to establish a relationship. How can his interest be captured? If you try hard enough, this relationship will become evident. More than likely, it will begin during a play time.

We are trying to establish an adult–child social relationship. When this begins to happen, other adults who have a high interest value can be used, especially those who are familiar to the child. These people will be willing to contribute either needed tangible materials or social interactions that are important as the child becomes a part of the community. Involvement of others will be necessary, as the child must not grow up in an isolated environment.

Most people are helpful. The local dentist can probably be persuaded to contribute an old set of false teeth to use for creating interest in the mouth or in tongue gymnastics. The policeman will happily let the child sit on the motorcycle for a few moments, and the fireman will turn on that wonderful rotating red light just for him.

Make It Fun

Create a situation that will be as relaxing and as much fun as possible, then all will enjoy it more. Learning to play is important to any child, and the severely and profoundly handicapped child will not learn unless he is taught. The playing may be a little like work and a lot like teaching, but if the atmosphere is fun filled, it can be an enjoyable experience. He may not seem aware of certain ideas and objects, but he will be aware of mood and attitude. If we struggle into a "playtime" because we feel we must, the child will know it quickly and respond accordingly. We sing, talk, play happy music, do whatever is needed to establish a happy, relaxed atmosphere, and the child's attitude reflects our enthusiasm.

BEHAVIOR

Analyzing Behavior

There are many things about a severely and profoundly handicapped child we would like to change. He makes strange movements with his hands and shows no interest in his surroundings. When we try to break through to him, he "escapes" by either screaming or withdrawing into his closed world. He refuses to do much that we require of him and seems to be making no progress. In public places, he usually attracts everyone's attention, which is often embarrassing. He will not eat, cannot go to the bathroom by himself, and is uninterested in learning. Much of this disturbing behavior can be used to help him learn. Some behavior is better than none at all, and with help he can and will learn new things. If we stop and analyze exactly what the child is doing and when, then we can make plans. When we recognize behavior, then we can begin to reach decisions as to the cause. We must then develop ways to change, stop, or use the behavior we see.

There are some patterns of behavior characteristic of these children. They, of course, are not exclusive to the group. These behaviors do occur both with children who are nonhandicapped and those who possess handicaps other than the ones considered here. The following discussion analyzes these behaviors and the approaches that have been useful in modifying them.

The behavior a child exhibits is often a good indication of his energy potential. For example, we may have felt that little Johnny needed a great deal of rest, yet when observing carefully we see much energy being put into self-stimulating activities and realize that this child is sensorily bored. He is finding ways to release energy. We must then find ways to put this energy to positive use and substitute what he is doing for more acceptable behavior that will enhance his development.

Anything that the child does is behavior. It can be appropriate or inappropriate. Some behavior stands in the way of learning. Also, behavior that is right for one person or in one situation may be objectional in another situation. For example, if little Ivy is independently feeding herself with a spoon and Jenny is picking up the peas with her fingers, we see differences in the eating behavior of the two children. Finger feeding may be a great accomplishment for Jenny. Possibly she has previously refused to feed herself in any way. For Ivy to pick up the peas with her fingers would not be appropriate. Another time, a child may complete a relatively difficult task and be allowed to go to the window where he happily makes finger shadows in the light for a few moments. This privilege is serving as a "reward." Someone walking into the room and seeing the child might feel the behavior is wrong unless the reasoning of the procedure is explained. He would not, however, be allowed to continue for long, as too much of this *will* obstruct learning, but for now it serves a useful purpose.

Using Behavior

Often we can *use* objectionable behavior. We use what the child likes to do as a reward for something we want of him. The goals set for a child make the difference as do the reasons we allow unacceptable behavior.

Opportunities to use behavior occur frequently. One child was re-
pelled by many textures, including soft or fuzzy toys, and never interacted with other people. In this case, we used a fuzzy toy to stimulate the interaction. When touched with the fuzzy toy, she screamed
and pushed it away. Soon she was only pushing it away, and many
days later we were all enjoying a push-play game similar to "I'm gonna
get you." Knowing the child's dislikes is useful information. Another
child may be obsessed with the desire to stare at the window light. This
behavior can be used by changing the window, so when he looks there
is more to see than sunlight. We decorate, paint, or tape pictures to the
window or put something outside for him to see. With another child
who constantly stares at her hand, rings, flowers, and body paint can
be used for stimulation and awareness.

One of the important reasons to stop or change a behavior is if it is
preventing appropriate learning. A behavior that is keeping the child
from constructive learning is one possibly in need of being changed, al-
tered, or replaced with more appropriate action. Staring at the ceiling
light all day can become one of these behaviors, particularly if several
ways of using it have been tried and failed. A child who does not want
to be touched, picked up, sat up, or interfered with in any way has
behavior that is obstructing learning. This kind of reaction will need to
be gradually changed by slowly altering his behavior. The child who
constantly flicks objects in front of his eyes is behaving in a way that is
obstructing learning. However, this activity is evidence of energy level
and is better than complete inactivity. Constant awareness of positive
ways to use behavior is important. Most behavior will change gradually
as the child moves on to a higher level of development. This depends
on the child, why he is behaving the way he is, and the effort made to
give him alternative ways to increase stimulation.

There may also be behavior that is personally difficult to handle;
this behavior must be changed or eliminated. Extremely irritating
behavior can cause a negative reaction, one capable of destroying the
relationship we have tried to build. Irritating behaviors can also prevent the establishment of this needed relationship, one conducive to
learning. If the child behaves in a way that is irritating and we cringe or
draw away, then we will be fighting a losing battle. He will recognize
our attitudes and feeling but may not know the reason for our reaction.
We convey a message that he is not loved, accepted, and respected as a
worthy human being. Behaviors we cannot live with, accept, or use
should be eliminated as quickly as possible. Keep in mind, however,
that if there are many of these things that are irritating, then possibly it
is us and not the child who must change. Perhaps we are being too

"picky" or demanding too much from the child by conferring our standards on one who is not capable of meeting them. A behavior cannot be changed merely for the sake of change. We must be aware, analyze our position, and, if possible, devise a way to use the behavior to accomplish some goal.

Changing Behavior

Some children can be reached by using behavior modification. A technique such as this is not the only way to approach behavior, but rather one method that has been successful in many instances. Observation and analysis of the child's likes and dislikes is important and will reveal much about the child. This information is also useful in devising a plan. What the child likes, such as something to eat, a hug, or to be twirled, held close, or tickled, can serve as a reward for something great he does for us. This is a "you do this and I'll give you what you want" approach. It can work well, but we must be alert to that situation and resist putting too much importance on rewards. Knowing the child's dislikes is also important, as we may find something that is interfering and begin to see the reasons for some of his actions. Also, the child's dislikes can occasionally be used to reach other goals.

A reward to one child is not necessarily one for another. This is important to remember. Some children love to be held close and cuddled; therefore this social reinforcement is a reward to the child. Others do not want to be touched, so to touch or hold this child will actually be punishment. Some children love candy, others do not want to eat. Many like shiny objects and flashlights and others respond well to "time out for good work."

What happens to a child when he does something is important and will greatly effect whether he repeats that behavior. If he likes what happens to him, for one reason or another, then it will probably be repeated. If he does not, then the opposite will be true. What does happen must be immediate—at the very earliest possible moment following the behavior we are trying to influence. If we delay our reaction, we stand a chance of rewarding the wrong thing. The reward is used here as one way of communicating to the child that what he has done is good. Constant observation and analysis of behavior is required for successful rewarding.

When using tangible rewards, always accompany them with enthusiastic verbal praise and a tactile experience. For example, when a child performs some great feat, we may give him a taste of candy and pat him on the knee while we tell him he is wonderful, or give him a sip of juice and place his hands on our face as we nod approvingly and say "Good boy." Soon the tangible reward will not be needed; the verbal reinforcement and hug will be sufficient. By using praise consistently, he learns more quickly to discriminate between our negative and positive reactions. Eventually, the actual self-satisfaction of completing or accomplishing a goal will be a reward in itself. It should work this way. We do not recommend continuing with tangible rewards beyond the point of usefulness and necessity. He must move forward and should not become dependent upon rewards, useful only as an initial way of communicating with the child. Rewards can also be confusing and distracting to some children and, if so, are not useful as a way to establish a working relationship. Tangible rewards are soon phased out. The child must eventually depend on himself if he is to live in a normal society, which is one of our goals for him.

Whatever approach is used should be firm. We decide what we want and stick with it. Many children we see respond well to a dictatorial approach—"tell him what to do and see that he does it." As soon as possible, the child is offered choices. In this way, he learns to think of his alternatives. The teacher says, "Tom, stop it," and shows him that she means it; then, if he still persists, he will have to accept the consequences. For example, if Tom refuses, then he must sit on the chair for a while. He made the wrong choice, and he will have to learn over a period of time what this means.

Setting Limits

There is often a "testing" period. If the child has been in control for a period of time, he is not going to relinquish his position easily. Also, he will be testing constantly to see if we are still holding firmly to what we are saying. By doing the right things now and reacting appropriately often in the beginning, we shorten the testing period. If we are sure of ourselves and he knows it, this testing period will be shorter.

It is often necessary to be "boss" for a few minutes. We maintain a calm attitude and insist on what we know is best. If something is started, it must be finished. We do not want the child to see that we lack confidence in him. Also, he cannot make all the decisions anyway, so until someone better comes along, we must be the authorities.

Corrections and directions work better when they are positive rather than negative. Avoid saying, "Do not go up the stairs"; say, instead, "We are going to stay in this room for a while." Then insist that he obey. Follow-through is necessary, as is the offering of choices or alternatives. Carrying out a command may be difficult, but it is necessary. A little pulled hair or a bite can obviously be handled better now than next year—and it must eventually be handled.

Undesirable Behavior

We are often asked, "Why does he do so many funny little things?" For most of these children, body movement is soothing. It calms the child and relieves some of his frustrations. Self-stimulation is a way of entertaining. He needs to find a way to release energy, so he creates ways; and a severely handicapped child can be creative in his own way. Careful observation is required to recognize some of these mannerisms. Also, many of the activities he enjoys will require careful analysis, since what may look appropriate may not enhance development. Observe his favorite activity and discover why it is so much fun. An example of this is seen when the child appears to be looking at a book but is actually enjoying reflections created by the plastic-coated pages or flicking the pages against his nose for a sensation.

There are three recognizable groupings of self-stimulating behavior characterized by the fact that they are nonproductive even though they are stimulating to the child. These behaviors are stimulation to one or more sensory areas, motor release behavior, and movement patterns that frequently involve the whole body.

Stimulation of the sensory areas may involve objects, such as in gross visual stimulation. A spoon, flashlight, or other shiny object is used to make reflections and can thus be stimulating to the visual sense in a nonproductive way. These objects may also be used to stimulate other areas of the body, such as by clicking something against the teeth. Gross auditory stimulation may be evident when the child taps or scratches his hearing aid or turns the aid volume up and down for a feedback squeal. He may also make unusual noises or growling sounds to accomplish an auditory sensation or vibration. Still other stimulation of a sensory area may be obvious as the child repeatedly mouths everything he contacts.

At other times, stimulation may only deal with the child's ability to stimulate himself without the use of objects, such as thumb sucking, eye gouging, tapping his ear, clicking his tongue against his teeth, and others. The important fact to remember is that the stimulating activities are not helping the child to gain new information but are frequently being used as a means of avoidance. By so doing, he can avoid contact with people in his environment.

Many motor patterns, which have the same results, are also seen. Avoidance or self-stimulation may be recognized as the child persists in biting himself, banging his head, rocking, masturbating, snapping his fingers, or popping his finger joints.

Another type of avoidance behavior often seen could be called ritualistic. In some ways it resembles a self-designed ceremony. These behaviors are characterized by repeated movement patterns, frequently triggered by some environmental situation. For example, the child may ritualize when he hears his bath water being drawn and realizes it will soon be bath time. At this time, he may begin spinning around and waving his hands and arms in a peculiar fashion. Another child may be triggered by objects that turn or move, such as a fan, tape recorder, record player, or even the water swirling in the commode. We may guess that these rituals are always situational, as it is possible that when the actions do not appear to be triggered, it is merely that we have not been able to identify the event that set off the response.

Body movement occupies the child's time and provides him with some of the exercise he needs. It would be better, though, if he could be provided with other opportunities to keep busy, and therefore some mannerisms could be prevented. We must substitute, intervene, and teach him to use single or multisensory stimulation productively. This is another time when teaching is essential to break the pattern. It is much easier to prevent this behavior from developing than to change it once it does develop. Also, children sometimes resort to this kind of escape because what we are demanding of them is too difficult for now.

We try to stop the child before he makes a mistake, as he will often remember the mistake or inappropriate behavior and repeat it. Some children confuse what should be happening with what has just happened. Jeff was helping demonstrate to an adult group a teaching technique often used to teach manual signs. A group of objects was placed on the floor a few feet away. The teacher would give the sign for one of the objects in the group and Jeff would bring it to her. When "bell" was signed, he made a mistake and brought the key. Then, for what seemed like forever, each time "bell" was signed, Jeff would pick up the key and start to bring it, then after hesitating, he would put it down and get the bell. This pattern was finally broken, and Jeff got back on the right track. If he could have been stopped before the mistake was made and repeated, this could have been avoided. He was confused. Whenever possible, if we see a child begin to make the wrong choice, we place our hand on his and help him; then we give him another opportunity and see if he has learned the correct response. Unlearning comes slowly to all of us but is especially hard for children who are severely and profoundly handicapped.

Teaching can be complex. Many problems can only be solved as they occur; there is no magic answer. Think, plan, set goals, and analyze what is happening. Observe how much or how often a behavior occurs. It may seem that a child is masturbating constantly, yet when actually recording how much or how often this is happening, we may be surprised. Besides, if we are not aware of the extent to which a behavior is occurring, we will not be able to determine whether the child is doing it more or less at some later date.

The Learning Atmosphere

The atmosphere must be one of confidence, security, and structure. There are many reasons this is necessary. The child has probably been listening and watching for longer than we realize. He has picked up visual and auditory clues that tell him much about himself. He knows how others feel about him and that he may not be "OK." He has little confidence in adults and suspects that they have difficulty deciding what to do with him. He is unaccustomed to and intolerant of structure. Goals must be established and plans made for the child to accomplish these goals. Then he will begin to develop confidence. He may not readily appreciate these successes, but he must succeed. Eventually he will learn to enjoy cooperating and appreciate succeeding. As confidence develops, he will begin feeling more secure in the outside world and his self-stimulating inner world will not be as necessary. Progress toward adjustment will begin to move more smoothly as he develops and hopefully more rapidly.

As with the multihandicapped or other severely and profoundly handicapped children, talk constantly. This helps us treat the child more normally. Also, he is probably listening. We say, "I understand, Sam, you don't want to sit here with me, but we are going to sit here together for a moment, so let's relax and enjoy it." Then we brace ourselves for a smack and maintain firm control, as this is the time when aggression may surface. In several instances, we have taken a little one for a walk; a walk that was not welcomed. We walk anyway, moving forward holding hands with a little friend, which means his hand is grasped firmly as he drags the ground or swings from an adult's arm. As we walk, we talk: "I hear some ducks, Sammy." "Let's see if we can find the noisy ducks," and ignore his resistance. This may become quite a contest before it is all over, since once committed, we must follow through.

At times like this, it is good to offer alternatives. If he insists on swinging on your arm, say, "Put your feet down" once or twice, and if this does not work, turn him loose and drop him. Then grasp that tight little fist and try again. Watch out, this is when he bites. Right when we are beginning to win a little and gain more confidence in ourselves, he attacks. The next time it will be easier, and within a few days, pleasant walks can be enjoyed together without the necessity of holding hands. In the beginning, the same resistance may be confronted with eating, drinking, staying in bed, sitting in a chair, and almost every task attempted. In fact, if someone says, "Do it," no matter what the task, there may be a testing period. Each success is one step in the right direction, and makes the next task easier. Learning to live in a real world may meet with much resistance.

Behavior is learned. If it is not there, it must be taught. If it is wrong, we develop a way it can be used, then replace it with some that is more acceptable. The child needs to learn right from wrong and acceptable from unacceptable. We help him move from one level to another by using behavior. If he is persevering, continuing to do something repeatedly, we design ways to help him move gradually to a higher level.

The child's energy level should be observed. He may be expending energy inappropriately. Observe the amount of energy used for avoidance activities such as we have described. What he is doing is an indication of his energy level, and ways must be devised to put this energy potential to positive use through substitution. Also keep in mind that if he has excess energy, then it is inappropriate to require him to spend extra time in bed. As the child learns more, understands more about what is happening, and becomes more serious and interested, then he will gradually stop doing some of his "funny" things, but he needs help.

This child is dependent upon others and he knows it. He realizes he needs help. He is accustomed to decisions being made for him. He has been deprived of some experiences, others have been different. He may even realize that he is "different." Behavior and knowledge expected of others is not expected of him. Care should be taken with the use of reward and punishment, as we do not want the child more dependent upon us, and we want him to be as much "like others" as possible. Rewards can be used, however, to communicate to the child that his actions are good and appropriate. In this way, we help him develop a feeling of confidence and acceptance. Remember, say "yes" more often than "no."

Punishment

How do we punish him? This depends on the child and also on us. Some children respond best to being ignored. Others do well when they are removed from the action. We sometimes use a little "time out" room. The child can stay in the room for a few minutes when he needs time out for bad behavior. Some children are funny, trying to peep under the door or through the keyhole to see what they are missing. This is real punishment, and five minutes is a long time. Angie responds well to being put in the corner. There is nothing worse than to be away from all of the activity—she tries to peep around and see what we are doing. Sometimes it is best to remove the wrong stimulus. If the child is playing with an object in an unacceptable way, we take the object and replace it with another more acceptable one, but also watch how this one is used. For some, a 12-inch ruler or small switch may work best. This weapon should be used appropriately and with caution. Remember that once we spank a child, we may have lost the fight. There are almost always more effective methods of control. It takes little planning to pick up a ruler, and there is no connection between the seat and the mind. There are some children, though, who have had this used so much that it may at first be the only way they can be "reminded" that they must change.

It is much more effective to restrain the child who is acting out. Since the teacher is bigger and stronger than the child, he finally gives in and has gained nothing by screaming or attacking. Few children like to be held tightly and calmly as they are told "I'll hold you until you are finished and then we have other things to do." When restraining a child, we hold him tightly for a few seconds until he relaxes or changes behavior. Then, when released, if he persists in the unacceptable behavior, we hold him again. If he throws himself on the floor and screams and kicks, we may imitate him. This way he learns how he looks, and he also fails to accomplish his task, which may be to show how bad he can be. Most children react by changing their behavior. Of course, imitating the child's bad behavior cannot be done often as the child will begin doing things to see us "act out" or possibly accept this kind of behavior as appropriate.

There are many approaches effective in working with children. This discussion has been concerned with those procedures that have worked on troublesome behavior exhibited by severely and profoundly handicapped children. It is most important to be flexible, although not to the point of inconsistency. The child must be observed, and the behavior which is of concern should be described. This allows for evaluation of success or failure at a later date. An approach can then be outlined to change the problem behavior. If there is no description and no prescription, then it is impossible to determine what effect one approach may have over another.

These methods are applicable to all areas discussed in this chapter. Our purpose has also been to suggest a process for determining procedures for working with the child. This allows for modification in methods and also for the teacher or parent to be an individual and capitalize on his own strengths. Throughout the chapter, we have discussed those areas that are recognized as important before a child can fully profit from an academic program.

There are many questions that need answering and many other areas of importance that must be considered by those responsible for a child's development. When the child is severely and profoundly handicapped, there are few sources for answers, and no one even to consult to determine if the appropriate questions are being asked. Chapter 3 discusses some of the areas that must be considered as a child develops and as others become involved.

BIBLIOGRAPHY

Abel G, Hatlen P, Lowenfeld B: Blind Children Learn to Read. Springfield, Ill, Thomas, 1969
Arnheim DD, Sinclair WA: The Clumsy Child: A Program of Motor Therapy. St. Louis, Mosby, 1975
Auditory Training Handbook. Northampton, Mass, Clarke School for the Deaf, 1971
Barraga N: Increased Visual Behavior in Low Vision Children. New York, American Foundation for the Blind, 1964
Bartel NR, Hammill D: Teaching Children with Learning and Behavior Problems. Boston, Allyn and Bacon, 1975
A Basic Course in Manual Communication. Silver Spring, Md, National Association of the Deaf, 1975
Becker W: Parents Are Teachers: A Child Management Program. Champaign, Ill, Research Press, 1971
Breen J, Cratty B: Educational Games for Physically Handicapped Children. Denver, Love, 1972

Cratty B: Perceptual and Motor Development in Infants and Children. New York, Macmillan, 1970

A curriculum guide for the development of body and sensory awareness for the visually impaired. Springfield, Ill, Illinois Office of Education, 1974

Doctor PV (ed): Communicating with the Deaf. Washington, American Annals for the Deaf, 1963

East San Gabriel Valley School Project Staff: An educational program for multi-handicapped children. Los Angeles, County Schools Los Angeles Duplicating Center, 1972

Eisenson J: Aphasia in Children. New York, Harper and Row, 1972

Fant LJ Jr: Say It with Hands. Silver Spring, Md, National Association of the Deaf, 1972

Findlay J, et al: A Planning Guide to the Preschool Curriculum: The Child, The Process, The Day. Chapel Hill, NC, Chapel Hill Training-Outreach Project, 1975

Finnie NR: Handling the Young Cerebral Palsied Child at Home. New York, Dutton, 1968

Flowers AM: The Big Book of Sounds. Danville, Ill, Interstate Printers and Publishers, 1974

Fulker M, Fulker W: Techniques with Tangibles. Springfield, Ill, Thomas, 1968

Furth HG: Deafness and Learning: A Psychosocial Approach. Belmont, Calif, Wadsworth, 1973

Gearheart BR: Learning Disabilities: Educational Strategies. St. Louis, Mosby, 1973

Gearheart B, Litton F: The Trainable Retarded: A Foundations Approach. St. Louis, Mosby, 1975

The Georgia Center for Multi-Handicapped: A Guide to Education and Services for the Multi-Handicapped. DeKalb County, Ga, DeKalb County School System, 1974

Ginott HG: Between Parent and Child. New York, Avon, 1961

Gowan J, et al (eds): The Guidance of Exceptional Children. New York, McKay, 1972

Groht MA: Natural Language for Deaf Children. Washington, DC, Alexander Graham Bell Association for the Deaf, 1958

Guldager V: Body Image and the Severely Handicapped Rubella Child. Watertown, Mass, Perkins, 1970

Gullion E, Patterson G: Living with Children. Champaign, Ill, Research Press 1968

Harris GM: Language for the Pre-School Deaf Child. New York, Grune and Stratton, 1971

Haycock GS: The Teaching of Speech. Washington, DC, Alexander Graham Bell Association for the Deaf, 1972

Karnes MB: Helping Young Children Develop Language Skills: A Book of Activities. Washington, Council for Exceptional Children, 1968

Karnes M, Kirk S, Kirk W: You and Your Retarded Child. Palo Alto, Pacific
    Books, 1955
Kirman BH: The Mentally Handicapped Child. London, Thomas Nelson, 1972
Kolstoe OP: Teaching Educable Retarded Children. New York, Holt, Rinehart
    and Winston, 1970
Long J, Rosenzweig L: Understanding and Teaching the Dependent Retarded
    Child. Darien, Conn, Teachers' Publishing, 1968
Lorton MB: Workjobs. Reading, Mass, Addison-Wesley, 1972
Lowell E, Stoner M: Play It By Ear! Los Angeles, Calif, John Tracy Clinic,
    1963.
Lowenfeld B: Our Blind Children. Springfield, Ill, Thomas, 1964
Lowenfeld B (ed): The Visually Handicapped Child in School. New York,
    Day, 1973
Mager RF: Preparing Instructional Objectives. Palo Alto, Fearon, 1962
Meyen EL: Developing Units of Instruction for the Mentally Retarded and
    Other Children with Learning Problems. Dubuque, Iowa, Brown, 1972
Mindel E, Vernon M: They Grow in Silence. Silver Spring, Md, National Asso-
    ciation of the Deaf, 1971
Robbins N: Speech Beginnings for the Deaf-Blind Child. Watertown, Mass,
    Perkins School for the Blind, 1963
Robbins N, Stenquist G: The Deaf-Blind Rubella Child. Watertown, Mass,
    Perkins School for the Blind, 1967
Robins F, Robins J: Educational Rhythmics. New York, Association Press,
    1967
Van Riper C: Speech Correction: Principles and Methods. Englewood Cliffs,
    NJ, Prentice-Hall, 1972

3
Family Concerns and
Other Considerations

INTRODUCTION

The severely and profoundly handicapped child has at least some of his disabilities identified early in life. This early diagnosis can be beneficial if records are available to aid adequately in an effective approach to the problem. This section considers the functions of available resources and the specific considerations that could be prescribed.

Figure 5 illustrates the relative responsibilities to the child by those systems that are essential to his development from birth to adulthood. Initially, it is the child's family or surrogate family (in the case of an orphaned child) who has most responsibility. While advice and some specific treatment may come from certain areas, such as physicians and private or public agencies for the handicapped, responsibility for implementation rests with the family. With the severely handicapped child, the family is called upon to make an overwhelming number of decisions and must exert tremendous physical energies to carry out even the most rudimentary program.

The community, represented by social service and other tax-supported agencies, also includes the educational program. If a child were ultimately placed in an institution, the community or state would assume almost total responsibility for management. If the family were intact at adulthood and the child was not adapted to society, then family and community would share responsibilities. If the handicapped adult were socially and vocationally adjusted so that he could maintain

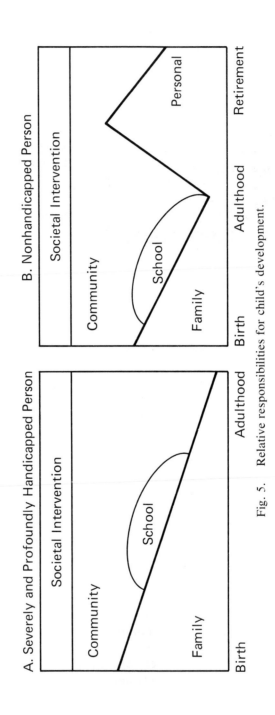

Fig. 5. Relative responsibilities for child's development.

himself in the community, then he would retain the major share and control over his management. This model may generally be applied to all persons, but it becomes especially significant as a means of identification of responsibility for the severely and profoundly handicapped.

Another essential factor influencing development of the handicapped is "societal intervention." This factor is particularly evident with the existence of a minority group, especially one related to the handicapped. For the purpose of identification, it should be recognized that this factor is one over which the affected person has little, if any, control and who frequently does not know that pressure is being exerted. The fact that a child is not placed for adoption or an adult cannot find an apartment in a certain area or get treatment in a special hospital may be the result of this societal influence. Also, in some countries and even areas in the United States, marriage is illegal, sterilization may be prescribed, or property confiscated for individuals with certain abnormalities. Thus, the possibility of such influence should be recognized whenever and wherever one person maintains responsibility for another.

Application of this responsibility model allows for the time and personal commitment of others to be placed in perspective. However, the relative influence of each area may, of course, vary. For example, the total school time is quite insignificant in relation to one's life, yet the results of the school period may be quite significant. Also, a comparison of responsibilities assists in making recommendations as to adequacy of commitment in certain areas. Any time one makes a complete assessment of these relative commitments, it will be possible to determine relative energy expended by all persons involved.

The comparison of relative responsibilities becomes more evident with Figure 5b, which displays the responsibility of the family and community of a nonhandicapped person. This shows a much larger personal involvement as adulthood is reached, with family intervention decreasing and community control varying with the person's ability to handle his own life. There is still a societal factor, but even this is probably diminished for the self-sufficient adult. It is our goal to provide whatever program is necessary for the responsibilities to approximate, as much as possible, those of the nonhandicapped citizen in any community.

If we are to capitalize on these factors and realize the maximum potential of each toward treatment of the multihandicapped child, then careful attention must be given to the prescribed program. While the school program is an important element in the prescription, it should be evident that other considerations are necessary long before the child is ready for such formality.

A directed program is necessary in the home as early as possible. Most families can do much at this time; with some organized efforts, they can do more than merely meet the child's immediate needs. With each step of advancement, the family can better organize its own thinking and identify and plan for future needs.

Readiness for school is an important part of such general program planning. So is concern over preparation for adulthood. There are also other factors that are important to consider. The nature and organization of those factors will be discussed in the remainder of this section. It is necessary at all times, however, to have some responsibility model in mind. This allows for a clearer delineation of duties and establishment of the priorities necessary so that decisions may be made around the child's development. It also hopefully makes possible recognition of the child's rights and any abuse of them that may exist.

In addition to the responsibility model as presented in Figure 5, there should also be a model representing the characteristics of a child's functional ability. In order for such a model to be complete, it should include categories related to the total living environment. It should also represent the interrelationship of the several environmental situations experienced in the daily life of the child. One system of categorization based upon a functional model has been developed relative to a behavioral observation protocol (Curtis and Donlon). The characteristics of this model were described in Part 1. These characteristics formed an outline that was used in Part 2 to detail the specific techniques and procedures necessary for meeting many of the needs of severely and profoundly handicapped children.

Our purpose in the following pages is to outline some factors that contribute to the treatment of the handicapped in any community. We also hope that some suggestions for action will be obvious where services and community organization do not exist.

Mobilization and Development of Family Effort

In order for a family to maintain itself and keep in perspective the nature and needs of the severely and profoundly handicapped child, it is necessary for them to obtain assistance and counsel during several key periods in the child's growth and development. When a diagnosis of multiple disorders is made, the family is naturally confused about any plans that might be presented. At this time, it is necessary for specific objectives to be made clear with accompanying time limits for their accomplishment. For example, toilet training can be accomplished in a shorter length of time if one either knows the steps leading to development of this skill and how to carry them out or if advice can be obtained from one who has this knowledge. Then, given the child's readiness for toilet training, goals can be sequentially designed that lead toward independent toilet behavior. If these goals have time limits and there is periodic reporting to an "advisor," much quicker and smoother progress is achieved.

The process for obtaining such specific advice may be difficult. Frequently, the professional "advice giver" feels qualified to make diagnostic statements which lead to referral into another setting but do not account for the development of an objective program. This only serves to remove the child from the advisor's responsibility, which is unstated and perhaps unrecognized by the one giving advice. All too often, this person has little knowledge of a child's developmental processes and is primarily concerned with his ideas of what the diagnosis represents rather than an analysis of the child's traits as represented at that time. Several questions should be answered before taking such advice.

The questions will vary with each situation, but there should be clarification as to how much follow-through would be available from the advisor, how long the advisor would be involved, the reasons for setting certain goals, ways to actually go about reaching these goals, and specific ideas that have been helpful in other cases. These questions should be related to specific goals which might be accomplished by the new advisor. Also to be considered is the familiarity the advisor has with other programs. If there is no evidence of considerable knowledge about programs, then it might be best to rely on one's own common sense instead of the opinions of another less-committed person.

Quite possibly, the reason services and program plans are not recognized is that appropriate questions have not been formulated in a specific manner. The structure of such questions may be based on the categories in Part 2. For example, if a parent can go to certain persons requesting specific information about daily living skills or communicative behavior, then answers from the clinician can more immediately be evaluated and the qualifications of this person to go further in program goals may be better assessed. If, then, in the case of the specific questions being asked about daily living skills, no suggestions are contributed that prove to be helpful, there is no need to continue utilizing this person as a potential source for this kind of information.

Ideally, a family should have a consultant available who would be a clearing agent for advice received from any "specialists." This person could play a role in analyzing such advice and could also assist in selecting goal priorities to start the child in the right direction. The consultant would also define and evaluate results of "advice" as a basis in further goal setting. A variety of persons may be identified to serve the function of clearing agent. It would be good if there were a professional group whose training suited them for the role, but of course this is not the case. Such a person would act as an advocate for the child. (This concept is discussed in more detail in a later section.)

It would also be good if one person could follow a child's progress for several years, but this also is frequently an impossibility. The family, therefore, must have a system for recognizing the need for such service and for identifying the characteristics of persons or agencies who can provide it. The importance of the need to set up specific questions cannot be overemphasized. A sure sign of a person who is not useful for this purpose is one who will not approach the problem by attacking specifics but rather uses vague general terms in describing problem areas. One might think that the professional training for psychologists and social workers would be ideal for this purpose, but frequently these people have not had the important and intense exposure to children necessary to analyze and recognize their needs at this level. Perhaps one of the most informative rules to follow when identifying persons who can help is evidence that they are presently in close contact with children. Persons who are specialists in handling parental attitudes and guilt feelings are important, but they are not crucial to the program needs as outlined here. If one cannot rapidly recognize and evaluate progress over relatively short periods of time, then some aspects of the program cannot be fulfilled.

A "specialist" who has some ideas as to what should be done but cannot offer usable suggestions as to how to accomplish the task is of no help; nor is an "authority in the field" who has training and position yet has not recently worked intensively with handicapped children. Ideas from such a person may seem appropriate but may not be what is actually needed. Also, the "specialist" may dwell on his own area of interest and concern and overlook the major problem needing attention at the moment with this child. An example of this is the speech therapist who knows how children can be taught speech and promises to initiate a program as soon as the child has learned to sit still.

One element of importance in establishing a program is the identification of someone who will assume responsibility for carrying it out. This person may be responsible for one very specific part of the program, such as providing glasses or a hearing aid, or his range of responsibility may be broader. The important consideration is that such responsibilities are outlined and understood by all parties, and there is a clear definition of the conditions by which they are to be met.

Family Needs Must Continue

"Crisis" may best describe the climate of a home following the realization that a child is severely handicapped. Most parents look forward to the birth of a normal child with confidence. Fleeting thoughts that the child could be imperfect are short-lived. Even knowing the child may be imperfect as a result of some condition of the pregnancy may fail to prepare parents.

The news may come in installments. More than a few parents have been told their child has a severe "visual problem," only to learn a few weeks later that there are other problems. A year later, their fears are confirmed, and they are told the child may not walk. Others hear that retardation is suspected. In some cases, the news may be thrust upon the parents in one big dose. Whatever way the news is given, the results are probably the same: shock, disbelief, grief, hostility, horror, and guilt, resulting in experiences that cause a crisis in the family.

From this point, life within the family will undergo many adjustments. Major decisions involving the entire family can bring much frustration. It may seem necessary to sell the home and move to another city where help is available, or the mother may not be able to return to work. Situations requiring decisions arise rapidly and additional pressures are placed on the family unit.

The situation within the family cannot ever be exactly as it was. One could generalize that any new arrival into the family causes changes; however, the arrival of a handicapped child makes the changes more dramatic. Some of the problems now facing the family may seem insurmountable and even the best adjusted family may fall apart, at least temporarily. Feelings of confusion, frustration, fear, and unacceptance may be partially caused by circumstances accompanying the birth. For example, hospital staff may isolate this new mother from other mothers, perhaps hoping to protect her. The baby may be placed so that he cannot be seen in the "peep window." Comments and suggestions from acquaintances further frustrate the new parents. Friends may not visit because of a lack of confidence in their ability to communicate with the mother about the new baby. The attitude of the parents may change, and they may isolate themselves. This reaction often results from an unfounded feeling of shame or a desire to protect the child. They may be saying, "If I stay to myself, don't see anyone don't go anywhere, and don't encourage others to come, I won't be hurt more."

The emotional climate in the home is one of the determining factors in predicting the future success of the child. If the child is to make maximum progress and if the relationship within the family is to remain on a stable base, the atmosphere within the home must be as nearly normal as possible. There are no magic solutions to the existing problem of what to do with the child. Even with the additional pressures that cause situations to change, all cannot fall apart. Certain segments of home life must continue.

Although some adjustments will need to be made, the child must eventually fit into the family. He cannot overturn the balance within the home completely. To try to change life within the home continually so that every condition will be ideal for him, without consideration for other members of the family, can only lead to frustration and discontent. The child must be accepted into the home. Some adjustments will be needed, and these should be made realistically. Everyday life will not be smooth for the family, but years of development in home life routine cannot be sacrificed in hopes of creating a perfect situation for one child.

This child does deserve a place, acceptance, and love; but he must also learn to realize that he is a member of the family and accepted. If he feels he is being treated differently, his adjustment will be affected. He needs to feel equal to, not different from, others in every way possible, and we want him to feel he is a worthy member of society and capable of contributing to that society. We often speak of our responsibility to the child, but we cannot forget that the child also has a duty to the home. By helping him learn that he has certain responsibilities, we will be assisting him in developing the kind of confidence and independence that will be necessary if he is ever to find his place in the home, the school, and the community.

Being Realistic

An attitude of realism involving acceptance of the child should be integrated into the home atmosphere as soon as possible. This attitude will include the "acceptance" of certain positive truths about the child's condition and of diagnostic statements as they have been made about the child. This information will be correct to some degree. For example, obvious evidence of cataracts, spasticity, or a crippling condition indicates certain problems, some of which may be corrected. After correction, we cannot linger on what "might have been." The child's future adjustment may depend heavily on the realistic attitudes assumed by those within his environment at this time. When an accepting attitude is transmitted to the child, he knows all is well. A negative attitude tells the opposite. There are, however, certain statements made about the child that should not be accepted as truth, at least until proven. Unfortunately, it is often the case that parents may be told that there is "nothing that can be done." This does not always hold true. Many times in the case of medical, educational, or social diagnosis, there is more that can be done than is realized. The situation of providing parents with negative information is not necessarily a result of professional incompetency but may be due to a lack of experience with children who have compound problems. One must realize that unless the professional seeks out such children, he will come in contact with comparatively few severely and profoundly handicapped individuals during a whole professional career.

Therefore, care must be taken when accepting statements made about the child's future, his potential, or his needs without securing further and probably much more useful information from one who is more experienced. It is relatively simple for a professional to describe an obvious problem and then offer no direction. It is difficult to seek ways to find help and relay them to the parents. Some suggestions on ways to secure and evaluate professional help are included in other sections of this book.

The future for this child depends on what happens now. A positive attitude must be developed. The child needs the best efforts available. Such problems as to where he will go later and what kind of help can be obtained will continually recur as he develops. Each new step forward brightens his future potential. There are programs developing new ways to help severely and profoundly handicapped children. New techniques for teaching are being devised. Some of these techniques are being practiced by people now in the field. We all must look toward the future and plan. By the time the child reaches school age, he must have been given the experience that will make his potential for getting help much brighter.

COMMUNICATION TO PARENTS

Severely and profoundly handicapped children have a multitude of special needs. If this were not the case, then a variety of programs would previously have been developed, and this discussion would not be limited to general statements of a few basic program types. When dealing with the severely handicapped, it is necessary for a third party to participate. Such participation must be on several levels. First, parents need a counselor and confidant as a sounding board for their feelings about having a handicapped child and one who will discuss implications of decisions that need to be made about programs and placement. A third party is also needed to intervene for both family and child when the community or society does not understand the child's needs, or when his rights are being violated. Finally, third party participation is needed to coordinate the complexities of program development and secure appropriate changes when necessary. One person cannot serve all of these functions. It is our feeling that many persons should be used and that their availability needs to be assured in a variety of ways. The remainder of this section will be directed to a discussion of the process by which this can be accomplished.

Since congenital sensory handicaps are usually identified early in the child's life, the family needs information immediately about the future. While decisions regarding educational programs are not necessary at this time, the questions are. There is an urgency by most parents to know, not so much whether the child is educable, but where he can be educated. Will a move be necessary? How will he learn to talk? Who will pay for it? What kind of work will he be able to do at graduation? These questions are important because there is no referent system to call upon past experiences. The parent and frequently the community have no experience with a severely and profoundly handicapped child. It may be relatively easy to discover what cannot be done but finding alternatives is much more difficult.

First it is necessary to identify those areas needing immediate attention. Medical considerations are certainly important. Frequently, however, questions in this area may be formulated and answers obtained more directly than is the case in other areas. This is true because medical technology is advanced to a point where evaluation can be completed without verbal communication with the patient.

Other areas are not as easily attacked. The importance of infant learning is one that has only recently been recognized as important to the handicapped child. Systems of communication also need to be recognized and developed early in the child's life. Often a parent may feel that because a child has a disability, he is especially fragile. This may result in a lack of emotional bonds being formed simply because others are afraid to touch, fondle, cuddle, or otherwise develop a physical closeness to the child.

Many other areas need attention for the young, severely handicapped child. We have considered these in more detail in Chapter 2.

Beyond these considerations, though, is the value of a coordinating person to analyze areas that are not being considered and to secure services and advice about these and other needs. Those areas that are either partly developed or totally left out must be recognized and incorporated into child's life plan.

Making Parents Aware of Services

The task of specifying and identifying services is difficult. When the severely and profoundly handicapped child is involved, there is almost never a time when the desired services are available, especially for the child with certain combinations of handicaps. Therefore, it is necessary to identify services on the basis of what they do rather than what they say they do, and then match these services with those that are needed by the child and his family. There is almost never a time, for instance, when a preschool program is available for the severely handicapped child. There are, however, situations in nearly every community that could solve parts of certain problems with some extra help. For example, a local day school could accept a child needing the experience of relating to other children. The situation resolves itself to finding specific ways to meet the immediate needs in the best way possible. Solve one problem at a time. It is important, especially in identifying specific services, to maintain an attitude of flexibility in locating them. This is not necessarily the case when one is searching for longer term services relating to education.

The process of matching a child with a school program may still be misleading if one searches for programs limited to certain diagnostic categories. For example, two programs treating the severely and profoundly handicapped, having the same stated goals, may be entirely different. One could be appropriate and the other ineffective. This is one more reason why immediate goals of any program should be specified. There can then be agreement by the family and the school as to the areas of the child's development that will be attacked first.

At this time, some programs for the severely and profoundly handicapped child are funded by the United States Office of Education, Bureau for the Education of the Handicapped. This allows for some coordination between communities and states and also makes it possible to obtain information about functioning programs as well as new programs that may be coming into existence. This office is a good resource when it is necessary to consider possible placement situations for a child.

Regional offices collect information on programs functioning in each area. They also have information about children who are not in programs but may be receiving services in the community. Since this information is always changing, it is important to make a personal contact with the regional and state coordinators. It is also important to be familar with as many agencies as possible who provide services to children.

There may be existing programs within the community that can be useful. The most obvious examples of a community service are Head Start and other early childhood programs. Head Start is being required by new regulations to accept a percentage of handicapped children. Many private early childhood programs are happy for the opportunity to integrate these children. Another kind of service may be provided by the clinic for physically handicapped children. Community, church, charity, civic, and fraternal organizations may be able to provide some help. For example, the Sunday School departments of larger churches may have leaders capable of directing children with specific needs, such as group activity and socialization. Special classes within the city and county school systems may be led to accept a severely handicapped child. Day-care centers operating under the Office of Economic Opportunity may accept a handicapped child if his needs can be specified and met. Private day-care and kindergarten centers may accept the child, particularly if there is adequate staff, and they realize they will not be required to take responsibility for all of his developmental needs. College-associated programs will often take a special child on a daily basis. Developmental learning centers will accept some responsibility for evaluation and placement. Also, interested groups may be challenged to develop a "program," particularly if a handful of children needing help can be identified and interest can be inspired. A group of parents or motivated individuals may be stimulated to form volunteer programs, such as "grandparents for the retarded." Interested individuals can also stimulate interest so that help can be obtained for a child with specific problems. Community programs often have someone who has had experience with handicapped children, even though their stated purpose is to work with the nonhandicapped.

There are several groups and organizations that come to mind when thinking of help to be offered in any community. Specific charitable organizations are generally available and willing to help those persons who have the type of disorders specified in their charters. Many groups are also able to work with children who have different disorders and so have much more flexibility in their programs. Most organizations dealing with the handicapped work only with the handicapped, so if our goal is for integration, these programs may not be tailored to the needs of the total population. In these cases, the handicapped child would always be separated from the nonhandicapped, unless specific goals can be described and carried out that lead to integration. These organizations are usually easily identified and when contacted are willing to help in any way possible.

Other times, services may be offered only to children with specific handicaps but may be restricted to one diagnostic category. Agencies doing this do not usually advertise the fact that they will work with children who have other handicaps. In fact, many times there are rules in their charter or conditions stated from their funding sources that prohibit this. Fortunately, and frequently, those who make such rules are seldom around to enforce them. Also fortunately, those who administer the programs have more empathy for the needs of the handicapped than those who wrote the rules.

These groups do not see themselves as having the ability to work with this population but quite possibly can be synthesized to do an excellent job. Services and programs vary within communities and perhaps within neighborhoods. Generally, they will not be listed in a telephone book or other directory as being interested in working with the severely and profoundly handicapped. A person who is familiar with the community will probably know some of these groups. This is not always the case, however, and frequently it will be necessary to get acquainted in the neighborhood where the severely and profoundly handicapped person will be before contacts can be made.

There are times when a small group of people, perhaps in a church congregation, will be interested and willing to offer their help. For young children, there are times when a private, preschool program will be willing to accept this child. Many times, an individual with sensitivity and empathy for the problem will serve as a focus to begin the process of acceptance if he is willing to allow a person to be around for several hours a day and has some means of communication so that at least simple directions can be given. This experience may go a long way toward giving the person exposure in a community and thus promoting acceptance. Some groups who meet regularly about other topics may encourage some of their members to go out of their way and serve a handicapped person. If there are special needs, the person may be available to volunteer their services to meet these special needs. This is especially the case when transportation may be needed, when readers are necessary for persons who cannot read, or when sewing, arts and crafts, or music would be a valuable addition to a community program.

Perhaps one of the most important reasons for maintaining perspective of available services and activities to meet the needs of the handicapped is to be found in professional and citizen advocate groups. Both types of organizations are actively involved in recognizing the needs of each population they serve. Their prime goal is usually to provide service and act as consultants in developing these services. Citizens' advocates groups, such as the National Association for Retarded Citizens and the United Cerebral Palsy Association, have been instrumental in developing and supporting model programs to serve mentally retarded and cerebral palsied individuals. Various professional organizations such as the Council for Exceptional Children and the American Association on Mental Deficiency encourage research and provide a forum for communication and development of those who are professionally dedicated to the field.

Recently the American Association for the Education of the Severely/Profoundly Handicapped has been formed. In its first year of operation, it has grown rapidly and received the support of many leading professionals. With continued growth and dedication, this organization should provide much needed energy and emphasis to a group that has been too long neglected.

Considerations for Placement

When anyone is looking for possible placement opportunities, it is important to be specific about the needs of the child and his family. One should also be careful not to label the child as belonging to a certain diagnostic category when talking to persons working in the program. Labels such as "deafness" and "cerebral palsy" may have meanings to another person that are not at all true for the particular child in question. The use of labels may have been instrumental in keeping children out of the certain programs, yet children with behavioral characteristics similar to the labeled child are often seen in these same programs. For example, a very active child with a hearing loss may have been labeled "emotionally disturbed" and therefore not "qualified" for a program, whereas another child labeled severely and profoundly handicapped might be accepted. Caution should be used in placing a label on the child. Also future developments, such as surgery, reevaluation, or maturation, may invalidate the label, yet it may be difficult to remove once recorded.

Ideally, a program could be developed that would meet all needs of the child as they exist in the home, school, and community. Such a *total* program would be made effective by an experienced and qualified staff who work together as a team. Presumably, the staff in such a program would be made up of representatives from various disciplines who could work together to help the child progress in all developmental areas.

At this time, let us assume that such a program is not available and that we must recognize and deal with specific needs. It is through this process that several programs may be brought together so that each may attack specific problem areas. The challenge at this time is to recognize and define a child's needs in behaviorally oriented terms so that they may be communicated to persons in another program. Persons in these programs can then relate the child's needs to their own past experiences with children who may have entirely different problems. If we can describe our severely and profoundly handicapped child's needs so that a person in a cerebral palsy clinic can identify his characteristics with their children, then there is a good chance they will accept him for at least a part of their program. Or, if we can describe a child with an expressive language development problem to a program designed for the deaf child, and can identify similar needs, then he may be accepted. There is no question but that it is a difficult task to match services and needs in this fashion, but the results more than make up for the effort when it is successful.

The important point to consider in obtaining this kind of service is that the program does not have to assume full responsibility once they accept the child. If the administrators can be assured that someone else is willing to assume a large part of the burden, then they are often more than willing to take over a well-defined portion. In this way, the residential school may be willing to accept the child if their specific goal will be to get the child into a routine (i.e., alter an irregular sleeping pattern) that will make his management easier. But the school might not be willing to accept the child into a "classroom" because of the lack of a program designed to meet the other needs of this child. Therefore, specific parts of the child's immediate needs might be met by this placement. In another case, a school might be willing to accept responsibility for socialization, mobility training, or preschool-type opportunities offered during a half-day program and yet not be willing to accept responsibility of the child on a 24-hour basis. Carefully outlining the child's specific needs and requesting the school to accept only partial responsibility in detailed portions can be advantageous in getting help.

Perhaps one of the most important considerations in promoting acceptance is for someone to have a plan and to be specific about needs. If a person (or group) can then be approached and not be overwhelmed, he will see a beginning and end to his involvement. Our goal is to provide a variety of experiences within the neighborhood and to make as many experiences as rewarding as possible.

Getting Parents Aware of Laws

Children have "rights" to education. In most states, these are becoming more and more inclusive so that the school is required to educate a child regardless of his degree of handicap. Laws are passed frequently because parents and organized parent groups have made legislators aware of the fact that some children are not receiving the benefit of tax-supported educational services. These laws may mandate that programs be established within the school system. They may also provide extra funds for schools offering such programs. In other cases, tuition may be paid from state funds which allow children to attend special schools.

In addition to laws, there are also rulings by agency directors such as commissioners of education. These rulings have the power of laws until contested and are more difficult to locate since they are not generally publicized. There is no effective system capable of monitoring all applicable laws and rulings at either the state or federal level. Such a system is technologically possible, especially with equipment dedicated to data storage and retrieval.

There are other ways of maintaining contact with new laws and with new interpretations of old ones. The information collected by agencies and persons interested in specific handicapping conditions can be made available if one knows whom to ask. Persons working with children in a treatment capacity or in a clinic frequently have up-to-date knowledge of trends and even proposed legislation. It is regrettable but true, however, that much of the burden for obtaining information in this area rests with the parents. This can only lead to fragmented and uneven administration of services and monies which are legally available. A clearinghouse is definitely necessary on a broad basis. Project Closer Look is one attempt to attack this problem. Information about programs for the handicapped throughout the country is available. Parents of a handicapped child can describe his problem, and a computer search will be made to identify programs and professionals in their immediate area. This is a good first step. Much more needs to be done, however, to locate and monitor programs after placement has been obtained.

Another possible procedure was suggested by Sanzi after participating in a survey of facilities for the multiply handicapped in Massachusetts (Sanzi and Donlon).[1] Interdisciplinary groups could be formed who would maintain familiarity as part of their professional experience

[1] Unpublished study contracted by Syracuse University School of Education, Division of Special Education.

with programs, laws, and anything else related to the handicapped. Their role would be to apply this knowledge toward the solution of problems of individual cases. Persons in this group would function as information givers and probably would not have direct contact with the child or his family. Information about various programs would be provided to those supplying direct services to the child and his family. A representative from one of these services would analyze the information obtained and serve as coordinator of the responsible service groups and programs.

For example, according to some reports, a child may be doing "well" in an existing program yet obviously not getting all he needs. The representative would gather information about other programs that are available and analyze his findings. By contacting the selected people and asking specific questions, he would quickly have a clear picture of the alternatives and be in a position to make decisions about the child's future. It might be decided that, although the existing program is not good, others offer less. Then it would be necessary to decide how changes can be made in other ways.

There are systems available for storage of information which could be applied to data obtained. The use of these data could be amplified considerably if the committee of experts were made part of the collection and retrieval process. Questions asked of the data are important, but the selection of the questions is at least equal in importance. Much must be done in the area of categorizing information as well as establishing models, so that repeated items of information will be placed in the same cell. With technology in this area expanding so rapidly, it is extremely important that those working with the handicapped should have access to these procedures.

Financial Help (Funding)

Along with the recognition that specific programs are not available for the severely and profoundly handicapped child, the need for financial assistance is probably the most chronic and perplexing problem for the family. If, by some chance, a suitable program is found, usually one of the first items of information about that program is its cost. Frequently, the stated annual cost for these children is more than the combined annual income of the family. Similar financial burdens occur even though the child does not have a full-time program. The frustration and hardship experienced by families attempting to meet the financial needs can be overwhelming. There are several areas, however, where some, if not all, of these costs can be covered by other sources.

Frequently it is difficult to determine which funds are available for any particular child. It is almost impossible for one who is not familiar with regulations governing these funds to obtain all that are appropriate. Rules governing allocation of funds change frequently. There are also cases where new interpretations of the law make funds available for previously excluded groups. Constant research and review is necessary to obtain perspective on the availability of financial aid to families at any given time.

Some federal funds and direct grants to state and regional programs are available; however, unless they are earmarked for a specific population of children, they are not used for direct services. They may be used for obtaining extra staff and for including special populations in an ongoing program. An example of this would be funds to provide a special teacher for the severely and profoundly handicapped in a Head Start program. Some funds are also available because of the unique aspects of a region such as Appalachia, for the purpose of working with the deprived as well as the handicapped. Funds of this nature may be available to any of our children provided those who are receiving them can be convinced that they should be allocated for this particular child. Sometimes extra funds are available to a program if they are used for a certain group of children. This is especially good information to have when approaching a program director for your child.

Other federal funds are supplied to state programs. Frequently it is left to the discretion of the state as to how these funds can be used. There are usually some guidelines, however, making it mandatory that handicapped children should receive the bulk of these funds. Sometimes it is necessary to advise state and local program directors of these conditions.

It should be remembered that most states have or are getting right-to-education legislation. This usually says that the state, through its various public school programs, has mandated responsibility to educate all children, regardless of handicap. Again, where this legislation is in force, it is also sometimes necessary to advise the local programs of their responsibility. The more knowledge a person has about individual cases who have been served, the better opportunity for suggesting that services be provided for a particular child.

There are other funds available earmarked for specific purposes. These are usually distributed through other than the educational agencies. Medical rehabilitation funds, for instance, may be used to buy hearing aids, glasses, and other equipment. Other funds are available for medically treating disorders that prevent a child from functioning at his maximum potential. Money is available from social service departments for a variety of treatment programs if the family cannot pay for this program without going through undue hardship. While these funds are frequently administered by welfare departments, it is not required that the family use all of its available funds before applying for this assistance. Some social services departments may be overzealous in their interpretation of needs. At these times, the family should receive aid and counsel about their rights and should be aided in going through necessary appeal procedures.

If a school district cannot provide certain services, the state may make funds available through that district so that it can contract with a privately operated program that does provide these services. It is not difficult to recognize these funding sources when contact is made with the private school, since a good proportion of the funding for the school is usually provided by these sources. Still, there are times when those responsible for the program are not fully aware of the variety of funds and services available. The fact that talking books, supplied by the Library of Congress, are now available to children with handicaps other than blindness is a case in point.

Many programs, especially private schools, are the recipients of endowed funds which may be used as tuition grants for some children. Since these funds vary with each individual school, it is often necessary to approach these schools on a case basis in order to determine if they apply.

As the child grows older, and especially after the age of 16, vocational rehabilitation programs have considerable flexibility in the ways they can help their clients. This program can be as specific as providing a prosthetic appliance to make a handicapped person look more presentable or as general as providing for a totally subsidized college program so that the handicapped person may reach his fullest potential as a professional.

There are times when some non-tax-supported funds are available. These may come from a variety of sources. Foundations sometimes have funds that apply, but more generally fraternal organizations will meet specific needs of a child upon request. Clubs and organizations in the community, such as Rotary, Lions, Shriners, or the Y.M.C.A. will sometimes make donations to help with a specific case.

Other times, programs that receive voluntary contributions from the public, such as March of Dimes, Crippled Children Associations, Red Cross or the United Givers Fund, have available funds. Funding from the latter group is limited and seldom of benefit to the individual child and his family so far as an actual program is concerned. These agencies will, however, when approached, often provide for specific needs, such as a hearing aid, money for orthopedic braces or corrective surgery, or transportation to and from an out-of-town medical facility for outpatient clinic services.

There are programs that provide material useful to the handicapped. American Printing House for the Blind, Regional Centers for the Deaf/Blind, and the various state and regional Instructional Materials Centers are examples. These latter programs catalog and make equipment available to the handicapped in a variety of ways. State education department divisions for handicapped children are usually the best source of information on availability of these materials.

While the availability of physical and professional services often seems nonexistent, it is almost always possible to find some alternative that can be arranged, providing there is a willingness on the part of many people to look for these alternatives. It is a challenge to the person who is responsible for providing a program to look at all possibilities. There is considerable reward when a successful program has been arranged and effective results are observed.

The existence of schools implies that teachers will be involved with children within these schools. Therefore, whenever one looks at a school and its program, the major concerns should be with the practice of teaching as it exists there. This would seem to be a logical statement without any need for clarification. Yet, it is so often the case that a person, when visiting a school, talks only to the administative head and seldom sees the teacher. If contact is made, it involves only a few minutes of classroom observation or a conversation about class size or materials.

Teachers of children, especially those children who are our concern here, must be intrinsically involved with the child's growth and development through a broad spectrum of areas. If these areas are not related to the child's needs during school hours, then the program is wrong. For example, written symbols or numbers should not be taught unless the child has a reason to count. Recognition of word symbols or even picture symbols is also of little value until the child has sufficient words in his inner vocabulary to be able to use them in a meaningful manner. A quick tour through the school that gives one the impression that the children sit at desks and perform school tasks tells little about the school. If the child is working at a task yet does not have the skills or the need to learn the task, then it might be best to avoid this particular school.

Those children at the level discussed here must experience a variety of stimulating situations that promote interpersonal and physical involvement. These experiences must be sequential so that one logically leads to another and another until the child is ready for even more complex learning tasks. If such conditions are not evident in a school program, and this evidence may not be obvious, then careful investigation should be carried out before allowing the child to participate. The picture of children sitting quietly at desks working may be so encouraging to a parent or interested person that the appropriateness of this activity for a particular child is forgotten when evaluating the complete learning situation.

KINDS OF PROGRAMS

Educational programs are classified in several ways. One is based on the length of time a child spends in the program each day. This could be rather brief as in the beginning or preschool situation where, to allow for adjustment, the child is only involved for a few minutes a day; or, as in the case of residential schools, the child could live in the facility for a large portion of the year or even his entire childhood. There are strengths and weaknesses in each. When it comes to the severely handicapped, the options are minimal and often there is only one. This does not mean that others cannot be devised. Frequently, there are programs existing in a community, without labels for specific handicaps, producing good results for the child or children involved.

Residential School Programs

Residential school programs have been the most prevalent in this country. Those working as educational programers have often been devoted to severely and profoundly handicapped children with sensory disorders. Here, a child is enrolled for the school year which usually begins in the early fall and ends in the late spring. There are usually one or two vacation periods such as Christmas and Easter. Several programs require children to go home more frequently, sometimes as often as every weekend.

Residential school programs for the severely and profoundly handicapped are considered here because they have most recently been developed. Many of these have been connected with schools for the blind. In the past few years, there has been a trend to develop other programs connected with medical centers, child development programs, and new projects sponsored for the specific purpose of working with the severely and profoundly handicapped. Many of these are combinations of day and residential programs. Their newness makes them difficult to describe, but they hold much promise for the future.

Activities in the residential school should be all-inclusive for the child. Staff members teach daily living skills as well as academics. They must also fulfill the children's need for love and affection, which, because of the distance from home, cannot be fulfilled by the child's own family. Usually, there are two groups of adults working in these programs. They are divided by responsibility so that the time span beginning shortly after breakfast and continuing to mid-afternoon is devoted to "education," with remaining time supervised by other personnel. Sometimes an additional group such as teacher aides or recreational staff take over between the end of the day and the evening meal.

Ratios between adults and children may vary considerably in these programs. This is an important consideration since this ratio could be as low as one-to-one in the school program and five-to-one, or more, at other times. With the severely handicapped, a prime teaching concern may be for the child to learn effective eating habits. If teaching of this skill is not consistent, then much delay can result, and the child can actually be retarded in development because there is not a total and coordinated effort put forth. Lack of communication between those working with the child could, for example, be indicated by the fact that during breakfast, the child is learning to eat independently, yet during the other two meals, the major concern is to accelerate his eating so that the staff can be served.

It is possible, of course, for the various staff groups to be in close communication and for the child to go from one place to another in his development at peak efficiency. This is the ideal of the residential programs. It is possible, and it is even happening in some instances.

Careful attention can be paid to many areas of health, education, and child development in the residential unit designed specifically for the child with severe multiple handicaps. These areas have been considered in Part 2. We are not concerned with a discussion of negative features of any administrative plans offered. These factors exist and should be recognized and changed when possible. Educational methodology for these children is rapidly changing. Ideas and techniques that were not considered feasible some years ago are now incorporated in many programs. There are many children today recently identified that have led to the need for new programs and to the development of new models for teaching which, although they may have no recognized validity, are getting results. In the near future these models may solve some of the unsolved problems of the past related to working with these children.

Day School Programs

These programs have not been strongly in evidence in past years, especially for the low functioning child. Those children too young to attend residential programs have been enrolled in day programs for children with other handicaps and even in some preschool programs for nonhandicapped children. Generally, schools for children with a single handicap, such as day programs for the deaf or emotionally disturbed, have not offered to take the multiply handicapped into their regular classes. Sometimes one suspects this has been a matter of definition and stereotype rather than functioning, since when one observes children in those special situations, multiply handicapping conditions can be recognized. On the other hand, programs for the physically handicapped and some for the mentally retarded have accepted severely and profoundly handicapped children. In many of these programs, though, there has been an emphasis on teaching around a specific disorder with little knowledge of or consideration for other handicapping conditions.

Day programs allow the child to be with his family and in his community environment whenever he is not in school. If functioning in an integrated, nonhandicapped society is learned, then one could say it must be learned through experience and constant interaction with that society. We feel this can be accomplished much easier in a program where the child is at his home everyday and is functioning in his community regularly. *When* these experiences should happen is the problem facing educators. The climate within the home may dictate the "when" of this experience; it varies between children. All educators seem to agree that it should occur some time before adulthood is reached.

One major concern about day programs is the lack of experienced teachers having the special skills necessary for working with severely handicapped children. This shortage occurs because there are not enough children unless the program is located in an area with a large enough population base to support it. Because of the low incidence of severely and profoundly handicapped, this could only occur in a large metropolition area.

It is possible, however, that some children's needs are not such that they require the constant, intensive attention of a specially trained teacher. In fact, as an alternative of segregated placement, one could consider the possibility of a community-oriented program where the handicapped child lives and learns in his home environment. In some cases, this could be with foster parents. This arrangement would allow all parties in the community to adjust together to a person who will have certain individual differences but, by and large, will be able to function with a minimum of supervision.

It may be best that these children would have a home environment for specific intensive experiences in certain skill areas such as communication. But, even in this area, if some adjustment is necessary by all parties in the communication process, then one might assume that the adjustment should take place as these parties learn together. Perhaps a neighborhood could be challenged enough by such interaction so that all members would be stimulated toward forming even deeper relationships with these and other handicapped members of their community.

There are often advantages to this approach—cost is certainly a factor. This is particularly true when long-term costs are so high. Some members of the group could be merged with other children who have similar problems. In these instances, one could work with a heterogeneous population in the specific area of most common need. Perhaps the greater advantage is the fact that as children grow in their community, they learn to live within it. That community can then both educationally and socially make the necessary preparations to provide for the most appropriate modifications on a step-by-step plan.

SEVERELY AND PROFOUNDLY HANDICAPPED IN THE COMMUNITY

Most of the educational goals of the handicapped as well as the nonhandicapped are directly related to community adjustment. In fact, the effect of an educational system may be judged by the effectiveness of its graduates in society. If we assume that the severely and profoundly handicapped person will be living in a community that is primarily made up of nonhandicapped persons, then the educational system must relate most of its curriculum to the needs this person has in being a participating and contributing member of that community. Most of these areas have been discussed in Chapter 2. We are concerned here with the recognition of those other factors and their importance in community life.

Any person functioning outside of an institution receives some degree of supervision. Those who are in institutions, of course, are there because someone feels they need almost total supervision. We who are not institutionalized are usually willing to accept the fact that the police will not allow us to commit certain acts that are harmful to others. Moreover, other agencies are dedicated to supervising our health and education. If we are not able to be economically self-sufficient, then for the price of even more supervision, we are given amounts of money so that we may remain in the community. There is then considerable latitude in the behavior and abilities that allow a person to remain in the community. Certain stated limits, if surpassed, lead to exclusion through expulsion or total supervision. For example, when disaster strikes and we are no longer self-sufficient, we can get supplementary assistance. We feel that most severely and profoundly handicapped persons can remain within the tolerable limits prescribed by society and participate in community life. Educational programs should have stated goals that clearly recognize these facts. It may be useful here to identify at least the end results of some of these goals.

Activities of Daily Living

Most severely handicapped children, when they first enter an educational program, are inadequate in many activities of daily living. Self-care skills—dressing and toilet habits—usually require special attention. This is true whether the child is in a residential or day program. Since most of the children are functioning at a lower level, there also needs to be much consideration given to their eating habits. While the development of these skills is of direct concern early in the school program, the fact that the children have several limitations makes it necessary to be more specific for longer periods of time so that their living habits can become culturally acceptable. It is, for example, difficult for most of us to enjoy gross eating behavior in public. Motor patterns, especially those related to blindisms, identify the persons as being abnormal and are socially objectionable. Unfortunately, these behaviors are often neglected by teachers of the handicapped and persist into adult life.

The educational program should be concerned with the difference between the necessity for exploration, such as finger feeding, at one developmental stage and the need to replace it with more culturally acceptable skills when it is no longer needed. In the same way, tactile exploration, such as when the child is encouraged to examine an adult's facial features, at an early developmental stage might be appropriate, yet as the child moves to a higher level, this kind of exploration will not be necessary. The initial curiosity, however, must be encouraged and developed if the child is to progress. Later, development can gradually be channeled in a direction that would lead to behavior more appropriate for community living. Timing here is important. Careful consideration should always be given to the fact that children with severe handicaps frequently need more time before they are ready to change.

Progress must continue, however, and the child should not be maintained at one developmental stage indefinitely. Motivation may be high in certain settings to assist the child in learning daily living skills that make supervision easier, such as when the child learns to feed himself independently in any manner. However, the child must not be allowed to remain at an elementary feeding stage and must move on developmentally beyond the point at which he is less trouble to those supervising him. Gross skills that may be acceptable in some settings will not be so easily accepted by the public in a normal community. Behavior desired or required in different situations must also be recognized. We may all be messy when eating a watermelon, yet we do not put our faces in food at a restaurant.

Leisure Time

The adult with no interests and no ways to use leisure time is allowed to remain in the community, but he does so as a social isolate. Most of our friends are related to outside interests and hobbies rather than employment. Often our self-concept is enhanced by these activities, which is not always true of our employment. If we consider the real possibility that the severely handicapped individual will have less years of employment, then it is even more important for him to have challenging and self-fulfilling leisure activities to occupy his periods of unemployment.

The school plays an important part in providing experience in many alternate ways for the person to use his leisure time creatively. In addition to the fact that a person with many interests and skills has a more well-rounded personality, it is also quite possible that when specific vocational training has failed, further development of an avocation will lead to an acceptable new vocation. For example, a handicapped individual may receive vocational training during his teens and adult life that prepares him to work as an auto mechanic. Later, he may not be able to secure or to keep a job requiring this skill because he cannot communicate with his employers or is unable to follow specific directions. It may seem more appropriate for this individual to find another way to use his time and also assist in his support. At this point, he can be led to rely more and more on other skills he has developed and finds enjoyable. It might be advantageous for him to try mending mechanical toys or repairing bicycles at his home. If he has developed a hobby, such as making crafts, another solution might be available. In this case, items made in his home could be sold at a local store, thus using skills developed for better use of leisure time for financial gain and self-reliance.

Another important reason for the educational program to teach the use of leisure time is the need for healthful physical activity. Unless the importance of this is stressed in an educational program, the handicapped person may easily neglect the need for physical fitness. Handicapped adults can and often do present an image that appears physically unfit. Visual problems may inhibit physical activity and lead to poor muscle tone and weight problems. Motor problems may cause similar symptoms. Lack of social acceptance may bring isolation and cause the person to be more comfortable inside the house with the television or record player or just sitting.

Lack of physical ability causes loss of fitness at a rapid rate. We have but to be hospitalized for a few days to realize the speed at which our strength deteriorates. The handicapped individual must be taught ways to keep physically fit and motivated to do so throughout his life. In doing this, he will present a healthier and more normal image as he mixes with those in the nonhandicapped society.

Good physical condition can also make life easier for any individual and is especially needed for the handicapped person. Good coordination and well-developed reflexes can help stimulate correct motor responses in emergency situations. For example, crossing the street or moving around the house and yard may present situations that require quick movement without thinking. Stimulating physical activities will lead toward development of quick reactions which, when used in practice, are available in emergencies. Therefore, the fact that a school program includes courses in health and physical education should not be considered enough for the severely and profoundly handicapped unless there is careful consideration for their specific needs.

Economic Needs

The economic needs of a handicapped person are related to many aspects of community living. Whether the community is large or small, urban, suburban, or rural, or rich or poor has a direct bearing on the type of integration any person may attain. The amount of cash available may be important in one community and quite insignificant in another. There are communities where cash transactions are very limited and the economy is based on barter. There are also situations where economic needs are met by a pooling of labor and sharing of produce. Most of us are familiar with the economy that is based on wages earned

and expended. This is also the economy that is prevalent for most severely and profoundly handicapped. It may not be necessary for a
person to earn an hourly wage since income may be gained in a variety
of ways, but it is quite essential that every person be able to spend
amounts of money wisely. A person may receive money from social
security, aid to the handicapped, veterans' benefits, and a variety of
other means. It is usually important to the community that this peson is
able to spend these sums in a responsible manner. This skill must be
taught and perhaps overtaught. Many people in society today are not
able to do this even though they are not handicapped.

It is also important that the handicapped be taught to deal with
material possessions. These, of course, are different from cash and
also have a variety of values depending upon the community. Objects
that might be considered important in one community could also be rejected in another. The person who does not realize this may well be rejected in that community. Certain animals, such as horses and goats,
can be considered prized possessions in a farm community and yet be
unacceptable in another neighborhood. In the same way, the purchase
of an expensive suede coat can be appropriate or extremely inappropriate, depending on the community value placed on such an item. An
independently functioning person should be able to make the right decisions and correct choices as to how his money can best be spent to
provide him with services and possessions necessary for survival and
appropriate for his individual situation.

It is important that all programs serving the severely and profoundly handicapped have some goals related to each individual's
needs. If a child is in a residential program far from his home, this can
be extremely difficult. It is not possible, though, and with some consideration, many ways can be found to modify a program for each child.

Social Needs

Social adjustment in a community should be a major goal of any
educational program. Careful consideration must be given to the essential factors that lead to this adjustment. Some of these essentials are
daily living skills, use of leisure time, and economic ability and are considered in Chapter 2. Additional characteristics that might best be included as social are also essential.

At times, in a school or home setting, it may be possible for a
person to have almost 100 percent of an adult's attention, yet this is not
always possible or appropriate. If the handicapped person has been demanding and receiving attention most of the time, then he will be frus-

trated when he does not get it. Social adjustment and acceptance will be made easier if he gradually learns that he cannot always dominate others or maintain himself as the center of attention. A well-adjusted person also needs the ability to observe others and fashion his dress and behavior appropriately for different situations. Before this can happen, he must learn to analyze situations and act accordingly. Pajamas are worn in bed and bathing suits are for swimming; warm clothes are worn in winter and heavy garments are not needed on a warm, summer day. Behavior at a picnic or party is not the same as at church or a quiet dinner. Laughter at times is certainly appropriate but not if it continues past a certain point. A phrase may be funny at one time, but constant repetition will make it objectionable. The ability to adjust to these and numerous other situations must be taught, and it also must be based on practice which comes from considerable experience.

The ability to communicate is important. Functional communication is perhaps the most significant path to acceptability. It is not necessary for a person to be totally verbal to function in nearly any community. There are times when individual community members may feel especially important in being able to "talk" to a handicapped person. When an individual has needs or desires and can communicate this to another person in any manner then the communication is useful. Inability to communicate brings social nonacceptance. Failure of the community member to understand the handicapped individual reinforces the feeling that there is no place for such a person in society, as his needs cannot be met and no one can understand him. On the other hand, if the nonhandicapped person understands what is being asked of him, the success he has in meeting another's needs will be reinforcing and lead toward other attempts to understand.

Provisions for a variety of experiences designed to expose the handicapped person to those in the community is one step toward practical use of functional communication. The parent or teacher, by being aware of this need, will be able to create situations leading to acceptance in the community. By constantly demonstrating communication in natural environments, the community members can gradually become aware of the way communication can and does take place and their responsibility in making the necessary effort to understand. Such learning experiences can begin with merely exposing the handicapped person to the grocery store, restaurant, or general store and those persons he will see in such places. Later, as skill and confidence develop, more responsibility can gradually be left to the handicapped person, and he will finally learn to order a meal, eat and pay for it, or collect the groceries and go through the total process involved in getting the groceries from the store to his living quarters with no assistance. If the adult responsible for teaching persists in translating communication attempts or accepts total responsibility for all the steps that must be learned in order to go through this process, then the child and the community member will learn only what is necessary.

Travel experiences must be carried out in the same way. A child living in a residential school, for example, eventually will need the skills necessary to move from one place in a town to another independently. Therefore, the school must provide opportunities for this skill to be gained. It is relatively easy for the school to group students and transport them from place to place; it is more difficult to create situations requiring the learner to get on a bus, pay the proper amount of money or get change, sit down by a stranger, and then get off the bus at the correct station. This could present various needs for communication. This knowledge will come gradually and can be learned only if there are many experiences structured so that these specific goals can be reached over a period of time.

There are alternatives to the kind of communication that we normally use in transferring a need to another person, and these alternatives must be taught to the handicapped individual and sometimes to the community. A gesture or pantomime that relays a thought can be as useful as a long and complicated sentence. Also, over a period of time, certain basic manual signs can be taught to the grocer, bus driver, drygoods salesman, and social worker, if these are the people who will need to communicate. It is not practical or necessary to assume that they will all need to take a course in manual communication in order to relate to a severely handicapped deaf person. A few basic signs, probably different ones for each type of service provided, will be enough. Others can be learned later if desired. The signs also vary considerably with the ability of the handicapped person to communicate. So, the grocer could learn signs such as "money," "have none," "pay," "come tomorrow," and a few food signs. The bus driver might want to know a sign or finger spelling for local towns or areas of town, "sit down," "off," "on," "where," and "stop." Signs such as "big," "small," "more," "money," "try," "wrong," and "pretty" might be useful for the clothes salesman. A nurse in the hospital might need only to know the signs for "toilet," "water," "eat," and "sleep." Also, many signs used by the deaf are used and understood by all. The wave of "good-bye," the beckon of "come," the shrug of "don't know," and nod of "yes" or "no" are examples of universal communication. Pantomime of such things are drinking, sleeping, crying, eating, and

angry are also easily understood and when accompanied by appropriate facial expressions can be very effective. When these ways to communicate can be taught to the child and relayed to community
members, a much more relaxed attitude of acceptance can be obtained.
Written communication also works well. A small tablet carried in the
pocket can be useful, and here again, only a few basic words are
needed. Also, all people desiring to communicate can do so if the handicapped person knows the alphabet and can print a few words in the
palm of another's hand with his finger. Further, technical developments are making communication between the deaf in one community
and another more accessible.

The approach necessary for communication with the deaf is used
here as an example of the need for community interaction to solve a
problem. Similar approaches may also be devised for working with
problems of those with other handicaps.

Finally, the need to keep communication appropriate for each different situation must also be taught. It is not useful or socially acceptable to communicate to the grocer at the check-out counter about a
broken window at home or to talk to the bus driver about Santa Claus,
or to the waitress in the restaurant about school. This is especially true
when communication is difficult and requires much effort on the part of
someone who is inexperienced. These kinds of behavior are detrimental to community acceptance.

LEARNING TO LIVE TOGETHER

Societies and members in each society must learn to live together,
and learning seldom takes place as an isolated activity. The severely
and profoundly handicapped child who spends much of his life with
little chance to interact outside of a completely controlled society may
face failure when the opportunity to integrate is offered. He may graduate magna cum laude from his school program with good skills in many
areas. However, unless these skills have been used and adapted to the
community, they will probably not be used appropriately. If practice
has not taken place over a long period of time, then the extreme adjustments necessary at graduation may not be possible. Many pitfalls
may be avoided through planning and learning. It is necessary for each
child to live a full and integrated life. Our only concern must not be
with brief periods such as the school years.

We must also realize that detailed planning for life in a given community is difficult, especially today when most communities have rapid turnovers in population, and even the most stable neighborhood may be destroyed through renewal projects or other "improvements." People's attitudes, interests, and values, however, do not seem to be unstable. These are factors that remain within broad categories of description. They may be well hidden in some communities, but when members of these communities communicate with those interested in the severely and profoundly handicapped, then attitudes become evident and may be used to establish future goals toward accepting a new member. If a particular community should not continue to exist, then fundamental and essential acts will have to take place so that integration into a new community will be easier.

As we recognize that communities and individual members of each community are in a process of constant change, it becomes even more evident that continuous participation is essential. The handicapped person cannot leave for long periods of time without needing much help to reintegrate. The longer a person is out of the community, the more difficult his adjustment will be upon returning. If a child grows up in a family that is part of the community, then there will always be someone to recognize and accept this membership.

Community Expectations

Any group of people who have been living together for a period of time has rules established that members are expected to follow. They will vary from group to group. Size of the community, ethnic background, income level, and geographical location all will have some effect upon the communities' expectations for acceptance of new members.

Some behaviors are, of course, dependent upon the age and development of the person. This will also dictate the amount of supervision required for the person to function. A young child, for instance, who is without parents will need supervision prescribed either by community members or by legal decree. An older person who is incapable of making decisions in certain areas will also need some form of help and at some time will need extra supervision. If this is not provided by family and friends, then again, the community will make provisions. Community members have a right to expect certain capacities and behaviors which conform within limits to those that prevail. Our goal for severely and profoundly handicapped persons is to have a maximum of acceptance with a minimum of extra supervision. So we must identify some of the behaviors that are generally seen as necessary for acceptance.

Guidelines for these categories of behavior and descriptions for these specifics have been discussed in Chapter 2. In this section, we have also considered in detail some goals that might be recognized for those adults who have completed their school program and have shifted their energies to those necessary for living in society. These broad categories of behavior as outlined should match with those requirements established by the community for acceptance.

It is quite possible through pressure and publicity to gain admittance into a community for almost anyone. This is the best way to gain acceptance and is one prime reason for increasing a person's experience within the community over a period of time. If the community is forced to accept a handicapped person, this will lead toward a kind of isolation similar to institutionalization. If the individual is to be isolated within the community, even though he lives there, then he is institutionalized. This isolation on the part of the community members is not an acceptable alternative and is useful to no one. A better way is to gain acceptance gradually, first by a few people perhaps for a few things. Then, exposure can be increased until the individual is an accepted and participating member.

When the handicapped person has not learned the skills necessary for social acceptance and has failed to have the necessary integrating experiences, then this isolation is assured, and his existence in the community will probably be temporary. At these times, it is easy and convenient for decisions to be made resulting in dismissal. If, for example, the handicapped person knows no way to spend his time appropriately and irritates people by constantly asking for money or other assistance, then he will not be accepted and most will want to have him put out of sight. Or, if over a period of time, the handicapped individual has been taken care of in his home, and the times comes that he must get his own meals but cannot, then again his chances of being placed in a situation of total supervision are increased. Likewise, institutional placement will probably occur if he cannot manage his time or money to some degree of acceptance.

If a person has the basic knowledge and skills for survival, then community acceptance is possible. Activities of daily living are important here. In adult life, he must know how to bathe and dress himself, secure and prepare food, maintain himself on a reasonable schedule, handle his money practically, entertain himself alone, and get help when necessary. Without these skills, extra supervision is needed. The community has a right to expect certain behaviors from one of its members, and we must see that these expectations are planned for and met so that the handicapped individual can eventually live among the nonhandicapped.

There is a wide range of acceptability available and suitable to those who exist in the community. Broad ranges of acceptability include the individual who can coexist as an independent member of society with little or no outside help. Also within the acceptable range is the individual who has needs that can be met by individuals or organizations operating within the community. A person can live as a hermit and although he foregoes certain social privileges, may be allowed to exist in the geographical community. Even though some cannot handle their own money, they can still exist in most communities, and with some supervision in this area, they may continue to function fairly independently. In the same way, a person who depends on others to help him move from one place to another can exist if these services can be provided. Providing help is much preferred to total supervision and, when possible, the provision of these services is realistic from a financial, social, and educational standpoint.

Many persons in institutions are functioning within the limits of acceptability for some community or at least were when placement occurred. There is a recognizable trend in the country to move even low-functioning people out of institutions. In fact, some states are closing institutions, especially those for the retarded, and mandating that communities assume responsibility for those who are released. If this trend persists, then much will be done to integrate the severely and profoundly handicapped. Further, the help of both professionals and paraprofessionals, so necessary for handicapped persons, would be provided. The result in the community could well be efficient use of service for a larger population, which would apply to this group of handicapped individuals. It could also lead to a community effort toward broadening the limits of acceptability.

Community Attitudes

If we plan to integrate a severely and profoundly handicapped person into a community, then it is important to have as much knowledge of that community as possible. This knowledge could come from a formal and detailed analysis carried out by skilled professionals. We are not recommending, though, that such an approach be used. We do feel it is important that a plan be established and carried out which will allow for some organization toward getting the person and community to adjust to each other.

Identification of groups functioning in a neighborhood is useful. It is also important to know which groups in the larger community might be of service if needed. Contact with these groups, whether they are benevolent organizations or casework agencies, may not be necessary, but if they are known before a need is recognized, then much time may be saved in making contacts at a later date. It is possible to make too many contacts and thus create anxiety over possibilities that may never occur. Someone should have a feeling for what can be done. There is no reason to push an issue in the wrong way or to get too many people involved when the same goal can be accomplished more smoothly. For example, much confusion can be created when a person demands that a six-year-old blind child be admitted to the local public school by writing the governor, state board of education, or his favorite congressman. When outside pressures are placed on the local system, the child becomes a special case before anyone has ever seen him. All are then put on the defensive, and additional problems are created. In addition, the local system uses all efforts to rationalize and justify a position that might not have existed if the situation had been handled differently. Contacts made earlier through the proper channels can prevent many such communication problems.

Other examples of delaying actions can be seen when a handicapped person is sent back to the community after 15 years of schooling without proper steps toward integration and placement having been made. At this time, perhaps someone will go to a local industry and present the case of the handicapped client who now has the necessary skill to work in the factory and will be returning home next month. The suddenness of this request and the unfamiliarity with the handicapped person puts the industry on the defensive. Then everyone searches for a reasonable explanation as to why it would be impossible for this person to be given a job in the factory. One excuse might be that labor has contracted with the industry to provide promotion after a set period of employment and that the handicapped person would not be qualified for that promotion at any time. If over a period of time the individual had been periodically in touch with the industry and personnel who would later be making these decisions, much of this rationalization could be avoided and integration would be smoother.

Our analysis, then, is to gain information and familiarity so that we can decide on the best alternatives when they are presented. We need to know who will be of positive help and who may be of negative value. We also need to know the areas of strength and weakness in service and attitudes.

Attitudes are probably the most difficult to measure. Many people will verbally state one feeling while they demonstrate another. If we can begin by objectively observing the behavior and be realistic in our expectations, then both positive and negative attitudes can be dealt with appropriately. Perhaps the greatest problem facing us in this area is to recognize potential sources of negativism before they become active. In doing this, it is possible to take steps so that we can change the attitude of those who are negative and hopefully recruit those persons as a positive force. Often all that is needed is a little information or for someone to become better acquainted with the problem.

While it is not essential to be aware of all groups that might work with the severely and profoundly handicapped, there are reasons for locating some, especially in the neighborhood. If we can find groups who will accept a person for specific activities, then a strong beginning has been made for that person to become integrated into community life. There are, of course, some groups and agencies whose duties and responsibilities require them to work with handicapped persons. These can be called upon to work for us. Frequently, however, it is necessary to be specific as to the amount of intervention. It is quite possible to take over a person's life entirely through scheduling. Groups can then be used for a variety of purposes and their capacities and weaknesses should be recognized and controlled.

VOCATIONAL REHABILITATION

One goal which is often stated for the severely handicapped is to make them as economically self-sufficient as possible. Although this is the objective, childhood educational programs often neglect to provide the means of attaining it. If we do believe that there is a capability for vocational placement, then some recognizable behaviors must be accomplished before this placement can become a reality. The term "vocational habilitation" implies an analysis of these behaviors in a sequence for their accomplishment. When dealing with a severely handicapped population where the individuals have never worked before, habilitation is a more exact word than rehabilitation. There are several mandated services, however, that are supplied by vocational rehabilitation agencies. These same services are mandated for those handicapped persons who have never worked before and perhaps never will be employable. In this sense, the term "vocational rehabilitation" is accepted and will be used. Lately, there is evidence that vocational rehabilitation services are giving priority to severely and profoundly handicapped persons, and there is relaxation of the strict interpretation that there must be reasonable expectation of employability. This will certainly be beneficial to the development of future plans.

Most employers in every vocational rehabilitation unit are interested and concerned about several specific traits of the individual who will be applying for employment. In fact, many rehabilitation programs provide courses designed to teach the handicapped these behaviors. The ability to handle funds, balance checkbooks, and be knowledgeable in the various payroll deductions are items taught in these courses. An effective educational program should, of course, have these goals, and a graduating student should be evaluated concerning this knowledge. It is our concern that most of these behaviors are easily analyzed and that programs are seriously defective if they do not have recognizable and sequential objectives throughout the child's educational career. We include some of these in this discussion, and we have alluded to others in Chapter 2. Still others should be evident even though they are not stated.

We feel that it is extremely detrimental to wait until a person has graduated before beginning an analysis of his vocational needs, interests, and capabilities. If a person lives in a community as a child (and many of the problems of acceptance are approached at that point), then the possibility for problems will be minimal. Persons who, as children, have had experiences in buying groceries, clothing, and school supplies, which lead to consideration of budget priorities, have the best potential for realistic learning. When these experiences are accompanied by even short periods of earning money, they become even more beneficial.

Observation for Potential

It is important to observe for work behavior in the most familiar environment so that abilities may be recognized under the best circumstances. There are many traits that are oriented toward task completion and are necessary in some degree for job placement. There is no reason to go through a long period of training until it is proven that the individual has the needed task-oriented skills. Some of these traits will be mentioned here. Motivation is one. A person of low skill level who is motivated to complete an assignment will often do a better job than a person of better ability who is bored with the task. Persistence and the ability to control boredom is good. Dependability is also important. The ability to receive and carry out an assignment without constant supervision is necessary for employment, as is dependability related to punctuality and attendance. A person who can follow directions, no matter how simple, without supervision is useful in many jobs. Cooperation is important. The attitude one has toward himself, his job situa-

tion, and those with whom he will be working greatly influences employment potential. The more of these and other job-related skills the
individual possesses, the greater his potential for employment will be.
Likewise, the higher the level of sophistication he reaches in these abilities, the more he enhances his potential for more skilled job placement
and success.

During periods of observation for job potential, it is also useful to
analyze the amount of supervision required for completion of assignments. The amount of supervision necessary must be known before
there can be a decision about when and where to place the individual in
a job. The amount a person can do independently influences the level
of job he can get. Most often, jobs of increasing difficulty and technicality are assigned in graduating steps as the levels of proficiency are
demonstrated. There is no reason to assign a person to a ''difficult'' position until he has demonstrated basic job-oriented traits and shown us
that he can accomplish easier tasks. He may be capable of a technical
skill but incapable of holding the job because of other learning gaps. It
is possible, however, for an individual to hold a job in a workshop
without being completely self-sufficient. For example, he may be able
to walk or ride to work independently, or he may need to be transported under supervision. The degree of supervision can be analyzed
and provided; then the individual can be assigned to a task within his
capability. Eventually, with leadership, more independence can be obtained.

Essential Behaviors for Work

Most rehabilitation facilities have a complete list of skills and
behaviors which they feel are essential for the handicapped person to
attain before he may be successful in a job placement. A review of
some of these may be useful for us to gain perspective and set goals for
the severely and profoundly handicapped. In doing this, it should be
possible to observe the beginnings of these behaviors long before the
individual is ready for work placement. Some skills necessary for
independent community living have been discussed earlier under social
and economic adjustment; other skills are needed for job placement.
Not all can attain a level of competency that would make job training
reasonable or useful. All will not have the attention span or the ability
to follow a plan and carry out a sequence of activities.

It is necessary for all of us to be able to receive instructions for
accomplishing a task. We must also have the ability to concentrate
long enough to accomplish the task. The task may be long and

complex, such as outlining a research project, which could continue for several years, or it may be as brief as assembling one unit on a production line or counting five potatoes to put in a sack for further marketing. In either event, if the job is to be completed, then the person must have the ability to attend to and carry out the task. Our concern, then, is to recognize this ability at whatever level so that the decision may be made as to whether it is adequate or whether further training would be useful or necessary. It is important to realize that there will be variations here as in all areas which are dependent upon the person's motivation and familiarity with the project.

Although economic self-sufficiency is a goal to be considered for the future, all severely and profoundly handicapped individuals will not completely reach this level. One important consideration of vocational rehabilitation services is habilitation to a setting that allows the handicapped person to exist in an environment of the least possible restrictional supervision. Therefore, skills important for homemaking either in a totally independent setting or a group home should be part of one's program. These life skills may be much more important to the severely and profoundly handicapped person than those considered work skills; however there is some overlapping. We recognize the importance of living on a schedule, accepting certain responsibilities, cooperating with others, and making decisions as skills needed both for employment and for daily living in a community. Other work skills also have a place in the training for independent functioning in a home. These behaviors and skills are included as part of the training program in a complete vocational rehabilitation facility and can be a valuable asset for the severely and profoundly handicapped.

Our basic concern when considering the vocational rehabilitation of the severely handicapped is that vocational adjustment and the rewards obtained complement the individual's total living. The best rewards that could be attained for those concerned with coordinating and developing the program would be to recognize and predict strengths of the individual as he is developing. The rewards to us come about when it is obvious that these strengths have been incorporated in his work adjustment and lifestyle.

ADVOCACY

When there is a well-formulated program, it should include contact with the home and community to interpret special needs and promote acceptance of the handicapped child. This task can be difficult, however. Unless the educational institution provides specifically for such a person, this part of the program may well be neglected. In addition to this function, other personnel are needed to perform a variety of services. As our experience increases in recognizing the needs of this group, many previously unrecognized problems are identified.

Most of the organizations needed by families and communities to accept these children are now available. There are times, though, when situations do not lead to this acceptance. There are also times when a community or a state may not be prepared through lack of information, appropriate legislation, or attitude. At these times, interpretations, education, or intervention may be needed by an outside individual or group. This person, or group may assume the role of a consultant, a teacher, or an activist, who after identifying and analyzing the problem, can state the necessary steps toward solution. One term used to describe persons endeavoring to do this type of work is advocate. The advocate's role must vary with the individual needs of each situation. It must be flexible enough so that results can be accomplished but cannot be so free that responsibilities of others are assumed. His role, therefore, varies with the locale and should be developed with a knowledge of programs and their defined and undefined purposes.

The advocate must concern himself with the energy available to help his client and with techniques he may use to obtain such energy at a given time. We are making some distinctions here between energy supplied by people for whatever purpose and the energy available to purchase materials necessary or useful to the handicapped person. Generally, the advocate is concerned with the energy supplied by people. The second type will generally be available as needed and frequently, as in the case of prostheses, there will be legislative or state-operated services to provide them. This does not mean that someone will not be needed to apply for such services. Even though there are clear legal statements, it is possible for misinterpretation by some agency or person which will exclude the handicapped individual needing these services the most. The advocate is especially needed to clarify these interpretations.

Before going further in this discussion, it may be important to state that to our knowledge, there is no advocacy program functioning for severely and profoundly handicapped children. In fact, there are few, if any, programs organized for any group. There are some developing. These are sponsored programs to demonstrate their efficiency for specific target populations.[2]

---

[2] The authors are indebted to John Pelosi, Ph.D., for his work and counsel regarding the principles and application of Child Advocacy procedures.

We feel that such programs should be started and that they could be effective. In fact, they are almost the only answer to assuring the fullest integration of a person into the community. Our concern here is for the severely and profoundly handicapped child, and this discussion will be limited to his needs. There is no reason, however, why many of the principles discussed would not apply to other groups.

The person who will be advocating for a child in the community should possess certain characteristics to assure acceptance, cooperation, and communication with the community. It may be preferable that the person live in the community, but perhaps more important is the number of interactions that there have been and the positive feelings generated by them within the community. The person who can move with ease from house to house and from home to church, to school, to the local policemen, and to other agency representatives possesses one important qualification of an advocate. Communication with these people in a manner that is meaningful to them and on topics that are of interest to them must occur before one can discuss the more emotional and stressful items related to the handicapped. An ability to communicate with these various individuals is difficult to come by. Many languages are spoken even though each is called English and the same words may be used. Smiling at a certain time in a conversation may have opposite connotations to the parents and the caseworker. The advocate may be able to aid the communication process by recognizing these dynamics.

Some feeling for the negotiation process is also essential. Little is accomplished by confrontation at any time. Respect for each other on the part of persons who differ will usually bring about results that are mutually beneficial. There are times when communication has been blocked because of differences. A third party may be effective in clarifying the reason for differences or even acting as an arbitrator to resolve them.

We do not feel that an advocate must know everything about the handicapped or that he be an expert or professional in any one area. It is more important to be able to analyze situations and determine the essential areas of conflict. It is also important to ask questions and to know whom to contact for the answers. Then after formulations are made and a plan is carried out, the advocate should be able to evaluate results and hopefully withdraw when they have been achieved.

At the end of this chapter, we will discuss roles that might be assumed by others who will also act as advocates but without such intimate knowledge of the participants. The person we are considering here is the one who knows the child and his problems and who will be entering into the plans for solution. He will be dedicated to principles and practices that are basic to the handicapped person living as full a life as possible in the community. His energy will be spent in making sure that this happens.

Application of Child Advocacy to the
Severely and Profoundly Handicapped

There are many programs, agencies, and interested persons in any community who can be of service to the severely and profoundly handicapped child. This is true even though the residents may be in an extremely remote area. It is necessary to know what services are available or could be made available when certain conditions are fulfilled. It is also important to have a specific plan of immediate and future needs. It may be as damaging for a child to have too much help as to have no help at all. If there is no outline of needs and priorities, then it is difficult to refuse service when it is offered in a way that will allow for the service to be accepted when needed.

We hope that an outline of specific needs will be dictated by analysis of the child's functioning based on suggestions given in Chapter 2. If such is the case, then the problem now is to translate the prescriptions from this analysis into practice within the community.

We may now deal with advocacy as an attitude that is practiced by many persons. It is almost always necessary for someone to ask for a service before it is provided. It is a rare occasion, for instance, when a person will walk in on a family and say, "I am an expert and will help you." In fact, our attitudes are such that we might well feel suspicious toward such a person and assume that he or she is not an expert but merely wants to sell us something. Yet, the person who does just that is truly being an advocate. He is offering something to someone who needs it.

The attitude we seek and try to develop is one that allows these offers to be made and accepted. They must also be evaluated for appropriateness and priority at the time of offering. The advocate recognizes positive and negative attitudes and works with them to the advantage of the child.

It is so often the case that negative attitudes have developed from lack of information about needs. A few statements or an incident may provide the information to change the attitude. "The child, because he is deaf and blind, cannot communicate." The belief that the child cannot communicate can easily be changed when people see him communicating. Those who interpret his behavior as hopelessly retarded believe otherwise when they see the child learning, and those who think he has no social awareness may change when he shows love.

Part of the analysis that must be done includes those attitudes and areas where change is needed. There are times when it is not possible for the family to alter such attitudes. At these times, advocacy is needed, and a planned strategy must be implemented before change can be recognized. Advocacy in this fashion takes the form of direct intervention close to the home—in the neighborhood. It can only partially be accomplished by an outsider. Such a person makes suggestions and some direct contacts, but unless he is a part of the immediate community, it is difficult for him to accomplish measurable changes. The help really comes from someone who can communicate and is familiar with people in that area.

Other things can be accomplished locally, however, and the persons needed here must use other skills and techniques to accomplish them. Again, the abilities to recognize a specific problem, to analyze it, formulate a plan for solution, and then implement the plan are important. There are times when a knowledge of services and agency functions is all that is necessary. The need is recognized, referral is made, and follow-up carried out to be sure that service has been given. Sometimes, however, services are not provided or referral is inappropriate. At these times, a more specific analysis of the problem is made and the advocate must assume a more active role. It is necessary now to know questions to ask and to have good resource people to question. It has happened many times that a child has not received a prescribed service, such as physical therapy, because the local specialists do not have the skills or equipment. At these times, it was necessary for the advocate to make further inquiries for referral or to clarify the prescription. The person did not possess the technical skill or even the vocabulary, but immediate recognition of the problem was important and alternate methods of solution were necessary. This is another important advocate trait. In this time of specialization in diagnosis and treatment, whether the problem is educational, social, or medical, it is increasingly important for someone to know when the individual has received proper service and when further questions must be asked and alternatives developed.

The example of physical therapy was specific. There are other more general problems that occur perhaps even more frequently. There may be problems of more importance to the family and even crucial to the child's future position in society. If we agree that the handicapped should be an integrated part of society, then the conditions that assure the integration must be specified as early as possible. A contract, in effect, must be drawn between the participants—the severely and profoundly handicapped individual and those in each society who participate in determining his position. Too often in the case of other groups, we have not recognized the importance of these contracts. To date, many in society have not truly considered the severely and profoundly handicapped as possessing these rights.

While the severely and profoundly handicapped are important to us, we must maintain a realistic stance as to what can be accomplished. This is not to say we should be overly optimistic, and certainly we do not counsel pessimism. It is important to be able to be specific, and when results occur, have a way to recognize them.

Who Can Advocate

As we consider the attitude of advocacy, we need to realize that there are persons in all walks of life and areas of government who can contribute. The possibilities of identifying a new ethic are intriguing, but in actuality, we are essentially reconsidering an old one.

The feeling of helping one's neighbor has always been with us. The concept of an ombudsman is identified in many societies and is closely related to advocacy. The application of these principles to the handicapped is not so easily found. Historically, the handicapped have been treated in a variety of ways. They have been worshipped, tortured, ignored, and incarcerated. We agree with many today who are saying that everyone should be able to live and move about in a world without bars and locked doors. Even though it is easier to rationalize putting people who are different in segregated conditions, it is, in fact, isolation for no legal reason.

There are signs that values are changing on this matter. The attitude of advocacy when it is applied by persons in all walks of life will not only bring this about faster but it will also provide a workable alternative. We are advocating for advocacy to include the severely and profoundly handicapped. In order for this to happen, it will be necessary to recognize those who are applying these principles to others. It may also be necessary for those dealing with such children to be leaders in encouraging the development of these attitudes and practices where they are needed.

Advocacy does not generally come about from conferences and committee meetings. Things happen for children when individual problems are recognized and someone does something about them. Many laws have been changed and many programs begun because one child needed it and one adult decided that something should be done.

Anyone facing the problems of the severely and profoundly handicapped is facing one of the most difficult child management problems imaginable. In addition to difficulties experienced in consistent and meaningful observation and evaluation of behavior with these children, the teacher must make plans based almost entirely on untried procedures. As was indicated earlier in this book, all the suggestions given have been tried with severely and profoundly handicapped children. They have worked for some child in some place at some time. With modification and the intelligence of a dedicated adult, we hope some of the suggestions may stimulate the interaction process between child and adult which will lead to the development of each. We also hope that ideas leading to effective change will be adapted and passed on. The eventual development of a model and methodology for educating the severely and profoundly handicapped is only possible if those persons who are dedicated to these children can and do communicate both success and failure to each other.

BIBLIOGRAPHY

Directory of Agencies Serving the Visually Handicapped in the United States. New York, American Foundation for the Blind, 1974

Directory of Programs for Exceptional Children. Boston, Porter Sargent, 1974

Goldberg I, Lippman L: Right to Education. New York, Columbia University Teachers' College, 1973

Massachusetts Study of Educational Opportunities for Handicapped and Disadvantaged Children, Burton Blatt, Director: A Study of the Massachusetts Advisory Council on Education. Commonwealth of Massachusetts, 1971

Mental Health Law Project: Basic Rights of the Mentally Handicapped. Washington, DC, 1973

Pelosi J, Neufeld R, Paul J: Learning about Child Advocacy: The Child Advocacy System Project. Durham, NC, The Learning Institute of North Carolina, 1974

Wright BA: Physical Disability—A Pyschological Approach. New York, Harper and Row, 1960

APPENDIX I
Behavior Rating Form
Communication Adjustment
Learning Instructions*

The videotape telediagnostic protocol was developed to aid in the early identification and evaluation of deaf-blind children and to assist in reporting observational data about such children for clinical, research and teaching purposes.

The protocol consists of the following specific procedures for videotaping and judgmental behavior rating. First, the subject is videotaped in eight 3-minute segments as specified. Second, the videotape is viewed and judged by one or more examiners who are part of the psycho-educational evaluation team. Third, the ratings become a profile of the child's communication, adjustment and learning skills which can be averaged and used as a consensus profile for the child's record or as an index to aid future viewers of the videotape.

Although this procedure was designed to be used as a flexible tool, it was constructed with the following procedural plan in mind.

The Subject. The child to be studied through this technique should be between the ages of three and eight years; he should be a member of the group known as severely multi-sensorily handicapped; he should be under evaluation to determine if he is a legitimate candidate for admission to a deaf-blind program. Ordinarily, this procedure is applied when a child shows such low levels of response on traditional psychological, educational, speech, hearing and vision tests that results neither

* Reprinted by permission from W. S. Curtis, Director, Speech Pathology and Audiology, University of Georgia.

provide a satisfactory base for characterizing the child as he is now nor permit reasonable prognostication.

Videotaping Procedure. A portable videotape recorder with camera-mounted microphone and zoom lens is the preferred equipment. Prior to videotaping, the conditions under which taping will be done should be inspected by the cameraman to be certain of quality recordings. Precautions mentioned in the final report should be observed to enhance the quality of the videotape recording.

The photographer should be a professional in the psycho-educational field since some of the effectiveness of the procedure undoubtedly rests on decisions made by the photographer as he chooses scenes to film and selects aspects of each scene to emphasize. The photographer's job is to try and characterize the child's real day through these brief scenes. Ordinarily, when a scene has been selected, it is photographed continuously for the time limit specified.

When videotaping, the examiner and photographer should comment on unseen events which are occurring in the videotaping situation. For example, if a strong odor is present it should be reported; if a sound or visual stimulation occurs in the nearby area but off camera it may be noted since the judges may wish to consider any such event as a stimulus for the activities of the child.

The child's schedule for the day should be known to the examiner and photographer who will prepare a videotaping schedule which should encompass the eight required scenes.

Behavioral Stimulation Procedures. The following eight brief situations have been selected by the research and conference process as useful conditions in which to observe and videotape.

CLINICAL SCENES

1. Unstructured Orientation (3 minutes): the child and examiner are alone in a relatively empty room. The examiner merely reacts.
2. Task Orientation (3 minutes): the examiner attempts to conduct basic traditional psycho-educational testing procedures near the child's ceiling.
3. Stimulus Orientation (3 minutes): the child is bombarded with stimuli at varied intensities and through many avenues simultaneously.
4. Interpersonal Orientation (3 minutes): the examiner persists in close physical contact such as holding, touching, and fondling the child.

LIFE SITUATIONS

1. Activity of daily living situation (3 minutes): the child is shown at bathing or dressing or toileting or self-care.
2. Eating Situation (3 minutes): the child is shown at his meal time.
3. Formal Learning Situation (3 minutes): the child is shown in class or at a lesson with a familiar person.
4. Informal-Social Situation (3 minutes): the child is shown at play or during free times.

The first four are the clinical situations (Unstructured, Task, Stimulus, and Interpersonal Orientations). There is no necessary required order for videotaping or judging the eight sequences of the protocol, with the exception that the four clinical scenes identified in the behavior rating forms are more easily photographed as a group in the order shown. The second four life situations (Formal, ADL, Meals, and Informal) should be videotaped as they occur in the child's day.

The four life situation scenes can usually be most expediently videotaped by arriving at the site as the child arises. We have found that in most institutions as the child arises it is possible to videotape him dressing, toileting and/or bathing; following which, he has a short informal social period representing a second situation. He then has breakfast, representing the third situation; following which he goes to his first formal class of the day, representing the fourth life situation. If this opportunity is not available those four life situations may be videotaped at any point in the day. If one is familiar with the children and situation and arrives properly prepared at the proper time, the entire videotaped sequence can be prepared in less than one hour per child.

Judging. Any number of judges may view the tape and judge simultaneously although their reactions should be independent. The judges need only be aware of the child's age.

Viewers should not be afraid to make judgments on behavior and activities for which they are not an expert. The classroom teacher may be reticent to rate some aspects of communicative skills; the speech therapist may be concerned about his ability to rate affective paraintellectual skills. Many judges will be unfamiliar with the "relationship pattern" rating procedure. In such cases be concerned; but try. It is our experience that after a short time using the forms, judges become remarkably adept at interpreting what they see and its meaning with respect to categories on the form. And, in the learning process the judges enhance their ability to share and communicate with other members of the evaluation team.

Judges may rate as they view or following the viewing of each scene. They are free to review within the scene and should change ratings on a given situation as necessary to arrive at the best rating to convey their observations.

Ratings may be highly variable from situation to situation. Normal communicative behavior may be seen in one scene and a very low level of communicative behavior in the next scene for the same child. Rate what occurs in each scene. It is only at the conclusion of the eight observations that judges are permitted to make a synthesized judgment of the child's ability from observation scores for all scenes.

The best way to learn to judge is to rate a child's tape which has been prejudged by several more experienced workers and to compare and discuss ratings with these criteria.

USING THE BEHAVIOR RATING FORMS

Judging Communication. The ratings require reaction to a five point scale from behavior which is "absent" to that which is "satisfactory." Think of the breadth of the scale as 100 per cent and make decisions as to a category from 1 to 5 on that basis. If the words "primitive," "emergent" or "usable" are of assistance it is only as guidelines rather than absolutes. They are generally defined as follows:

Category 1, "absent," means that an opportunity to observe this behavior was present but the behavior did not occur. For example, if a loud sound occurs in a room or the child's name is called, one has an opportunity to observe hearing. If no hearing occurs, one would indicate auditory reception as level 1, that is, "absent."

Category 2, "primitive," refers to behaviors that are primarily reflexive, vegetative or such infantile skills as often occur prior to six months age. Crying, coughing and choking are evidences of oral expression which are reflexive. Therefore, when such primitive oral communicative behavior is observed, it would be rated as level 2, "primitive."

Category 3, "emergent," represents behavior above the primitive level which is developmental evidence of progress beyond primitive reflexive behavior—beyond the level of reflexive and vegetative behavior. Such things in speech as babbling, such behavior in vision as eye-hand play, such tactile-motor skills as putting things in the mouth would represent emergent learned behavior. The criteria for distinguishing between "emergent" and "usable" is that emergent behavior shows evidence of a desirable future skill which is sufficiently present to warrant developmental aid and teaching to develop that skill.

Category 4, "usable," represents behavior which is sufficiently developed that although it may need considerable improvement, it is a behavior which can at the moment be capitalized on in developing and teaching other skills.

Category 5, "satisfactory," is checked when a child's skill is satisfactory in that modality for his age level. It does not mean that he is normal with respect to non-handicapped children, nor average nor better with respect to his own peer group of handicapped children.

Judging Adjustment. In rating the behavioral attributes under adjustment, the judge should be aware that the terms listed in the left hand column—such as "cooperativeness"—represent terms which are neither positive nor negative in their implication. They are words which can represent skills either as assets or liabilities under different circumstances and must be judged separately as seen. The judge's task is to note those behaviors which are observed by placing a checkmark in the proper column following words which represent observed behavior. When behavior has been observed and so indicated, the judge is urged to make a decision as to whether the behavior was a liability or an asset in that situation. Under some circumstances the decision regarding value of the behavior judged cannot be made, and it is legitimate to withhold further judgment at that point. The judge should make every effort to rate the quality of behavior observed as either a liability or an asset. He should place a checkmark in the column which most appropriately indicates his decision.

The rating of "liability" or "asset" should be considered as follows. The behavior which is being seen at the moment should be viewed as a liability or an asset in that situation rather than as a predictor of whether or not it would be a liability or asset at some other time. For example, if a child repeatedly goes through a toy box and the storage bins of the classroom while the teacher is trying to work with him, such activity might well be judged "curiosity" and "liability," because in that situation at that time curiosity was interfering with the educational tasks at hand. Such a rating does not mean that curiosity is always a liability or that it cannot become a greater asset.

Some items on the rating form will not be observed and are therefore, not ratable. It is not necessary that the judge rate every item on the rating form. In some instances there is a category—"observed"—for those occasions in which behavior was observed but could not be catalogued as "liability" or "asset."

The judgment of the interaction pattern is probably the most unfamiliar and complex part of the rating form to new judges. It is actually a relatively easy judgment to make and of considerable use according to those judges reacting in the research project. In each scene, the judge should identify a key segment of interaction which most characterizes the child in that scene. For example, it may be the child playing ball with another child, or it may be the subject being fed by a teacher. Whatever occupies the largest amount of interaction time and is most characteristic of the child in that scene should be rated on this segment although there may have been many other interactions occurring in the scene.

The judge's task will be to place one checkmark under each of the columns—initiator, mediator and recipient—with that checkmark indicating who or what served in that capacity during the interaction. For example, if the child is seated at a table and the teacher approaches the table, picks up a spoonful of food and puts it in the child's mouth, the judge should rate that the initiator of the behavior was an adult, that the mediator of the behavior was an object (the spoonful of food) and that the recipient of the behavior was the subject. Following the rating, the judge should write on the bottom line opposite the word "agent," and under initiator the word "teacher," under mediator the word "food," under recipient the word "subject."

Judging Learning. The learning behavior rating form is most familiar to the general observer and the format for rating is similar to that for adjustment. The judge, during and after observing the scene, checks those words which he observed as applying to the child in that situation under para-intellectual skills. He then attempts to determine whether or not that observed skill was a liability or an asset to the child in that situation at that time. He is urged to make that decision although it is acceptable to merely indicate that the behavior was observed without rating its value in the situation.

USING THE SUMMARY RATING FORM

At the end of the viewing and judgment of the eight behavioral observation situations, the judge is requested to make a series of summary ratings on communication, adjustment and learning. These summary ratings are similar to but different from those previously made.

Communication. The rating of communication level is accomplished with the same guidelines indicated above; however, it should be noted that the categories of behavior have been changed from a theoretical formal framework—such as "visual perception" used in the behavior rating forms—to such things as "oral speech" and "braille writing" which have a more direct bearing on educational planning and fit better within the framework of a summary judgment.

Adjustment. The adjustment summary rating form requires a decision on the judge's part indicating his composite reaction to the child in terms of the amount of supervision the child will need in a majority of daily living activities. The judge need only rate those observed. If no opportunity was given to observe the behavior, the judge makes no rating.

Learning. The judge is asked to rate under three major behavioral groups the child's amount of learning and ability to learn the kinds of activities that occur in that situation. The levels of learning have the same categorical values established in the five levels used under communication. Again, the judge may have seen either an amount of learning or an ability to learn and not both, and he is free to rate only what he saw. It is important to remember that no absolute standard of "satisfactory" is available for the judge anymore than an absolute standard or normal in real life situations is acceptable to most judges of human behavior. Thus, a relatively simple configuration can be shown for both the amount of learning and the ability to learn in three important situations, and the judge should take advantage of this opportunity even though his judgments cannot be based on absolutes.

Index

Academic environment, maintenance in, as goal, 4; *see also* Educational programs
Adjustment
 to community, 224–231
  daily living activities and, 225–226
  economic needs and, 227–228
  leisure time and, 226–227
  social needs and, 228–229
 rating of, 250–252
 self-sufficiency and, 47
Adults
 manipulation of, 60
 play activities while adults work, 187–188
 relative responsibilities for handicapped, 201, 202 (figure), 203
 See also Families; Fathers; Mothers; Parents; Teachers
Advocacy, 239–245
 applications of, 242–244
 who can advocate, 244–245
American Association for the Education of the Severely/Profoundly Handicapped, 214
American Association on Mental Deficiency, 214

American Printing House for the Blind, 220
Amplification, 6
 learning to wear hearing aids, 100–102
 speech training and, 175
Assistance and counseling, 204–206, 210
Attention-getting, use of objects and, 65
Auditory disorders
 behavioral components of, 1
 formation of body image and, 54
 manifestations of, 6–8
Auditory sense, stimulating and training of, 99–111
 awareness of sound and, 102–103
 case history, 109–110
 emphasis on, 71
 in infants, 51
 motivation and, 106–107
 need for, 99–100
 praising the child in, 110–111
 sound game in, 103–106, 108
 undesirable behaviors and, 193
 visual stimulation and, 93
 voice awareness in, 107–109
 See also Amplification
Avoidance
 developing substitutes for, 42

Avoidance (*continued*)
  energy put into, 196
  undesirable behaviors and,
      193–194
  vision used as means of, 6

Balance, sense of, 9
  learning to walk and, 119
  reflex movement and, 116–117
Baseline, educational planning, 37
Behavior rating forms, 246–252
  of Joe, 16
  of Sandra, 18
  using, 249–251
Behaviors, 188–198
  analyzing, 188–189
  behavioral components of various
      disorders, 1
  learned, 195–197
  modifying, 191–192
  punishment and, 197–198
  ritualistic, 7, 194
  setting limits and, 192–193
  target, 37–38
  types of, 12–13
    essential for work, 238–242
  undesirable, 193–195
  using, 189–191
  See also Avoidance; Imitation;
      Self-stimulation
Blind children
  tactile sense of, 8
  visual stimulation for, 85–86, 95
Blindness, defined, 85
Blowing
  nose, 148
  in speech training, 176–177
Body image formation, 54–60
  help needed in, 55–56
  language development and, 161
  motor development and, 122–123
  physical contacts and, 59
  spatial movement and, 124
  suggestions to help, 60–63
  visual stimulation and, 90–91
Boredom, self-stimulation as
      response to, 55

Brain-injury, behavioral components
      of, 1

Chronological age, developmental
      age vs., 44
Communication, 152–160
  adjustment to community and,
      229–231
  auditory disorders and problems
      of, 7–8
  finding methods of, 152–154
  judging, 249–250
  with infants, 50–51
  with manual signs, 155–156
  object-centered, 161
  to parents, 209–221
    on financial help, 217–221
    on laws, 216–217
    on placement problems,
        214–215
    on services, 211–214
  problems of, 9; *see also* Auditory
      disorders; Visual disorders
  rating, 251–252
  rewards and, 10
  self-stimulation and, 154–155
  self-understanding and, 55, 85
  suggested activities for, 158–160
  unacceptable methods of, 154–155
  See also Language development;
      Speech training
Community
  adjustment to, 224–231
    daily living activities and,
        225–226
    economic needs and, 227–228
    leisure time and, 226–227
    social needs and, 228–229
  relative responsibilities of, 201,
      202 (figure)
  social interactions and attitudes
      of, 234–235
  social interactions and
      expectations of, 232–234
Concept formation
  auditory training, 111

visual stimulation, 85, 90, 91, 98–99
Confidence
 need to develop, for spatial movement, 119–121
 in teacher-child relationships, 45
Cooperation needed in self-care skill development, 129
Coordination
 motor, 5–6
  poverty of, 9
  vision, hearing and, 9; *see also* Auditory sense; Visual sense
 movement in space and, 121–122
Council for Exceptional Children, 214
Counseling and assistance, 204–206, 210
Crippled Children Associations, 219
Crisis, defined, 207
Curtis, W. S., 204

Daily life activities, adjustment to community and, 225–226; *see also* Self-care skills
Day-care centers, 212
Day school programs, 223–224
Deaf-blind children, 6
 auditory training of, 99
 communication with, 157
Deaf children, auditory training of, 99
Defensiveness to textures, 8, 71, 73
Development age, chronological age vs., 44
Dressing, 141–145
 suggestions for, 142–145

Earphones, value of, 101
Eating, 135–141
 training in
  steps toward independence and, 137–139
  suggestions for, 137–139
Economic needs, adjustment to community and, 227–228

Economic Opportunity, Office of (OEO), 212
Education, Office of (U.S.), 211
Education of the Handicapped, Bureau for the, 211
Educational planning, 36–38, 204
Educational programs, 2–3, 221–224
 building, 47–48
 in day schools, 223–224
 location of, 4
 placement in, 211–212
  considerations for, 214–215
 residential school programs, 221–222
 role of, in adjustment to community, 225–227
Environment
 experiences with objects relating to, 63–64
 maintenance in academic and social, as goal, 4; *see also* Educational programs
 physical, 55–59
  being in touch with, 56–57
  body image and, 55–56
Evaluation
 observation for, 14–36
  observing Joe, 15–24
  observing Sandra, 28–32
  setting goals for Joe, 24–28
  setting goals for Sandra, 32–36
 teacher, 220–221
Expectations
 of community, 232–234
 of teachers, 44–45, 59–60
Experiences
 firsthand, 47–48
 of infants, 50, 51
 learning to see and, 84
 for movement in space, 122–124
 needed for language development, 163–165
 with objects, 63–70
  suggestion for, 68–70
 restricted by crippling conditions, formation of body image and, 54

Experiences (*continued*)
  tactile, 72–73; *see also* Tactile
    sense
  in training of gustatory and olfac-
    tory senses, 78–79; *see also*
    Gustatory sense; Olfactory
    sense
  in visual stimulation and training,
    94–95; *see also* Visual sense
Exploration
  tactile, 72
  visual, 91–92
Expressive language development,
  167–169
Eye-foot coordination, spatial
  movement and, 121
Eye-hand coordination, 5
  spatial movement and, 121
Eye glasses, 6
  visual stimulation and wearing,
    87–89
Eye poking, as self-stimulation, 87

Facilities, *see* Services
Families
  mobilization and development of
    family effort, 204–207
  need for, to be realistic, 208–209
  program planning for, 204
  relative responsibilities of, 201,
    202 (figure)
  satisfying needs of, 207–208
  See also Fathers; Mothers
Fathers, as teachers, 43–44; *see also*
  Teachers
Financial help, 217–221
Forward mobility, 117–119
Free time, observing use of,
  181–182; *see also* Play
  activities

Games, sound, 103–106, 108; *see*
  also Suggested activities
Glasses, *see* Eye glasses
Goals
  of auditory stimulation,

recognition of oral language
  as, 99, 108
behavior, 195
in experiences with objects, 65–67
for Joe, 24–28
language development as major,
  160–161; *see also* Language
  development
maintenance in academic and
  social environment as, 4
for Sandra, 32–36
Grooming, 145–150
  hair combing and nail care,
    149–150
  nose blowing and teeth brushing,
    148–149
  washing as, 146–148
Gustatory sense, 8
  stimulation and training of, 77–84
    basic elements of, 77–78
    creating interest and, 79–80
    experiences for, 78–79
    in infants, 53
    problem solving and, 80–82
    suggested activities, 82–84

Hair combing, 149–150
Handicapped adults, relative
  responsibilities for, 201, 202
  (figure), 203
Handicapped children
  characterized, 5–11
  locating, 4–5
  relative responsibilities for, 201,
    202 (figure), 203
Head Start programs, 212
Hearing aids, *see* Amplification
Homemade toys, 186

Identification of objects, language
  development and, 67–68
Imitation
  body image formation and, 58–60
  communication and, 159
  dressing by, 142
  inability to imitate, 10

motor development and, 122–123
spatial movement and, 124
in speech training, 177–178
suggestions to trigger, 60–62
tooth brushing by, 149
Immobile objects, tactile qualities of, 74
Independence
spatial movement and, 111–112
training in eating and steps toward, 137–139
See also Self-sufficiency
Infant learning, 49–54
Inner language development, 162–163
Instructional Materials Centers, 220

Joe (case study)
observing, 15–24
setting goals for, 24–28

Kindergartens, 212

Language, tactile, 76
Language development, 10
auditory disorders and, 7–8
experiences needed for, 163–165
of expressive language, 167–169
identification of objects and, 67–68
of inner language, 162–163
as major goal, 160–161
of receptive language, 165–167
self-understanding and, 85, 161
sequencing development and, 161–162
See also Speech training
Laws, making parents aware of, 216–217
Learning
attainment of self-sufficiency and, 3
infant, 49–54
rating of, 251, 252
to see, 84–86; *see also* Visual sense

to use objects, 67–68; *see also* Objects
See also Language development; Speech training; Stimulation
Leisure time, 226–227; *see also* Play activities
Lions Club, 219

Manipulation
of adults, 60
of objects relating to environment, 63–64
Manual signs, communication with, 155–156
March of Dimes, 219
Massages to stimulate reflex movement, 116
Memory, spatial movement and, 123–124
Mental retardation, behavioral components of, 1
Mentally disturbed children
characterized, 11–14
vision as used by, 7; *see also* Visual sense
Mobility
forward, 117–119
movement in space and, 113
visual stimulation and, 89
See also Movement
Mothers, as teachers, 43–44; *see also* Teachers
Motivation
in auditory stimulation and training, 106–107
to move, 113, 114, 118, 119
to problem solving, 112, 151
to be self-reliant, 55
for vocational rehabilitation, 237–238
Motor activity, undesirable behaviors and, 194
Motor coordination, 5–6
poverty of, 9
vision, hearing and, 9; *see also* Auditory sense; Visual sense

Movement
  in space, 111–127
    case history, 114–115
    coordination and, 121–122
    developing confidence and,
      119–121
    experiences in, 122–124
    forward, 117–119
    independence and, 111–112
    mobility and, 113
    orientation in, 113–114
    stimulating reflex movement
      for, 115–117
    suggested activities for, 124–127
  speech training and, 178
  tactile qualities of, 74

Nail care, 150
National Association for Retarded
    Citizens, 214
Needs
  adjustment to community and
    social, 228–229
  family, 207–208
Nose blowing, 148

Object-centered communication,
    defined, 161
Objects
  experiences with, 63–70
    suggested activities, 68–70
  perception of, 94
  tactile qualities of, 73–75
  See also Toys
Observation, 4
  for evaluation, 14–36
    observing Joe, 15–24
    observing Sandra, 28–32
    setting goals for Joe, 24–28
    setting goals for Sandra, 32–36
  importance of, 3
  learning to observe, 38
  of potential for vocational
    rehabilitation, 237–238
  of undesirable behaviors, 193–195
  of use of free time, 181–182;

    see also Play activities
  of use of objects, 64
OEO (Office of Economic
    Opportunity), 212
Olfactory sense, 8
  stimulation and training of, 77–84
    basic elements of, 77–78
    creating interest, 79–80
    experiences for, 78–79
    in infants, 53
    problem solving and, 80–82
    suggested activities for, 82–84
Oral language (speech)
  elements of, 179
  recognition of, as goal of auditory
    stimulation and training, 99,
    108
  training in, *see* Speech training
Orientation, 9
  limitations of tactile, 91
  motor development and, 123
  movement in space and, 113–114

Parallel play, 57
Parents, communications to,
    209–221
  on financial help, 217–221
  on laws, 216–217
  on placement problems, 214–215
  on services, 211–214
Participation in play activities, 184
Peer group interactions, lack of
    long-lasting, 10–11, 57
Perception
  concept formation and, 85
  of objects, 94
  visual, 92–93
Physical environment, 55–59
  being in touch with, 56–57
  body image and, 55–56
Placement, 211–212
  considerations for, 214–215
Planning, educational, 36–38, 204
Play activities, 181–188
  cleaning up after, 184–185
  parallel play, 57

participation and learning to play, 184
while adults work, 187–188
Possessions, care of, 150–151
Praises in auditory training and stimulation, 110–111
Private day-care centers, 212
Problem solving
  motivation to, 112, 151
  motor development and, 123
  self-care and, 151–152
  training of olfactory and gustatory senses and 80–82
  visual stimulation and, 90
Project Closer Look, 216

Reaching out
  stimulation of reflex movement and, 117
  visual stimulation and, 89
Readiness
  dressing, 142
  language development, 161
  learning, self-sufficiency and, 3
  school, 204
  toilet training, 131–132
Receptive language development, 165–167
Red Cross, 219
Reflex movement, stimulating, 114–115
Regional Centers for the Deaf/Blind, 220
Rehabilitation, see Vocational rehabilitation
Relatives, as teachers, 43–44; see also Teachers
Residential school programs, 221–222
Residual hearing, see Auditory sense
Residual vision, see Visual sense
Resistance and pressure, tactile qualities of, 74
Responsibility model, 201, 202 (figure), 203–204

Rewards
  accompanying visual stimulation and training, 87
  communication and, 10
  for learned behaviors, 196–197
  motivation to walk and, 118–119
  for movement in space, 126
  in speech training, 178
  use of objectionable behaviors as, 189, 191–192
Ritualistic behaviors, 7, 194
Rotary Club, 219

Sandra (case history)
  observing, 28–32
  setting goals for, 32–36
Sanzi, 216
Schools
  readiness for, 204
  responsibilities of, 203
  See also Educational programs; Teachers; Vocational Rehabilitation
Self-care skills, 127–152
  care of possessions as, 150–151
  dressing as, 141–145
    suggestions for, 142–145
  eating as, 135–141
    steps toward independence and, 137–139
    suggestions for, 139–141
  grooming as, 145–150
    hair combing and nail care, 149–150
    nose blowing and tooth brushing, 148–149
    washing, 146–148
  need for self-sufficiency and, 127–129
  problem solving and, 151–152
  toilet training as, 131–134
    suggestions for, 133–134
  when to start teaching, 129–130
Self-reliance
  encouragement needed to develop, 55
  motivation to, 55

Self-stimulation
   communication and, 154–155
   developing substitutes for, 42
   energy put into, 189
   eye poking as, 87
   forward mobility and, 117, 118
   during free time, 181
   and independence, 111, 112
   infant, 49
   lack of body image and, 55
   movement in space and, 111, 112,
       117
   with objects, 64, 69
   without objects, 11
   play and, 184
   to reach desired goals, 67
   as response to boredom, 55
   sensory deprivation and, 93; *see
       also* Auditory sense;
       Gustatory sense; Olfactory
       sense; Tactile sense; Visual
       sense
   with sounds, 7, 8
   tactile, 71
   undesirable behaviors and,
       193–195
Self-sufficiency
   adjustment and, 47
   as goal, 4
   learning readiness and, 3
   self-care skills and need for,
       127–129; *see also* Self-care
       skills
Self-understanding
   communication and, 55, 85
   language development and, 85,
       161
   visual stimulation and, 90–91
   See also Body image formation
Sensory deprivation, self-stimulation
       and, 93; *see also* Auditory
       sense; Gustatory sense;
       Olfactory sense; Tactile
       sense; Visual sense
Sequencing development
   of language, 161–162
   of vision, 93–94

Services, 11–13
   making parents aware of, 211–214
   See also Educational programs
Shapes and sizes, tactile qualities of,
       75–77
Shrines, 219
Signs, communication with manual,
       155–156
Sizes and shapes, tactile qualities of,
       75–77
Social environment
   body image and, 55–56
   maintenance in, as goal, 4
Social interactions, 231–236
   community attitudes and,
       234–235
   community expectations and,
       232–234
   peer group interactions, 10–11, 57
Social needs, adjustment to
       community and, 228–229
Socialization, free time activities
       and, 181–182; *see also* Play
       activities
Societal intervention, 203; *see also*
       Community
Sound games, 103–106, 108
Sounds
   awareness of, 102–103
   self-stimulation with, 7, 8
Specialists to assist families,
       205–206
Speech, *see* Oral language; Speech
       training
Speech training, 170–180
   amplification in, 175
   attitudes in, 179–180
   beginning lessons for, 177–179
   blowing in, 176–177
   devising total communication
       system for, 170–171
   obtaining results in, 172–174
   tongue exercises for, 175–176
Stimulation
   auditory, 99–111
       awareness of sound and,
           102–103

case history, 109–110
emphasis on, 71
in infants, 51
motivation and, 106–107
need for, 99–100
praising the child in, 110–111
sound games in, 103–106, 108
undesirable behaviors and, 193
visual stimulation and, 93
voice awareness of, 107–109
See also Amplification
of communication, *see*
  Communication; Language
  development; Speech training
gustatory and olfactory, 77–84
basic elements of, 77–78
creating interest and, 79–80
experiences for, 78–79
in infants, 53
problem solving and, 80–82
suggested activities, 82–84
in infant learning, 49
of movement in space, 111–127
case history, 114–115
coordination and, 121–122
developing confidence and,
  119–121
experiences in, 122–124
forward, 117–119
independence and, 111–112
mobility and, 113
orientation in, 113–114
stimulating reflex movement
  for, 115–117
suggested activities for, 124–127
visual, 84–99
auditory stimulation and, 93
emphasis on, 71
by encouraging independent
  travel, 89
exploring as, 91–92
in infants, 52–53
learning to see, 84–86
perception and, 92–93
sequencing development of
  vision and, 93–94
suggested activities for, 95–98

undesirable behaviors and, 193
using daily experiences, 94–95
using visual clues, 90–91
wearing eye glasses and, 87–89
Sufficiency, *see*
  Self-sufficiency
Suggested activities
for communication, 158–160
for dressing, 142–145
for eating, 137–139
for experiences with objects,
  68–70
for hair combing, 150
to help with body image
  formation, 60–63
for infant learning, 50–54
for stimulation of olfactory and
  gustatory senses, 82–84
for stimulation of visual sense,
  95–98
for tactile stimulation, 60–63
for tongue exercises, 175
for tooth brushing, 148–149
to trigger imitation, 60–62
for washing, 147–148
Summary rating forms
of Joe, 17
of Sandra, 19
using, 251–252

Tactile language, 76
Tactile sense, 8–9
limitations of tactile orientation,
  91
movement in space and use of,
  120
stimulation of, 57–58, 70–77
case history, 58–59
encouraging, 70–71
in infants, 51–52
materials for, 76–77
suggested activities for, 60–63
tactile qualities of objects and,
  73–75
by varying tactile experiences,
  72–73
visual stimulation and, 91, 93

Target behaviors, establishing,
    37–38
Teachers
    day school, 223
    evaluation of, 220–221
    expectations of, 44–45, 59–60
    need for, to get away,
        45–46
    selection of, 41
    who can be, 43–44
    residential school, 222
    self-care as taught by, 129–130;
        see also Self-care skills
    suggestions for building
        educational programs,
        47–48; see also Educational
        programs
Temperature, tactile qualities of,
    73–74
Textures
    defensiveness to, 8, 71, 73
    tactile qualities of, 75–77
    in training of olfactory and
        gustatory senses, 83
Tickling to stimulate reflex
    movement, 115–116
Toilet training, 131–134
    suggestions for, 133–134
Tongue exercises for speech
    training, 175–176
Tooth brushing, 148–149
Total body tactile experiences, types
    of, 72
Total communication system,
    170–171; see also Speech
    training
Toys, 183–186
    cleaning up, 184–185
    homemade, 186
Training, see Language
    development; Learning;
    Self-care skills; Speech
    training; Stimulation
Tunnel vision, defined, 85–86

Undesirable behaviors, 193–195
United Cerebral Palsy Association,
    214
United Givers Fund, 219

Vision, as major sensory modality,
    6–7
Visual disorders, 6
    behavioral components of, 1
    formation of body image and, 54
Visual sense, stimulation and
        training of, 84–99
    auditory stimulation and, 93
    emphasis on, 71
    by encouraging independent
        travel, 89
    exploring as, 91–92
    in infants, 52–53
    learning to see, 84–86
    perception and, 92–93
    sequencing development of vision
        and, 93–94
    suggested activities for, 95–98
    undesirable behaviors and, 193
    using daily experiences, 94–95
    using visual clues, 90–91
    wearing eye glasses, 87–89
Vocabulary development, see
    Language development
Vocalization, 10, 172, 174, 177, 178
Vocational rehabilitation, 236–245
    advocacy and, 239–245
        applications of, 242–244
        who can advocate, 244–245
    behaviors essential for work,
        238–242
    potential for, 237–238
Voices, awareness of, 107–109

Walking, 118–119
Washing (self-care), 146–148

Young Men's Christian Association
    (Y.M.C.A), 219